NEW YORK CAP PHOTOGRAPHY

NEW YORK
CAPITAL OF PHOTOGRAPHY

Max Kozloff

With contributions by Karen Levitov and Johanna Goldfeld

The Jewish Museum, New York
Under the auspices of The Jewish Theological Seminary of America

Yale University Press
New Haven and London

This book is published in conjunction with
the exhibition *New York: Capital of Photography*,
organized by The Jewish Museum, New York

THE JEWISH MUSEUM, NEW YORK
April 28–September 2, 2002

MADISON ART CENTER, MADISON, WISCONSIN
December 7, 2002–February 16, 2003

MUSÉE DE L'ÉLYSÉE, LAUSANNE, SWITZERLAND
April 10–June 9, 2003

Front cover: Sylvia Plachy, *Times Square*, 1993,
archival gelatin-silver print, © Sylvia Plachy, courtesy of the artist
Back cover: Andreas Feininger, *On the Staten Island Ferry
Approaching Downtown Manhattan*, 1940, gelatin-silver print,
© Collection of The New-York Historical Society, New York

NATIONAL
ENDOWMENT
FOR THE ARTS

New York: Capital of Photography has been supported by grants from The
Morris S. and Florence H. Bender Foundation, the National Endowment for
the Arts, Lynne and Harold Honickman, and other generous donors.

Endowment support has been provided by the Alfred J. Grunebaum
Memorial Fund.

This catalogue has been published with the aid of a publications fund
established by the Dorot Foundation.

Guest Curator: Max Kozloff
Exhibition Coordinator: Karen Levitov
Project Assistant: Johanna Goldfeld
Manager of Curatorial Publications: Michael Sittenfeld
Manuscript Editor: Alexandra Bonfante-Warren
Exhibition Design: Daniel Bradley Kershaw
Executive Editor, Yale: Patricia Fidler
Manuscript Editor, Yale: Laura Jones Dooley
Production Manager, Yale: Mary Mayer
Photo Editor, Yale: John Long

Credits for all photography are included in captions, except for the following
credits related to copyrighted copy prints made for reproduction: Addison
Gallery of American Art, Phillips Academy, Andover, Massachusetts (pl. 64);
Ben Blackwell (pl. 57); D. James Dee (pls. 71, 73); J. Paul Getty Museum of
Art, Los Angeles (pl. 59); The Jewish Museum, New York, photograph by
Richard Goodbody (Cover; Introduction: fig. 5; Essay: fig. 14; pls. 24, 34, 46,
53, 56, 63, 65), photograph by David Heald (Essay: figs. 12, 13, 15, 23;
pls. 16, 19–21, 28, 35, 39, 40, 43–45, 48, 49, 52, 66, 67, 68, 70, 72, 75, 80),
photograph by John Parnell (Introduction: fig. 6); David Mathews (Essay: fig.
6; pl. 17); The Museum of Modern Art, New York (Essay: fig. 20; pls. 10, 37,
41, 47, 77); National Gallery of Canada, Ottawa (pl. 74).

Designed by Daphne Geismar
Set in Celeste and Futura type by Amy Storm
Printed in Italy by Mondadori

Library of Congress Cataloging-in-Publication Data
Kozloff, Max.
New York: capital of photography/Max Kozloff; with contributions by
Karen Levitov and Johanna Goldfeld.
      p.;   cm.
"Published in conjunction with the exhibition . . . organized by the Jewish
Museum, New York . . . April 28–September 2, 2002"—T.p. verso.
Includes index.
ISBN 0-300-09332-2 (cloth: alk. paper)—ISBN 0-300-09445-0 (pbk.: alk. paper)
1. Photography, Artistic—Exhibitions. 2. Photography—New York (State)—
New York—Exhibitions. 3. Jewish photographers—New York (State)—New
York—Exhibitions. 4. Street photography—New York (State)—New York—
Exhibitions. 5. New York (N.Y.)—Pictorial works—Exhibitions. I. Levitov,
Karen. II. Goldfeld, Johanna. III. Jewish Museum (New York, N.Y.). IV. Title.
TR645.N72 K68 2002
770'.9747'1—dc21
2001006947

A catalogue record for this book is available from the British Library.

The paper in this book meets the guidelines for permanence and
durability of the Committee on Production Guidelines for Book Longevity
of the Council on Library Resources.

10 9 8 7 6 5 4 3 2 1

Contents

Foreword

Photography, once it moved from the confines of the studio, thrived on the spontaneity of life on city streets. In the hands of great artists, the camera captured the unpredictability and vibrancy of urban populations. Among the most influential of twentieth-century photographers were those who made New York City their subject. *New York: Capital of Photography* explores the work of men and women who focused on the quotidian drama of their fellow urban dwellers.

The subject of this exhibition was brought to The Jewish Museum by writer and critic Max Kozloff. In many ways his recommendation to us was a gift, offering the museum an opportunity to work with him to provide a fresh new context for the work of photographers who have previously been included in many surveys of photography as it emerged in America. Yet the exhibition has been a complicated one to consider, bringing out the challenges and possibilities that are embraced by a museum such as ours—an art museum dealing with Jewish culture in a way that is meaningful for people of all cultural backgrounds. What is it about these photographs that relates to Jewish culture? *New York: Capital of Photography* explores how artist and subject affect each other in ways that illuminate the Jewish vantage, particularly in New York City throughout the twentieth century.

Both the limitations and the opportunities afforded by living in New York generated new avenues of professional activity for people entering the field of photography. The photographers' subject was changing before their eyes as it was shaped by the very immigrants and artists who were contributing to its evolution. The interaction of these photographers with the life of New York's streets is palpable—one imagines the artists absorbing the world around them.

Like other descendants of immigrants, many Jewish photographers felt an affinity toward those on the margins of society, which is revealed in their poignant, humanistic images. Indeed, these photographers have frequently been in the vanguard of socially conscious artists throughout the modern era. The photographs gathered here are not distant recordings of unfamiliar places but intimate portraits that draw the viewer into their world. These images often express compassion for their subjects and in many instances draw attention to the plight of the underprivileged.

This volume brings a fresh perspective to the body of work in the exhibition. Max Kozloff's wonderful essay offers a striking narrative of life in New York as seen through the eyes of its street photographers throughout the twentieth century. Expanding the traditional chronology of street photography to include its later permutations, Kozloff examines the symbiotic relationship between photography and the city across the decades. In the last section of his essay, Kozloff examines the sensibility of Jewish photographers who had successful careers in New York. Assistant Curator Karen Levitov's insightful introduction focuses on the photographic concepts at play at the beginning and end of the century. She suggests that the work of the photographers represented here can be viewed in light of interpretive strategies central to Jewish tradition. Both essays speak to the dynamism of New York as a city of astonishing contrasts and vitality, as seen in the captivating images in this catalogue.

Many thanks to everyone who contributed to the realization of this exhibition and publication, particularly the curatorial team of Kozloff and Levitov. They have been assisted by Michael Sittenfeld, Manager of Curatorial Publications, who brought insight and care to the creation of this handsome catalogue. Further thanks go to Ruth Beesch, Deputy Director of Program, for her oversight of the project and her many substantial contributions.

The funders of *New York: Capital of Photography* have been generous in their support, and we are immensely grateful. I wish to acknowledge the generous support provided by The Morris S. and Florence H. Bender Foundation, the National Endowment for the Arts, and Lynne and Harold Honickman. Endowment support has been provided by the Alfred J. Grunebaum Memorial Fund. This catalogue has been published with the aid of a publications fund established by the Dorot Foundation.

Everyone at The Jewish Museum has a role in the success of an exhibition—from those who help raise funds to those who ensure that the exhibition receives adequate publicity. I thank all of the staff members,

who, as always, show extraordinary dedication to the museum's mission.

I wish to express my appreciation to the members of the Board of Trustees for their constant support of projects that break new ground and question preconceived ideas. It is always a pleasure to work with them. And final thanks to The Jewish Museum's Photography Acquisitions Committee, chaired by Jack Stern. This group has inspired the museum's heightened interested in photography and made us particularly aware of the development of this art form in relation to the American Jewish experience.

As I write this foreword, New York City and the rest of the nation are recovering from the horrifying attacks on the World Trade Center and the Pentagon, an apocalyptic moment of tremendous loss of life. The deeply felt connections of New Yorkers to one another and to our city sustain us and contribute to our ability to find some balance again. To a great extent, it is pictures of the city's people in the aftermath of the recent catastrophic events that have shown the world New York's resilience. Perhaps the photographs in this catalogue will have a special resonance for readers who love the city for its remarkable and unshakable spirit.

JOAN ROSENBAUM
Helen Goldsmith Menschel Director
The Jewish Museum, New York

Acknowledgments

Among those whose assistance to this book has been most intimate, Alexandra Bonfante-Warren, my editor, has my deepest thanks. Her oversight of the writing was exacting throughout and helped me to avoid many errors.

For her essential role in every aspect of the exhibition and catalogue, I'm grateful to Karen Levitov, Assistant Curator at the Jewish Museum. Michael Sittenfeld, Manager of Curatorial Publications, and Johanna Goldfeld, Project Assistant, did outstanding work in making this project possible. I am most indebted to them. I am grateful, too, to my agent, Alison Bond, who provided much sound advice.

For stimulating discussions of issues related to the content of this book, I want to acknowledge Bob Shamis, Mel Rosenthal, Maria Morris Hambourg, Phil Lopate, William Klein, Walter Rosenblum, Howard Greenberg, Alan Trachtenberg, Morris Dickstein, Charles Traub, Morris Engel, George Gilbert, and Bonnie Yochelson.

Many people were most courteous and professional in making their photographic collections accessible to me. The tireless help of David Staton, at the Howard Greenberg Gallery, was memorable and extremely generous. Others who enabled me to track down valuable pictures include Stephen Daiter, Jan Ramirez, Julia Van Haaften, and Anne Tucker.

The absence from these pages of images by Diane Arbus, Roy DeCarava, and Robert Frank is not an oversight. They have contributed significantly to the history of New York photography. But Doon Arbus refused to allow publication of her mother's work, unless she could read the manuscript—and this was unacceptable. Messrs. Frank and DeCarava categorically refused permission to let their photography be published in this catalogue.

I would like to dedicate this book to the photographers who, with great magnitude, described and evoked New York in the twentieth century.

MAX KOZLOFF

The dynamism of *New York: Capital of Photography* is owed in great part to the insight, energy, and determination of its guest curator, Max Kozloff. I would like to thank him for his engaging essay and his selection of a remarkable group of photographs.

This exhibition could not have been realized without the support and encouragement of Joan Rosenbaum, the Helen Goldsmith Menschel Director of The Jewish Museum, and our Board of Trustees, in particular the Exhibition Committee, chaired by Axel Schupf and Francine Klagsbrun. We are grateful to those lenders, public and private, who welcomed the idea of the exhibition with enthusiasm and to the funders who made this exhibition possible.

Ruth Beesch, Deputy Director for Program, was integral to this project from its inception and played a vital role throughout its development. Michael Sittenfeld, Manager of Curatorial Publications, dedicated himself to every aspect of the catalogue, which benefited greatly from his expertise. Johanna Goldfeld, Project Assistant, contributed in crucial and invaluable ways to the realization of the book and exhibition and wrote the informative biographies for this catalogue. I also greatly appreciate the advice and suggestions of my husband, Tom O'Brien, and of Norman L. Kleeblatt, the Susan and Elihu Rose Curator of Fine Arts at The Jewish Museum.

Numerous other colleagues at the museum and their respective staffs provided their expertise and advice, particularly Susan Spencer Crowe, Program Funding Manager; Debbie Schwab Dorfman, Director of Merchandising; Tom Dougherty, Deputy Director for Finance and Administration; Jeffrey Fischer, former Director of Development; Jody Heher, Coordinator of Exhibitions; Al Lazarte, Director of Operations; Nancy McGary, Director of Collections and Exhibitions; Linda Padawer, Director of Special Events; Grace Rapkin, Director of Marketing; Marcia Saft, Director of Visitor and Tourist Services; Anne Scher, Director of Communications; Aviva Weintraub, Director of Media and Public Relations; Stacey Zaleski, Merchandising Manager; and Carole Zawatsky, Director of Education.

My appreciation goes to Alexandra Bonfante-Warren, who edited the catalogue with intelligence and perception. Many thanks also to Cara Zwerling, Publications Intern, who volunteered her time and energy to the details of this catalogue, and to Ellen R. Feldman for her expert proofreading of the manuscript. I am grateful to Patricia Fidler, Mary Mayer, Laura Jones Dooley, and John Long at Yale University Press for their enthusiastic efforts on behalf of the catalogue. The graceful design of the catalogue was created by Daphne Geismar. Last, I wish to thank Dan Kershaw for his sensitive design of the installation and Sue Koch for her elegant design of the exhibition graphics.

KAREN LEVITOV
Assistant Curator
The Jewish Museum, New York

Donors to the Exhibition

New York: Capital of Photography has been supported by grants from The Morris S. and Florence H. Bender Foundation, the National Endowment for the Arts, Lynne and Harold Honickman, and other generous donors.

Endowment support has been provided by the Alfred J. Grunebaum Memorial Fund.

This catalogue has been published with the aid of a publications fund established by the Dorot Foundation.

Lenders to the Exhibition

Addison Gallery of American Art, Phillips Academy, Andover, Massachusetts
Lisa Ades, New York
Amon Carter Museum, Fort Worth, Texas
Deborah Bell, New York
Center for Creative Photography, Tucson, Arizona
Eli Consilvio, New York
Keith de Lellis Gallery, New York
Dreyfus Corporation, New York
George Eastman House, Rochester, New York
Larry Fink, Martin's Creek, Pennsylvania
Fogg Art Museum, Harvard University Art Museums, Cambridge, Massachusetts
J. Paul Getty Museum, Los Angeles
Ralph Gibson, New York
George Gilbert, Riverdale, New York
Howard Greenberg Gallery, New York
Marvin Heiferman, New York
International Center of Photography, New York
Jeff Jacobson, Jersey City, New Jersey
The Jewish Museum, New York
Kimmel Cohn Photography Arts, New York
Laurence Miller Gallery, New York
Magnum Photos, Inc., New York
Mary Ellen Mark, New York
Matthew Marks Gallery, New York
Jeff Mermelstein, New York
The Metropolitan Museum of Art, New York
Museum of Fine Arts, Boston
The Museum of Fine Arts, Houston
The Museum of Modern Art, New York
Museum of the City of New York
National Archives, Washington, D.C.
The New-York Historical Society, New York
New York Public Library, New York
Ruth Orkin Photo Archive, New York
Sylvia Plachy, Woodhaven, New York
Private Collection
Walter Rosenblum, Long Island City, New York
Mel Rosenthal, New York
San Francisco Museum of Modern Art, San Francisco
Barry Singer Gallery, Petaluma, California
Syracuse University Library, Syracuse, New York
Sandra Weiner, New York
Whitney Museum of American Art, New York

Picturing the Streets of New York

KAREN LEVITOV

Introduction

For street photographers, New York is a teeming urbanscape filled with the lives of its diverse inhabitants—from Italian-American revelers at the San Gennaro festival on Mulberry Street to African-American teens on Harlem sidewalks to Jewish merchants on the Lower East Side. These photographers have pictured New York not as a city of monuments but as a dynamic metropolis of distinctive neighborhoods, constantly in flux. For *New York: Capital of Photography*, guest curator Max Kozloff has selected images by both famous and lesser-known street photographers, particularly members of the so-called New York School from the 1930s to the 1960s, most of them Jewish, and their predecessors and successors. These images had a tremendous impact on the perception of life in New York throughout the twentieth century. From Lewis Hine's 1905 picture of recent immigrants at Ellis Island to Nan Goldin's portraits of her friends over the past thirty years, these photographs disclose the true vitality of New York. At a time when avant-garde artists were exploring abstraction, street photographers captured the multiplicity of New York through its people and their communities.

In his memoir *A Walker in the City* (1951), Alfred Kazin recalls his youth in New York in the 1930s through the fragmentary experiences of walking— where scenes and people change from step to step and block to block. In describing the elevated subway tracks, the pushcarts loaded with herring and pickles, and a distant ferry starting out from the Battery, Kazin reflects on the familiarity of his working-class Jewish neighborhood in Brooklyn and observes that "everything just out of Brownsville was always 'the city.'"[1] In spite of the consolidation of the five boroughs— Brooklyn, the Bronx, Manhattan, Queens, and Staten Island—into one city, communities within each borough, such as the Brownsville of Kazin's boyhood, continued (and still continue) to affirm their individual identities. Yet the people like Kazin who move between neighborhoods are affected and transformed by the dynamic life they encounter, and these interactions are what give the city its energy.

Kazin's memories are in many ways similar to the subjects of street photographers. His meandering glimpses of the city reveal a polyglot urban population, a place where wealth and poverty, change and tradi-

Anonymous, *"Before and After: Saving Heartaches with a Dash of Powder and a Comely Skirt,"* 1926. Ludmila K. Foxlee Papers, National Park Service Collection, Statue of Liberty National Monument, Ellis Island Immigration Museum. Gift of Joyce Pratt

tion are defined by their smells, sounds, and appearances. This vigorous existence was the New York that intrigued the scores of street photographers who attempted to capture the changing face of the city throughout the twentieth century. Kazin's recollections remind us that these photographs are not just static shots of time past but affirmations of lives lived, full of incident and motion.

Circa 1900: Influx, Immigration, and the Fixed Image

The modern photographer emerged at a time of intense change in New York's geographic, ethnographic, and visual identity. In the aftermath of the consolidation of the five boroughs in 1898, the 1900 census revealed a population of nearly three and a half million people. This was a bustling metropolis of people from all corners of the world, with German, Irish, and Italian immigrants making up a substantial portion. A second wave of immigration was bringing in newcomers from Eastern Europe as well as an influx of African-American laborers from rural communities in the South. The new inhabitants helped to shape the particular identities of New York's neighborhoods — Chinese and Italian immigrants settled primarily

in lower Manhattan, a large percentage of the African-American population moved to Harlem after the race riots of 1900, and Jewish immigrants lived first in the Lower East Side and later in Harlem, the Bronx, and parts of Brooklyn. Diverse and often separate, the ethnic communities were nevertheless integral to the formation of New York as we know it today.

At the turn of the twentieth century, photography became accessible to a greater number of people, thanks to the development of smaller cameras, simplified technology, and less expensive processing. And pictures were in great demand with the public. While art photography was gaining stature — notably through Alfred Stieglitz, who in 1903 founded the art photography journal *Camera Work* and in 1907 the 291 gallery of the Photo-Secession — most photography was used for recording facts. Descriptive photography took several forms, including portraiture, photojournalism, criminal identification, anthropological photography, and social documentation. For newly arrived immigrants, commercial photography studios provided affordable mementos: portrait photographs were made into postcards to send back to relatives in the old country with letters proclaiming high hopes for success in the land of opportunity. But the realities of immigrant life were not always the same as the expectations, as observed by an Italian immigrant: "I came to America because I heard the streets were paved with gold. When I got here, I found out three things: first, the streets weren't paved with gold; second, they weren't paved at all; and third, I was expected to pave them."[2]

As they entered the United States, immigrants of all ancestries came into contact with photography. Beginning in 1892, the majority came through New York's harbor at Ellis Island. Pictures of newly arrived immigrants served as news, as propaganda, and as official documents. A 1926 article published a before-and-after photograph of an immigrant mother and child who had been "transformed" through clothing into modern American citizens for a reunion with the woman's husband after many years (fig. 1). The article focused on a social worker on Ellis Island who took it upon herself to save "Heartaches with a Dash of Powder and a Comely Skirt." Immigrants were also photographed during health inspections that determined their eligibility to become United States citizens (fig. 2). In addition to their function as historical documents, the photographs taken on Ellis Island revealed the exoticism of the subjects to established citizens, defining the new immigrants as "different." Prejudice and fears over these visible differences haunted Italians, Roma, Jews, and Eastern European immigrants, as well as Africans, Asians, and Pacific and Caribbean islanders.

Public apprehension centered around not just contagious disease but also poor moral character, both thought to be visible on the body. According to nineteenth-century science, small hands indicated a penchant for crime, an attached earlobe or a widely separated big toe betrayed a tendency toward degenerate behavior, and a low forehead revealed feeblemindedness. Physiognomic findings of this kind served as grounds for deporting immigrants. Adherents of physiognomy believed that photography was uniquely able to capture the telltale traits of moral degeneracy. In 1883, the Frenchman Alphonse Bertillon devised a system of cataloguing photographs of criminals accompanied by measurements of their ears and skulls for police files, while the Englishman Francis Galton attempted to identify types of criminals based on composite photographs of pickpockets or burglars. Later, anthropologists and colonial explorers adapted these systems to document their observations of people in indigenous societies. This anthropometric photography promoted stereotyping of individuals or groups based on cultural myths of the time. Even into the twentieth century, the belief that photography could demonstrate the difference between so-called advanced and inferior peoples persisted. This notion appears in sources as diverse as Edward Curtis's twenty-volume collection of photographs that he began publishing in 1907 and that documented in an aestheticized style what he considered the dying race of Native Americans, and Nazi filmmaker Leni Riefenstahl's famous photographs of German athletes in the 1936 Olympics highlighting their "ideal" Aryan features as proof of their physical and racial superiority.

In spite of this sometimes uncomfortable history, photography is also renowned for its role as a positive tool in social activism, as exemplified in the pioneering work of Jacob Riis. His illustrated book *How the Other Half Lives* (1890) opened the eyes of middle- and upper-middle-class citizens to the squalor in which so many New Yorkers lived. Riis and his assistants surprised his subjects with the explosive flash of magnesium powder that illuminated their dim and often crowded homes, and even sent some jumping out of windows fearing a gun had been fired. Although Riis's writings reveal an ethnic prejudice toward some of his subjects, the

FIG. 2
Anonymous, *Physical Examination, Ellis Island*, c. 1895.
Gelatin-silver print, 8 x 10 in. (20.3 x 25.4 cm).
National Park Service Collection, Statue of Liberty
National Monument

FIG. 3
Lewis Hine (1874–1940), *Ellis Island (Children on Playground)*,
c. 1915. Gelatin-silver print, 4¹¹/₁₆ x 6³/₄ in. (11.9 x 17 cm).
George Eastman House, Rochester, New York. Gift of the Photo
League, New York: ex-collection Lewis Wickes Hine

photographs nevertheless exposed the dreadful living
conditions on the Lower East Side and served as a
document for social reformers to take action against
the appalling conditions.

Just as effective in rallying social awareness, and yet
more empathetic, were Lewis Hine's photographs motivated by the teachings of the Ethical Culture School
in New York. The school's ideology inspired students such as Hine to use photography as a tool for
assailing prejudice against immigrants from Eastern
and Southern Europe. Hine's Ellis Island photographs
portray people as individuals rather than as generic
and interchangeable subjects from immigrant countries
(fig. 3). Riis and Hine were precursors of the scores
of socially conscious photographers, especially those
who worked for the government during the Depression, documenting poor farm and urban conditions for
the Works Progress Administration and the Farm
Securities Administration. Most of the photographers
represented in this volume were either immigrants
or first- or second-generation citizens themselves; their
subjects were also largely newer immigrants and
others on the margins of established society. The social-
documentary tradition of street photographers encouraged them to individualize rather than categorize
their subjects.

Jewish Photographers, Jewish Interpretations

Max Kozloff's essay in this catalogue illuminates the historical and social context of street photography and, in the last section, examines the nature of the work of Jewish photographers in New York. Indeed, of the hundreds of professional photographers in New York throughout the twentieth century, an overwhelming number were Jewish. With the international success of such photographers as Stieglitz, Helen Levitt, Weegee, Robert Frank, and Diane Arbus, a question arises: why were so many of these photographers Jewish and what significance does that have for the way we now view twentieth-century New York? As one of the few trades Jews in nineteenth-century Europe were permitted to practice, photography was an immediate draw for Jewish immigrants in the United States. Whereas early Jewish tradesmen supplied film, paper, and chemicals to professional photographers, later generations of Jews became photojournalists and artists themselves. A great number also became filmmakers, as shown by the number of photographers in this exhibition who also created films.

The largest wave of Jewish immigrants came to the United States from Eastern Europe between 1881 and 1924, and by 1918 the United States had the largest Jewish population in the world. Like other recent immigrants, Jews tended to settle in urban areas densely populated with others of the same ancestry. The Jewish residents of the Lower East Side lived in tiny tenement apartments, built cheaply and quickly with small, poorly lit rooms. Sanitation was inadequate and disease rampant. In spite of these hardships, however, Jewish culture flourished. Numerous synagogues were built, Yiddish theater companies and literary societies thrived, and social and mutual-aid groups came into being. Jewish immigrants opened shops and restaurants, while many earned their living through the garment industry. Alongside all of these professions, the Jewish photographer flourished, too.

Still, Jewish photographers of the early and mid-twentieth century often did not define themselves as such. At a time when anti-Semitism was commonplace and post–World War I society was increasingly secular, many people privileged their professional identity over their religious or ethnic heritage. In addition, Jewish photographers tended to roam, covering the streets from Harlem to the Bowery and from the Bronx to Coney Island with equal empathy toward their Jewish and non-Jewish subjects. In light of the

pressure to assimilate and the photographers' wide-ranging subject matter, how might we think about the relation of their ethnicities to their images? If some aspect of Jewishness is revealed in these pictures, it is perhaps a Jewishness not of subject but of interpretation. In contrast to the early notions of photographic objectivity, an alternative approach might focus on the cumulative interpretative strategies that are part of Jewish tradition. Just as the pages of the Talmud offer successive, sometimes conflicting, commentaries, perhaps photographs do so as well, their meaning enhanced by layers of interpretation based on the biography of the artist, knowledge of the subjects, and an understanding of the politics and events of the moment. The many possible dimensions thus enliven historical images with renewed relevance and vivacity, and provide an ever-richer context.

For many Jewish photographers of the twentieth century, the streets were texts offering multiple readings, their denizens people with complex identities. For contemporary viewers, photographs may open themselves to various interpretations. French critic Roland Barthes, for example, wrote that photography is about death—about the preservation of a moment that has disappeared into the past.[3] Considered in this light, perhaps a Jewish mode of interpretation brings photographs to life, or at least illuminates their multiple meanings. As the scholar Laura Levitt has written in reference to Jewish family albums—but her insights are applicable to all family albums—photographs provide access to the moment of their creation and therefore provide proof of existence in the face of loss.[4] In other words, the subjects of photographs are overshadowed by the photographs' function as documents from the past, and by looking at them again, we add new layers of meaning.

Circa 2000: Roots, Routes, and Reinterpretation

Henri Cartier-Bresson, famously, coined the term "the decisive moment"—the exact fraction of a second when the most artful or interesting of what passes in front of the camera's lens is caught on film. But what about the moments previous and to come? The notion of a "decisive moment" produces a single frame, a single form, and perhaps a single meaning. All of the events before and immediately after the photograph do not appear. In order to reanimate the subject of photography, it is worth considering routes as well as roots as alternative means to interpret past masterpieces.[5] In other words, although the identities of the photographer and subject are significant, it is also useful to think about the successive layers of meaning brought to the picture by the viewer, the context in which the picture is presented, and the changing views of history. A consideration of the meandering pathways of interpretation parallels the liveliness and animation of Alfred Kazin's strolls though Brownsville and his surrounding neighborhoods.

This exhibition provides a new context in which to view twentieth-century images of New York and thereby offers viewers the opportunity to ask what

these pictures might have meant when they were taken and what they might mean now. Consider the work of contemporary artists who remain fascinated by historical photographs. Conceptual artists Sherrie Levine and Vik Muniz, for instance, give new meaning to past masterpieces by challenging—and indeed multiplying—the definitions of photography. Levine's *Untitled (After Walker Evans) #2*, of 1981 (fig. 4), and Muniz's *Steerage (After Alfred Stieglitz)*, of 2000 (fig. 5), both appropriate historical photographs by artists in *New York: Capital of Photography* but imbue these works with very different connotations. Sherrie Levine's rephotographing of Evans's picture displaces the notion of white male artistic genius by substituting a Jewish woman as the artist. In formal terms, the photograph is the same, but its implications have been questioned—a contextual interpretation has been added to the formal composition. In Levine's picture, a sense of time has replaced timing. Rather than a decisive moment, we have layers of different times: that of the original photograph, that of Levine's rephotography, and that of the viewer's engagement with the picture. Contemporary Brazilian artist Vik Muniz re-creates Stieglitz's famous 1907 photograph *The Steerage* (fig. 6), which portrays the fluid movement of immigrant arrival or departure. Muniz redesigns the formal elements of the image by drawing the composition with chocolate syrup, which he then photographs, creating another picture that appears almost the same as the first, but not quite. Muniz's work provides another way of thinking about Stieglitz's art as it plays with notions of media, time, perception, illusion, and photographic reality. In Levine's and Muniz's appropriated photographs, supplementary meanings and new interpretations encourage a new vision of historical photography.

New York: Capital of Photography offers a revealing look at the past century as it contributes to the continuous reinterpretation of extraordinary images. The photographs in this exhibition depict slices of life from different times, places, and vantage points and portray the variety and texture of an urban life that thrives because of the city's people. The city itself becomes a protagonist that constantly interacts with those who walk its streets. Engaging with the city and its people, New York photographers created a world of iconic images that continue to reverberate into the twenty-first century.

FIG. 5

Vik Muniz (Brazilian, b. 1961), *The Steerage (After Alfred Stieglitz)*, 2000. From *Pictures of Chocolate* series. Cibachrome, 40 x 30 in. (101.6 x 76.2 cm). The Jewish Museum, New York. Gift of Melva Bucksbaum, 2000-74. © Vik Muniz/Licensed by VAGA, New York

FIG. 6

Alfred Stieglitz (1864–1946), *The Steerage*, 1907. Photogravure, 13⁷/₁₆ x 10¹/₈ in. (35.4 x 25.7 cm). The Jewish Museum, New York. Museum purchase; Mr. and Mrs. George Jaffin Fund, 2000-6

Notes

1 Alfred Kazin, *A Walker in the City* (New York: Harcourt Brace, 1951), 5–6.

2 Quoted in Ivan Chermayeff, Fred Wasserman, and Mary J. Shapiro, *Ellis Island: An Illustrated History of the Immigrant Experience* (New York: Macmillan, 1991), 56. For additional information on photography and immigration, see the insightful essays by Vicki Goldberg and Arthur Ollman in *A Nation of Strangers*, exh. cat. (San Diego: Museum of Photographic Arts, 1995).

3 Roland Barthes, *Camera Lucida: Reflections on Photography*, trans. Richard Howard (New York: Hill and Wang, 1981), 78–79.

4 Laura S. Levitt, "Photographing American Jews: Identifying American Jewish Life," in *Mapping Jewish Identities: New Perspectives on Jewish Studies*, ed. Laurence J. Silberstein (New York: New York University Press, 2000), 66.

5 Paul Gilroy, *The Black Atlantic: Modernity and Double Consciousness* (Cambridge, Mass.: Harvard University Press, 1993), 15–19.

NEW YORK CAPITAL OF PHOTOGRAPHY

MAX KOZLOFF

The Three New Yorks

New York has probably drawn more attention from the camera than any other city in the world. Yet the city, despite its magnetism, is hard to grasp. It's too big for anyone to take its measure, except at a remote distance, which reduces the city to a collection of famous spires. And it shuffles, obliterates, and reconnects its appearances with such haste that it disorients the viewer at closer hand. We quickly appreciate which version of New York is being looked at: the visible citadel of collective power, or the disjointed patchwork of neighborhoods, spasmodically reassembled as if by local powers. What starts as a choice by the photographer about frame and topic carries with it, along with any other meanings, a political implication.

Jane Jacobs makes a broad distinction between "car people," who tend to generalize and synthesize their experience of the city, and "foot people," who value a much slower and more particular contact with the urban place. Among New York photographers who could be called "foot people," Jews figured in large number. The effect of their ethnic sensibility upon their photographic vantage is one of the themes pursued in this book, particularly in the later chapters.

How often has the metropolis been treated as a setting of discordant peoples in volatile re-creation of new social boundaries? Long before it took place elsewhere, ethnic-racial displacement churned through New York precincts, with more energy, flair, and conflict. This city of provocations on all fronts was necessarily photographed from contending points of view. "A famously hard environment," writes Phillip Lopate, "New York inspires both stoic pride and chagrin."[1] Its prodigious scale, its density of aspects, and its inexhaustible supply of events, all these defied even as they encouraged the photographer's eye. That these protean features were in addition affected by tensions between the host culture and minority cultures, and across class strata, ensured a body of images at considerable variance from one another.

As such variance was historical and social, it also showed itself to be ideological. In quick enough order it became aesthetic as well. The multiple realities of New York were argued in all media, and with much heat. But in photography, the process of argument was carried through the act of witness. A city is of course unknowable on the basis of only a limited

FIG. 1

Byron Company (1892–1942), *T. E. Fitzgerald Bar*, 1912.
Gelatin-silver print, 14 x 19¼ in. (35.6 x 48.9 cm).
Museum of the City of New York, Byron Collection, 93.1.1.17847

visual encounter. With their repeated contacts, their principle of selection, and the development of urban types, photographers became eloquent in sustaining long-term ideas about New York.

It's not just that the image describes, it also draws out certain features, to which later photographers respond in kind. As it builds, this dialogue becomes an imaginative continuum that attributes notions of worth and consequence to even a humble human settlement. It would be fair to call these notions the beginning of myths. Even when myths are partially grounded on fact, they uphold the dream a people has of itself. As New York was never a humble place, its myth could hardly be modest.

For it mattered that Americans a hundred years ago already considered the place the central metropolis of the age, treatable as an icon of the century to come. By 1898, the four other boroughs had been officially added to the metropolitan area of Manhattan, confirming it as the largest city in the United States. The next year, a parade was held on Fifth Avenue for Admiral Dewey, victor at Manila Bay. Many photographs show the Dewey Arch, a plaster Beaux Arts marvel, which climaxed the march at Twenty-third Street and Fifth Avenue. What awaited this site of imperial triumphs in the future was obviously of even greater magnitude than its considerable past.

By World War I, such a perception was worked out in three distinct and memorable photographic programs. One accomplished a material inventory of streets, interiors, and milieux; another evoked a poetic mood, simultaneously anxious and heroic; and the third was dedicated to the most vital issues of social justice.

"It is becoming clear that our ever changing, ever modern metropolis is in fact an older city, with ancient byways worn by the passage of generations."[2] E. L. Doctorow was referring to the familiar look of the New York infrastructure in early 1900s photographs from the Byron Company (1892–1942). Joseph Byron, the firm's founder, specialized in photographing the stage, and the appearance of the Victorian theater affected his outdoor as well as indoor tableaux of New York life. He treated people as a huge cast of characters, their roles demarcated, while the accoutrements of urban life around them have the air of props. Everything is for show in a repertoire of images that extends from the Bowery to the public parks and skating ponds, from tenements to business offices, from dock repair to sporting events, from flophouses to the salons and mansions of the very rich. Regardless of the social class represented, formality of behavior, and with it a distinct self-consciousness, are the order of the day. Even when the tripod-mounted camera ventured to observe unposed activities on the streets, the view assumed them to be veritable demonstrations of themselves. The candidness of the shot introduced only a slight rustle in what was still meant to be a presentable flow.

All the better to deliver the concrete information for which the firm was known. Proficiency in interior lighting was a Byron hallmark, one more artifice that contributed to the exposition of artifacts. As befits the output of a commercial studio, satisfying a business market, and later, as a historical archive appropriately donated to the Museum of the City of New York, these images emphasize plush textures, hard edges, and material amplitude. One can tell precisely what kind of Persian carpet decorated Mrs. So-and-So's drawing room in 1904. Rooms are described as, above all, enclosures for things, and if the room is populated, it's by a gallery of human specimens. Together, they betray the unconvincing exactitude of dioramas. Simply as images, Byron photographs have about

them a kind of prolix and stuffy magnificence. In that, they also develop a particular sociology.

These picture makers leave the viewer in no doubt of the competence and purpose of a society that they treat everywhere with a civic pride. As to what motivated that pride, the key to it is found in approximately a hundred matter-of-fact photographs they took of bank vaults. Manhattan, which the elite of Brooklyn condescended to as having a vulgarian and ostentatious culture, was the repository of wealth, an unparalleled nexus of cash. Services, amusements, and fine clothes were described as goods that the bourgeoisie, its funds nesting in those vaults, simply took for granted. In painting, William Glackens and George Bellows picked up the theme of the fashionable boulevards, with a conspicuous dash. In literature, we have Theodore Dreiser's vivid descriptions of the Broadway theater district, an ironic bouquet inserted in the tragic tale *Sister Carrie.*

The complacency of the bourgeois perspective, which the Byrons shared, led them to photograph manual workers, beggars, and ethnic groups as colorful elements within the city fabric. As photographers, they liked the motley effect of the spectacle such people provided. In *T. E. Fitzgerald Bar* (fig. 1), of 1912, a man who looks as if he were a Latino or Italian meat packer has wandered into a middle-class saloon, where the much-better-dressed clientele appears to accept him or at least to ignore him. Some visiting Native Americans, in full-feathered regalia (including tepees!) pose on the roof of the Hotel McAlpin, in 1913 (pl. 1). We could imagine this episode, in other photographic hands, as a study in displacement or a meditation on the frontier past. Here, apparently, the incongruous presence of these "outsiders" is intended as a humorous occasion. However, the Byrons also rendered the upper classes as "others," with a curiosity that we might mistake as droll were it not for the respect lavished on their possessions. On the basis of the images alone, from which all obscuring shadow has been banned, an auctioneer would have no trouble assessing the value of each item.

In fact, the camera eye of the Byron studio was an appraising eye, and its method of survey was accumulative. We would expect neither a synthetic nor an analytic approach from a studio that practiced with such a linear attention to the city, and in fact facades, neighborhoods, scenarios, one by one, accrete into an opulent catalogue of miscellany. Consult it for the look of Belle Époque streets, courtesy of scrutinies gathered in depth, but do not expect it to have a reflective spirit. A democratic ethos, of sorts, does manifest itself in the tendency to regard all prospects of small or larger import with the same, expensive precision. In this wide-angle spectrum of community genre, people exist only as passersby or types—for their actual lot in life is unexamined. Here was a photographic campaign that noticed people's disparities of fortune but drew no inferences from them. The leveling effect of the Byron catalogue results only from the aim to include everything on the horizon. We are left with a record that is nonjudgmental, good-natured, urbane, and philistine.

All this, in retrospect, had a reassuring function. "The urban photographic tradition," according to Peter Bacon Hales, "had been born out of a tremendous cultural need, the need for an essentially agrarian society to come to terms with the process of industrialization . . . which was . . . threatening the myths which sustained and defined the culture."[3] When we refer to the Byron archive, we see places that are quite populous, but never unsightly with congestion, except for the (mostly Jewish and Sicilian) Lower East Side (pl. 2). New York's rank as a metropolis is simultaneously a given fact and understated. Only the town's transportation network—specifically, its elevated trains—suggests a grandeur of scale, though even there, industrialization does not make its presence known. The hinterland could take comfort in this vision, little realizing how unstable was the world it portrayed.

In truth, the Byron craftsmen did not point out that New York was an international depot, an unprecedented hub of trade, a world-class port; that its skyline, as a result of these assets crowded into narrow quarters, was reaching astonishing heights; or that its people had never heard of the status quo. It fell to a small group of very different photographers to meditate on this state of affairs, inflecting the history of their medium as they did so. They were not content to *observe* the culture around them but wanted to make a new culture. Joseph Byron, born in Nottingham, England, in 1847, had the outlook of an artisan with entrepreneurial talents. Alfred Stieglitz (1864–1946), who came from a wealthy German-Jewish family in Hoboken, New Jersey, was a man of independent means who announced himself as a cosmopolitan aesthete and a messiah of photography as a fine art.

His circle (known as the Photo-Secession) numbered, among others, Alvin Langdon Coburn (1882–1966), Edward Steichen (1879–1973), and Karl Struss (1886–1981). As Stieglitz's bohemian protégés,

and, at the same time, as his competitors, they exhibited their pictures in international shows and published in *Camera Work* (1903–17), a deluxe magazine with a small circulation, run by Stieglitz to promote an ideal of artistic freedom. That is, the photographer's subjectivity must be just as free an agent in interpreting the visible world as, say, the industrialist's will in controlling productive forces.

Among so many mandarins, Stieglitz was the alpha male. They shared a loyalty to Walt Whitman's apostolic vision of America's grandeur, if not his egalitarian ethos. For their subject, they chose New York's growth, manifested through an efflorescence of towers just then rising before their very eyes. In their intellectual temperament, they were Symbolists, devoted to "a higher reality." In their artistic sympathies, they were Tonalists, indebted to Camille Corot, James McNeill Whistler, and George Inness (whose late work at Montclair, New Jersey, is a direct precedent of Steichen's landscapes). So, the first thing to notice when looking at the work of the Photo-Secessionists is its paradox: a eulogy to the most up-to-date urban forms visualized through a pastoral style.

This "Pictorialism" acted as a filter that transformed a drab urbanscape—at least critics thought it drab, even ugly—into picturesque schemata. The filtered effect was realized through muted shades and half-lit zones, although Steichen also used a soft-focus lens to achieve his poetic goal. A tremulous, waning, crepuscular light affects this pictorial vision of the ultramodern. It was a sign of their precious taste that the Pictorialists executed their imagery through the exquisite modulations made available by platinum prints. They added simplicity to refinement through a compositional sense, influenced by Japanese woodcuts, that flattened the volumes of motifs, rendering them as dark silhouettes in a twilight sky. The subject existed for them as something desired, but not actually contacted.

Had the Stieglitz group confined its picture taking to natural scenes, the characteristic sense of time suspended would suggest an unexceptional reverie. But when the subjects are buildings with names like Morgan Guarantee Trust and Singer, the discord between a reflective, ageless mood and recent construction draws attention to itself. These photographers identified themselves with "progress," which they correctly divined as the spirit that moved through the financial district. It was the chief subject worthy of being evoked by their "genius," a word they often applied to their own project. At the same time, they were antimaterialists who held in contempt the rapacity of Wall Street's behavior in the market. This ethical aversion subtly worked itself into the production of the Pictorialist photographers and skewed its otherwise affirmative spirit.

Nevertheless, they were good artists—despite their self-approval; if anything, their ambivalence about New York made their work more tense and expressive. Rather than producing cityscapes, for instance, they created an elusive genre of their own. Peter Conrad criticizes the Pictorialists for a "tricky smudging of sight," "a . . . mis-seeing of New York."4 But the escapist aesthetic he disparages had its reasons.

The Stieglitz group was enthralled by the phenomenal vagaries of atmosphere, which they used to cast a veil over subjects that were potentially alarming. In low visibility, and exposed to chilly weather, they conjured an idealized New York. Some of Karl Struss's vistas nevertheless betray the solitude of one who looks across almost empty streets, in a communion that is also apprehensive. In *Trolley, Horse-drawn Vehicle & El., N.Y.C.* (pl. 3), of 1911, Herald Square, a hectic crossroads with streetcars, seems only to murmur in a pall of light. Struss's perspective up West Forty-second Street, culminating in four shockingly outsized stacks of a liner, is an anxious vision (pl. 4). Intermittently, he notes that the creaturely life of the New Yorkers was dwarfed by these ominous and crushing structures.

Yet, as mist shrouds or night falls, the feeling the Stieglitz group most often transmitted is laudatory. If anything, their ship comes in to a land of pleasure. Alvin Langdon Coburn affirmed the city's greeting: "As I steamed up New York's harbor . . . on the liner that brought me home from abroad I felt the kinship of the mind that could produce those magnificent monsters . . . the suspension bridges, with that of the photographer of the new School . . . [who] blends chemistry and optics in such a way as to produce a lasting impression of a beautiful fragment of nature."5 It was elegant of Coburn to liken a conception of engineering to his feeling for nature. In fact, his sentiments chimed with those in books that toasted the gossamer and twinkling enchantment of the city's nocturnal life as something that came with the weather. Coburn had first discovered those indistinct visual seductions in London, and he translated them to Broadway in the years 1909 and 1910.

In this act of superimposing a European sensibility upon his photography of New York, Coburn was also legitimating the American place with accents of an old-world culture. Already, a visit to the Grand

Canyon had suggested to him that our natural wonders were prototypes for our urban pinnacles. Now, he placed a more recent past of European monuments in relation to the present, apparently to salute the monumental New York future. By a curious twist, however, this relation seems to have been inverted in his imagery—and in that of his like-minded colleagues.

Not only does the pictorial veil obscure the forms of the tower and other "monsters," it effects an emotional distance from them as well. There's more than a hint of nostalgia in this distance, for the disembodied banks and buildings appear to recede in time, as if, together, they comprise a profile that will have to be remembered. The scrim through which they're perceived acts as the gauze of memory. Though animated by steam and smoke, the Lower Manhattan of Stieglitz's *City of Ambition* (pl. 5), of 1910, has a spectral quality that does not augur confidence in the scene to come. His was a metaphorical treatment of a subject that he elsewhere observed in literal terms: the sight of new construction, not yet finished, lording it over the smaller and older buildings of the street. Even when Coburn handles the topic of the city creating itself, as he did in *The Tunnel Builders* (pl. 6), of 1908, the design may be heroic, but there's no interest in the physical labor itself, and the tone is retrospective.

It's hard to escape the impression that the very present they wanted to herald was problematic for these artists. In visualizing the mechanical marvels of downtown, everywhere sprouting up among them, the Stieglitz group used such techniques as the application of gum-bichromate to their prints, which emphasized their handiwork ethos and also their backward glance. It's true that they had not yet found a visual language expressive of the technological moment, but then neither had the skyscrapers. Their symbolism of American power and the technology that sustained it were radically out of joint with each other. The tallest edifice of its time, Cass Gilbert's Woolworth Building, which opened in 1913, is a showcase of Gothic revivalism. Lacking a culture of its own, corporate capitalism adopted the trappings of traditional European high culture. As it happened, this development occurred at the dawn of Cubism, the revolution Stieglitz was gradually to present at 291, his gallery.

New York Pictorialism is a style suffused with misgivings. Some of these the artists could not acknowledge because they posed a threat to their identity, to the group's investment in a spiritualist consciousness that they were aware American society as a whole had left behind. At the same time, these photographers' stake in their subject was clairvoyant. To gain an idea of their prescience, read Lewis Mumford, from "The Myth of the Megalopolis": "By a process of substitution and forced growth, mechanical processes had supplanted organic processes . . . and the total result was to displace living forms and to encourage only those human needs and desires that could be profitably attached to the productive mechanism."[6] No wonder, then, that the Pictorialists hesitated before such a prospect, maybe because of a delicacy of feeling or a failure of nerve, but certainly with a tremor of vision that was exquisite.

As a powerhouse on a phenomenal rise, and as a national symbol, New York had an identity problem. For many Europeans, twentieth-century Manhattan epitomized the America of their dreams, the signature metropolis of the New World. From the vantage of Middle America, though, the island often looked like a foreign enclave. As the United States broadened westward into regions without recorded histories, one retroactive effect was to intensify New York's history as a Euro-Atlantic outpost of styles, cultures, and ideals. Certainly, by the late nineteenth century it had a foreign character, polyglot beyond compare. This was embodied by an inflow of poor Southern and Eastern European immigrants speaking a babel of tongues. Such were their numbers that the old processing center, Castle Garden, had been shut down by the 1890s, to be replaced by a new, larger port of entry, Ellis Island, in New York Harbor. More than ten million people—the figures vary—passed through there between 1903 and 1913. To Henry James, the newcomers were a class of people who exerted an unattractive pressure upon the fondly remembered genteel New York of yore. A photograph of the teeming vista up Mulberry Street, vivacious to our eyes, must have affronted his (pl. 7). But to Lewis Hine (1874–1940), the arrival of these newcomers signaled an opening up, a portent of cultural enrichment, and a welcome test of American democratic values.

Consider, for example, Hine's *Climbing into America* (pl. 8) (sometimes titled *Climbing into the Land of Promise*), of 1905, in which a group of people at Ellis Island are about to exit up a staircase. Though some of them glance at him momentarily, in the blaze of his magnesium light, all are eager to get out of the hall. They had been physically cooped during a long voyage; on arrival, they had filed in lines past inspectors— the forms they brandish and the chalk marks on their baggage tell as much. They don't know who the photographer is, and they are strangers to one another as well, a fact revealed by their clashing national dress. The central figure is possibly Italian, the man beneath him, with his sheepskin hat, a likely Eastern European. Their boat has just come in from whatever misery or hardship compelled them to leave their countries of origin. They have passed tests for disease or other disabilities that could have sent them back. They are about to make, or try to make, an uncertain life for themselves in a fabled land. The space they are in just now is a bureaucratic space, a limbo between two epochs in their existence.

Lewis Hine reckons with this episode as a dramatic situation. He closes with his subjects at short range—and, simultaneously, catches their collective surge, which will take them rapidly off-frame. The photograph mixes the group portrait genre with a dynamic journalistic report. This fusion of genres makes his picture original, while his attentiveness to people as vital individuals gives it life. In spite of its positive, even aspirational motif—the ascension of stairs—Hine's tableau is a tense rather than a happy picture. It comprehends the gravity of the occasion, a pouring in of ethnic thousands who will irreversibly change New York's demographics (and that of the United States). Maybe he was unsure that we Americans deserved the compliment of their faith in us. A flux of agrarian and traditionalistic peoples was about to engage with our civic institutions . . . and with our notoriously exploitative capitalist system.

Hine took many other pictures of immigrants at Ellis Island. In these images, he addressed himself to moments in which the voyagers, even as they face the camera, seem to be looking inward, their features luminously and tenderly modeled within an impersonal background. Many of them reveal a nervous dejection, characteristic of those obliged to wait around for unexplained reasons. In *Slovak Mother* and *Slavic Immigrant* detained women are loaded down with their few belongings. In *Young Russian Jewess*, the protagonist is seemingly transfixed by her solitude. The shadowy atmosphere emphasizes their feeling of transitory homelessness, loss, and hope. Hine extended himself toward such introspective phases, seeing them as states of vulnerability, and part of a historic adventure. Without concern for an entity called "New York," he nevertheless attended to a decisive stage in the evolution of its democratic consciousness. Hine was a practitioner of "enthusiastic endorsement of difference . . . viewed as a necessary condition of human flourishing, one that offers to individual men and women the choices that make their autonomy meaningful."7

Who was this man, capable of such generous pictorial response? The short answer is that he was a schoolteacher, using recently learned photography to provide children with a civics lesson at Ellis Island. Born in Oshkosh, Wisconsin, Hine worked at menial jobs as a boy and under sweatshop conditions in an upholstery factory as a youth. Later, he studied education briefly with John Dewey at the University of Chicago. A mentor of Hine's from Wisconsin, now the head of the Ethical Culture School in New York, imported him to join his faculty.

The Ethical Culture Society (originally called the Workingman's School) had been founded by Rabbi Felix Adler in 1876 as an instrument of Reform Jewish progressivism. The curriculum of its school stressed the acculturating of the children of immigrants to American ideals with a program that combined the appeal to social responsibility of the liberal Protestant churches and an emphasis on Emersonian self-reliance. This was, from the first, a pragmatic enterprise: the school not only offered courses in the sciences and humanities but ran workshops in trade skills.

If it did not derive directly from Dewey, such activism nevertheless accorded with Dewey's accent on the good and productive life as a heightening of experience. Experience was affected as much by individual motivation as by social upbringing, both of these in tension with, and sometimes critical of, institutional restraints. "Dewey's creed," writes Alan Trachtenberg, "became fundamental to Hine's photographic social work: a concern with the process of seeing within the larger process of social 'betterment'—the more conscious use of intelligence to achieve a more rational collective life."8 It should be added that, for Dewey, the rational was inextricably bound up with artistic consciousness, in a common aim to discern meaning through the intensified experience of people acting for and with one another. On that score, Dewey's philosophy was interestingly convergent with the Jewish understanding that beauty is defined, above all, through moral behavior.

Hine might not have put it in such terms, but he endowed the stamina of the disenfranchised under repressive conditions with a moral beauty that distinguished his own project. His intellectual background, though it no doubt inspired his work, remained schematic, and his notion of high art was conventional, even sentimental, as, for example, in his *Madonna of Ellis Island*. That notion began to fade when he left teaching to be a freelance photographer for the National Child Labor Committee (NCLC) and was further diminished by his forays into the sweatshops where immigrants worked. Thereafter, he became an investigative reporter in earnest, bringing out images and commentary in the NCLC's journal the *Survey* (1909–17), later named the *Survey Graphic* when Hine rejoined its staff in 1921.

A comparison with Jacob Riis, Hine's precursor in reform photography, sheds light on his achievement of the prewar years. Riis, a Danish immigrant who had gone through his own very hard time, began as a New York police reporter on a campaign to expose the squalor and filth of an underclass that menaced its own health and that of the city. To dramatize those necrotic conditions—published in *How the Other Half Lives* (1890)—Riis employed a team of photographers who burst into downtown tenements, hovels, and basements, often at night. Within a degraded habitat, they photographed hoodlums, drunks, derelicts, waifs, and beggars, all of whom needed to be deloused and rehoused. Riis was a decent man who analyzed the conditions that impeded poor people from realizing their potential as citizens; at the same time, he was on the side of municipal authority, and his paternalistic view of his subjects was colored by racist stereotypes.

Often, a thrill of abhorrence runs through Riis's images, which trample the dignity and privacy of human beings with the same spirit with which they ignore pictorial conventions. Through his writings and his slide-illustrated lectures, Riis opened a door on a verminous existence, a civic stain that was to indict the conscience and offend the propriety of his bourgeois public.

There is a psychology of space implied in these revelations: Riis intended viewers to sense the sordid world he described as threatening to impinge on their own territorial way of life. For Hine, by contrast, the industrious poor did not comprise the "other" half at all. In his work, he sided with them and he centered them, casting the bourgeoisie to the social margin. He would disclose their burden of long hours, low pay, brutal production quotas, and dangerous conditions as a grief imposed on them by the self-interests of the real *others*, the invisible employers profiting from an unregulated economic system. Seeing his subjects suffering under this system, Hine concluded that theirs was a besieged environment. He rendered it as a physically coercive and socially abandoned space. This was especially true of the employment of children, whether "newsies" or breakerboys in mines, who were deprived of the right to education—in Hine's book (and those of others), a process indispensable to the development of individuals.

Given that the campaign to reduce or do away with child labor was on the national agenda, Hine chose to hit hard and be personal. His pictures show one man's encounter with kids in private factories (where he had to be as transgressive as Riis) and in public streets. In *Mendicants, New York City* (pl. 9), a seated blind man seems to peer at the photographer more intently from behind his shades than does the small girl, eyes half closed, who shields him a little. More than Hine's other scenes taken across the country, this one has a confrontational quality. But it's nuanced by the hesitancy of the child, in mid-step, as well as by the dark, out-of-focus girders of the El, the locale of shadowy, well-dressed figures literally cut off by the frame.

This distinction between acutely described subject and sketchy background has a technical explanation —the shallow depth of field of Hine's lens. More significantly, however, the optical contrast expresses his idea of the relationship between the sentient individual and the indifferent, amorphous city. Hine's workers (a term that includes mendicants) are isolated not only physically but in their consciousness of being on their own within an urbanscape of other purposes. Like a kind of sad music, that consciousness plays across the faces of a group of men in a Bowery mission breadline at two o'clock in the morning (pl. 10). For Hine, the impact of the metropolis, like that of the workplace, is manifested not by architecture but through physiognomy.

Once again, it's worth contrasting this human atmosphere with Riis's. For what purpose were Riis's downtrodden to be cleaned up and their slums cleared, if not to assume their proper humble place within an accepted social order? In that light, Hine shows himself to be a more radical figure because he questions the order. The issue is brought out in his systematic critique of the conditions of labor, especially piecework in tenement homes and in shops. There, a huge subproletariat of immigrants does preindustrial work, nut shucking or lace making, for pennies a week. Hine's commentary makes clear that such rates barely permit survival, but the pictures show only diligence, diverting our attention from faces to what is done and how it is done—a subject of keen interest as it reveals the labor that actually goes into products everywhere taken for granted.

The greater the city, the less likely the contact between producers and consumers or, for that matter, warmth and connection between inhabitants. Though his piecework scenes were nominally pictures of alienated production, Hine often treated them as moments of solidarity—frequently with a familial character (fig. 2). But this treatment could not be extended to the larger arena of the struggles between the unions and capital. The progressive unions decried the influx of unorganized immigrant workers, the profit-hungry employers welcomed them, and both for the same reason: the cheapness of their labor.

This reduction of individuals to numerical coefficients was a natural outcome of the U.S. money interests, concentrated in New York. The sociologist Georg Simmel had already insisted upon the entirely impersonal, even heartless foundation of metropolitan life. In a famous essay of 1900, he linked the perceptual challenge of big city living—hyperstimulation of the nerves—to the problem of enduring the schematic uprooting and deindividuating regimen of "How much?" Simmel thought that such an atmosphere of "inconsiderate hardness" develops in city denizens an attitude of reserve. He wrote: "The inner aspect of this outer reserve is . . . a slight aversion, a mutual strangeness and repulsion." And then, by a leap, "What appears in the metropolitan style of life directly as dissociation is in reality only one of its elemental forms of socialization."[9]

Lewis Hine apprehended those forms in day-to-day New York existence, but he was able to see them from the inside, as a ferment that infiltrated even as it gave poignant meaning to the camaraderie that was his subject. The melancholy of his work, the product of his observation, was held in check by his faith in the future. The wistful or occasionally even sad mood of the Pictorialists, in contrast, stemmed from their elegiac program, their seemingly almost involuntary mourning for the past when confronted by a future they were not yet ready to embrace. Stieglitz and his friends lived in a closeted, salon atmosphere. They were socially and emotionally indifferent to the life of multitudes, whom they depicted as nameless crowds. Although Hine's stance and Stieglitz's position would appear to have been incompatible, between them passed one person who, learning from both, changed the emotional weather of the photography of New York.

Paul Strand (1890–1976) had been a student at Ethical Culture and a member in 1907–8 of a camera club organized by Hine. Stieglitz's 291 gallery was an appreciated stop on the club's field itinerary. Though

Lewis Hine (1874–1940), *Flower Makers in a Slum
Apartment*, 1912. Gelatin-silver print. Library of Congress, Prints
and Photographs Division, FSA-OWI Collection

imbued with Hine's ethical principles, Strand did, in fact, come of age as a latter-day Pictorialist. Such was his progress that by 1915 Stieglitz regarded him quite accurately as someone who would take Photo-Secession to a more advanced level.

In his famous photograph of Wall Street, taken that year, Strand applied an astringent vision to Pictorialism's interest in the financial district. Where Struss dealt with the stock market crowd as a jumble of optical points, at most a lively passing throng (fig. 3), Strand appears to have seen them from closer in as scattered loners. In *Wall Street, New York* (pl. 11), of 1915, they're walking left, out of the picture, heads bowed against an early morning light, trailing long shadows in their wake. Perhaps because we read left to right, the people appear to be moving against a current. Like other views that Strand made of pedestrians taken from above, this picture is a study in tones. It also has a protomodernist organization of planes and shapes and what Maria Morris Hambourg nicely calls Strand's "downy quality" of surface. Instead of Struss's reassuring colonnades, however, he counterpoints his New Yorkers with the four gargantuan black voids of the building's windows. *Wall Street, New York* introduces an atmosphere of fatality into the depiction of the urban workplace, and the diminished figures who perform the work. For they are about to spend their day in what looks to be an all-too-solid mausoleum.[10]

The next year, Strand moved Hine's legacy of street portraiture into a new psychological region. However spontaneous the look of Hine's earlier work, it was still socially consented, still, therefore, a ritual where people adjusted themselves, in differing degrees, for the camera. Strand wrung this genre inside out. By means of a false lens attached at a right angle to his real lens, he was able to face away from his subjects, who were thus unaware that he was taking their picture within their personal territory. Hine continually maintained an equity of power between himself and his sitters; Strand gained a voyeuristic advantage over them, even at point-blank range. The result was a startling group of heads framed so close that, though they obviously breathe the air of the city, all physical evidence of the place itself has been removed.

Instead of a narrative about "conditions," subtly implied, we have the unaffected display of somewhat battered human organisms in random moods. The blowsy Irish washerwoman, the watery-eyed old Italian man (pl. 12), and above all, the awesome beggar woman in *Blind*—each bears the unreflective experience of that moment and no other. It is the apotheosis of the present, with all its "cruel radiance," to quote James Agee. Strand reduced story content in order to obtain an elemental rawness of view; his abrupt treatment of these underdogs confers on them a great power of earthiness and sorrow. To look at these stolen street portraits is to be drawn into an uncomfortable complicity with the photographer's voyeurism, yet even as his pictures effect a great intimacy, they short-circuit any feeling of connection—a very urban kind of dissonance. This tough approach may not have derived from any social judgment. Rather, it seems to have come to Strand as detachment, reflecting his claim to an asocial freedom of perception that could be developed only in the metropolis of strangers.

Such were the major arguments transmitted through the photography of New York in the first decade and a half of the twentieth century. They almost describe an arc, wherein a material triumphalism is aestheticized to an apex of etherealization, then rounds over to an accounting of the social and human costs of "progess," and finally descends to the pathos of life and the solitude of observation. There was a movement from the piecemeal consideration of things to an attempt to synthesize a whole in which such things were no longer visible parts, and then on to demotic contact with the citizenry itself, in the maw of its uncertain fortunes. Three New Yorks, based on myths and countermyths—of power and powerlessness—that often coincided with perceptions and expressed authentic feelings. Although it obviously varied its offerings of an affirmative, an ambivalent, or a tragic vision of the proceedings, this imagery coalesced in a sense that New York was an unfinished—and possibly unfinishable—piece of work.

Meanwhile, the city itself had gone through sociocultural transformations, with results that photography either could not show or could not explain, though they left their mark on the medium. The advent of movies—the film industry would be based in Astoria, Queens, until after World War I—galvanized the public's appetite for a high-speed spectacle of urban traffic, jangle, and confusion. Subways had extended democratic access to all the boroughs, at a fare of five cents that would hold for forty years. The horrid Triangle Shirtwaist Company fire of 1911, along with strikes by garment workers, sparked state legislation that eventually regulated some employment practices. New York pioneered new public health policies, and gave media and advertising on the streets and in publishing their major drive. In painting, the modern-

ism of adoptive New Yorkers John Marin and Joseph Stella described the city as an implicitly violent composite of simultaneous and shattering perceptions. Finally, World War I, which the United States entered in 1917, not only fostered huge war-bond rallies on Wall Street but revived memories of repression and discrimination that had brought European immigrants to New York in such numbers over the past thirty years.

In retrospect, the art of Lewis Hine proved to be a defining moment in the photographic view of the city. Though it sometimes fell behind and sometimes swam with the power of events, his work decisively influenced the terms of future photographic engagement with New York. For Hine determined urban photography's central issue: what is the relation of industrial capitalism to American democratic values? To the nation itself, and to the foreign-born or their children in New York, it was a pressing question.

Fallen Culture

During the 1930s, opinion polls developed a new sophistication, along with the social sciences and oral histories that examined the values of "ordinary" Americans in small towns. The advent of a mass commercial culture in the previous decade (powered from New York) opened up wider markets to more buyers than ever before. Now, after the Crash of 1929 and throughout the burnout of the Depression, when the corporate world seemed to have degraded itself, popular culture rose to the fore as both a familiar and yet an unexamined domain.

While advertising slogans hardly declined in currency, the enduring, earthy pleasures of vernacular expression gained in prestige. Photographers looked seriously even at graffiti. It was an age when many unpretentious artifacts that betrayed ignorance of high art were enthusiastically turned into candidates for aesthetic scrutiny.

By the end of the 1920s, expatriate American artists, bewitched firsthand by European "isms," were returning to the United States with the hope of developing voices and subjects on their home ground. Among them, the composer Virgil Thomson, who had already made a good transition from France back to the States, wrote of Aaron Copland's music that it is "American in rhythm, Jewish in melody, eclectic in all the rest."[11] After coming of artistic age abroad, American artists faced the challenge of reintegrating their now-hybrid aesthetic with the experience of their stay-at-home compatriots. One of these artistic transplants was Berenice Abbott (1898–1991), who reentered the United States after a successful career as a portrait photographer of the Parisian intelligentsia.

Abbott's timing (she returned in 1929) and her ambition (to reveal New York in pictures) were auspicious. The city had added several mighty new presences during her eight-year absence. Her work from 1929 to 1935 displays the architectural ensembles of Manhattan in the serrated configurations that are still familiar today. Mostly, it was a question of depicting the skyscrapers, those rhetorical embodiments of U.S. enterprise. Abbott was instrumental in establishing the bird's- and worm's-eye views as the characteristic vantages of New York gigantism. Her perspectives maintained for at least the following two decades a metaphor of American technological ambition, symbolized by New York and transmitted throughout the world. In each of the city's sections that she photographed according to a scheme for her book project *Changing New York* (1939), the place comes alive with a kind of demotic lordliness. Yet, for all that the rhythms of her photog-

NEW YORK: CAPITAL OF PHOTOGRAPHY

raphy were American modernistic, the genesis of her style was, strangely enough, French and antiquarian.

It is obligatory to discuss Berenice Abbott's work in the light of that of the Parisian architectural photographer Eugène Atget, a large part of whose image archive she bought upon his death, brought to America, and tirelessly promoted. Atget was a modest documentarian of his city's streets and buildings, an account of which he catalogued in ever expanding files for the use of historians, decorators, illustrators, and artists. Though there is little evidence for thinking that he regarded his output as anything other than good reference material, Abbott considered it to be epochal realism of a high order. Atget's status as a virtually unknown craftsman, combined with the precision of his method and what Abbott saw as the grandeur of his theme, led her to use his work as a model on which to base her own vision of New York. But since Atget had characteristically looked back upon his city as a museum of artifacts, Abbott's challenge was to translate Atget's retrospections into her view of an American metropolis metamorphosing within a dynamic system.

At the time, the photography of public Manhattan was in flux. To get some idea of it, consider Samuel Gottscho's (1875–1971) *Times Square at Forty-fourth Street* (pl. 13), and Walker Evans's (1903–1975) *Broadway* (fig. 4), of 1930. Though both pictures capture the city at night and are engaged with its glamour, they nevertheless belong to two different stylistic traditions.

The nocturne of Times Square still describes "the Great White Way" (so called because of the white effect of lights used before neon) that the Pictorialists enjoyed, but we can't speak anymore of the introspective mood of the photographer as the real subject. The lighted signs of the movies, and of Chevrolet and Pepsodent, have quite innocently replaced it. But if they've taken over New York with their promises of clean teeth, regnant cars, and talking films, in this picture by Gottscho, a refined architectural photographer, they've done it with finesse, through little flares and rococo logos. Evans will have none of such pleasure in consumer display. For him, Broadway mass culture, in this one instance at least, is a scramble of messages that have no physical support at all. They exist as semaphores of brag, overlapping in patterns that he superimposed from different negatives, a technique inspired by Bauhaus modernism. Acknowledging the age of radio and film, Evans reads Broadway's hype as an emission from space-eating media that are no longer site-specific.

Berenice Abbott (1898–1991), *Rockefeller Center Foundations, NYC*, 1932. Gelatin-silver print. © Berenice Abbott/Commerce Graphics Ltd., Inc.

By contrast with the Evans of *Broadway*, Abbott came to Gotham as an acolyte of nineteenth-century materialism. She renders every detail with a sharp factual insistence that is really implacable. Like Atget's, her insistence precludes any consideration of city dwellers as protagonists, let alone as figures who have an independent life, other than inadvertently being "there," on the street. The man about to buy a ticket, in *Lyric Theater* (pl. 14), of 1936, is an incidental presence compared to the sprightly, larger-than-life-size Charlie Chaplin poster, flanked by a barrage of film stills. Abbott sees New York overwhelmingly as an outpouring of information, not as a social organism. Her pictures are meaty with texts—her shopwindows are loaded with them and even the larger buildings seem to be "read"—so that the metropolis looks like some kind of inanimate but epic narrative, composed of story bits.

For that matter, the research program of the Works Progress Administration (WPA), which funded Abbott's New York expenses, provided her imagery with such contextual data for her work as "the koshering process for chickens and Boss Tweed's involvement in real estate transactions."[12] Because the camera gives a sunlit account of only one moment, she often framed tableaux to reveal developers' processes at work upon the city's structure. In *Rockefeller Center Foundations, NYC* (fig. 5), of 1932, a network of hard girders rises up from the obdurate rock. Houses from the Federalist period coexist with skyscrapers. The Automat, though it dates from 1919, makes a novel appearance. Atget had walked the streets, recording adjacent buildings, often in sequence; Abbott had to move her heavy equipment by car, which encouraged a tendency to search for climactic moments.

Well into this imagery, Berenice Abbott ceased to be an innocent about New York, yet it remained for her a catalogue of wonders. (Contrarily, when F. Scott Fitzgerald viewed New York from the top of the Empire State Building and saw that it was not a universe but only an island, he wrote of it as "my lost city.") To be sure, Abbott's subject was not favored with the pewter overcast of sky from which Atget drew so much poetry—and mystery—in Paris. Instead, she offered brand-new vistas at a moment when construction teams, organized with military precision, could take up the Empire State Building in a mere thirteen months. The aggregate effect of *Changing New York* speaks mainly of anonymous yet characterful civic growth. Here was an intelligent publication appropriate for use, finally, as a guidebook for visitors to the 1939–40 World's Fair.

To mark his arrival in New York in 1932, an emigrant from Germany took a few snapshots that are awkward and unpracticed, yet they rank among the most arresting pictures of the decade. Some of these photos from his first landing are harshly contrasted images filled with jumble and blur, such as his tipped views from the open top of the double-decker Fifth Avenue bus. But what could have been an exciting prospect of metropolitan traffic near Forty-second Street is here rendered as a discommoded glance into a boisterous and phantasmal space.

George Grosz (1893–1959) was clearly not a photographer. But he had been a pioneer Dada artist and, later, had become wonderfully notorious as a caricaturist who scourged nascent fascism in the Weimar Republic. Any resemblance between these few snaps by Grosz and tourist photographs of capitalist New York is not strong enough to be coincidental. Though he intended only to pay his respects to the famous city, he apprehends Manhattanites, among whom he was immersed, as dark blanks in unrelated configurations. It helped that he was a stranger, maybe a little lost but also exhilarated by the incoherence of the New York spectacle. The title of one of his pictures, *A Face in the Crowd* (pl. 15), of 1932, is a contradiction in terms, because the camera's shutter speed was too slow to catch the head of the main character as anything but a skull-like smear. A crowd, yes, but even one face, no.[13]

This effect may have derived from the misfire of an amateur, unprepared, as he said in his autobiography, for the tropical June heat of New York. The picture nevertheless awakens in viewers who walk the big city's streets the sense that they, too, have been of the crowd, but not *with* it. Such an impression of being alone even when pressed in among fellow citizens must already have been then a familiar urban experience to countless city dwellers. Only in the 1930s, however, did it become a touchstone of photographic vision.

New York photographers of the era, whether foreign-born or native, discovered that the act of framing placed them in a locale different from that of their subjects. That site was an imaginative space, a kind of mental stepping back that took place as they readied the camera to focus on a subject. At the moment of exposure, they were psychically outside the events they pictured. At the same time, many photographers had a need to get in close to their subjects, to be intimate with them as individuals enduring the heartbreak of the Great Depression.

The men and the few women who pictured this calamity—the defining event of the 1930s—evolved two principles of seeing that opened the street mode to its pictorial future. The first is an apparently artless manner; the second is an intensely voyeuristic approach. What made both possible was the advent of the Leica, a miniature, roll-film, rapid-fire camera manufactured in Germany. Unlike the unwieldy Graflex of Lewis Hine, this tool allowed for instinctive work. By means of the Leica, street photography, previously a cumbersome and conspicuous practice, was transformed into a genre of stealth. For the machine not only encouraged surreptitious behavior on the part of its operator, it often rewarded it.

A new style began to emerge: grabbed, notational, and intrusive. Instead of waiting for action to happen, or setting it up, the photographer could poke right into it. We have the feeling, with photographs taken by the Leica, that metropolitan life is no longer constituted by events so much as made up of a succession of sudden glimpses and ephemeral instants. And just as it atomized movement in time, this observational style also redefined social space. On the street, even though they were exposed to public view, people nevertheless moved—or assumed they moved—within their own private territory. They were not defended against the curiosity of others, but urban decorum at least required that it be circumspect. The new camera could and did violate that circumspection at will.

Ben Shahn (1898–1969) used the Leica as a flexible means of capturing the moods of people who, like him, were living through an impoverished era with empty pockets. He also wanted to record certain details that were visible only at very close range—for example, the difference between the way a twelve-dollar coat wrinkles and the way "a seventy-five dollar coat wrinkles."[14] Like Paul Strand before him, Shahn on many occasions employed the right-angle viewfinder so as not to adulterate the truth of the moment by any response his subjects might have to his presence. But he aimed at more than street portraiture—he shot faces in context, faces subtly or bitterly gripped by New York in hard times.

It was a world, said Irving Kristol, in which poverty was so normal that the poor did not even think of themselves as such.[15] Deprivation, hunger, and unemployment were everyday conditions afflicting huge numbers of people, from the ground-down to the deflated bourgeoisie to the once-richer classes. As soon as they woke up, the out-of-work were on the job. Breadlines, apple sellers, and shantytowns along the jetties and in Central Park were daily sights, and Shahn shared this normalcy of indigence with his subjects. Maybe that is why his photographs give an initial (but not constant) impression that most people, whatever their neighborhood, are on an equally disadvantaged footing, socially and materially.

Aside from conversation and window-shopping, of which he gave numerous vignettes, Shahn's main topic is people waiting. They wait at their stands for business that doesn't come; they loiter at street corners or on the steps of public buildings (pl. 16), or sit on park benches, frumpish and sour, with nothing to do, as in *Untitled (Seward Park, New York City)*, of 1932–35 (pl. 17). The distractions that they sometimes enjoy do little to alleviate an overall stagnation, the accumulated heaviness of time at vain disposal.

With so little gainful action to record, Shahn, for all his realism, articulated space as a dramatic agent. Generally, it speaks of New Yorkers' separateness from one another, even in proximity. People seem to experience a collective anxiety or discontent, but it fails to unite them. In Shahn's photographs, they're shown through their attitudes and body language as, at best, side by side rather than together. Sometimes little gaps open up between them, suggesting their introversion in different worlds. This is particularly true when the photographer included or focused on African Americans. Shahn caught an extra pang of worry in these faces, and he showed whites instinctively turning from blacks pictured in the same scene. With a startling freedom, he invented a neurotic, off-balance space that determines the human moment.

Such troubled moments exist, though with far less frequency, in the work of Shahn's close friend Walker Evans, the man who taught Shahn the rudiments of photography. Briefly neighbors in west Greenwich Village, they shared a studio and were antiauthoritarian free spirits whose backgrounds and artistic principles were poles apart. Sometimes subtly, often stridently, their records of comparable Depression topics take issue with each other.

Evans, who came from an affluent Midwestern WASP family, had been educated in Eastern prep schools. After a trip to Paris in the 1920s, where he studied literature and imbibed European modernism, he dedicated himself to becoming the complete photographer, a master of all but the commercial genres. Shahn was born in Kovno, Lithuania (then Russia), the son of an Orthodox Jewish carpenter who was also a social activist. Evans, a bohemian intellectual, broke with the upper-crust values of his family, while

Shahn honored and extended the political conscience of his heritage. By the early 1930s, Shahn had worked as a fresco assistant to Diego Rivera at Rockefeller Center and was making a name for himself as a figurative painter who memorialized martyrs to reactionary politics, such as Sacco and Vanzetti, and to bigotry, such as Alfred Dreyfus.

Photography was mostly a sideline for Shahn. He used it at first as a quick means of suggesting and authenticating details for future canvases. Much of his work is offhand, a defect that nevertheless accorded him certain intimacies. Later, with Evans, he joined the photographers who worked for the Farm Security Administration (FSA). There, exposed to the breakdown of American agriculture during the era of farm foreclosures and dust bowl migrations, they bore witness to gnarled faces, rickety shelters, and dirty children —sights uglier than anything they saw in the city. Both Evans and Shahn considered their photographic activity primarily as an observing process: in the one case as a testimony, in the other as an aide-mémoire of a world in stress.

Evans had definite ideas about the city as a crucible of modern perception; Shahn had distinct empathies for the lives of its citizens. Both friends were excited by the 1933 publication of *My Paris*, a photoreportage with Leica by the Russian journalist Ilya Ehrenberg, with whose account of squalor in France they felt a great affinity.[16] But it was the French photographer Henri Cartier-Bresson (b. 1908) who brought them decisive news of the camera's possibilities. At a 1933 show of his work at the Julian Levy Gallery, Shahn and Evans viewed images by one who, having absorbed the modern movements at close range, particularly Surrealism, then wandered through the dismal alleys and the ruin and poverty of two continents, surrendering his art memories to the contingencies of the lens.

It would be hard, also, to imagine Evans's early development without the passing influence of the Bauhaus and the enduring legacy of Atget, whose work was brought out for the first time in a 1930 monograph arranged by Berenice Abbott and published by E. Weyhe. It would also be pertinent to remember that Edward Hopper, that votary of regionalist solitude, worked in an imaginative zone parallel to Shahn's. Regardless of their disparate tendencies, the two photographers converged in their emphasis on the vernacular language of American signs, which became an archetypal setting in photographs throughout the decade. Evans and Shahn developed into masterful semioticians of poverty. Also, they liked the work of Lewis Hine a lot.

In New York, Evans photographed people eating in fast-food restaurants, visiting Coney Island, and working together or by themselves. "What I wanted to do," Evans reflected much later, "was to get a type on the street . . . grab a very natural snapshot of a fellow on the waterfront. . . . I could have done newsreel photography."[17]

It's true that Evans was attracted to the swirl of movement in the city, but he was drawn even more forcefully to place as an inanimate, built environment, a collection of immobile surfaces with idiosyncratic styling. Evans's interest in faces and manners is eye-droppered into his much grander involvement with American storefronts, fire escapes, empty interiors, and door moldings. Far from treating them as backgrounds in his imagery, he respected artifacts and arrangements as protagonists sitting for their portrait, under the gaze of an 8-x-10-inch view camera.

Evans's approach toward construction and handicraft was consistently respectful, unlike his contact with people—the 35mm machine he used for populated street scenes allowed him an occasional free play with what many friends agreed was his misanthropic temperament.[18] Still, to Evans's mind, human beings at their best could be depicted as memorably as things, whose plain presence he made beautiful in raking light. Each of his ordinary subjects is grasped in the particularity of its surfaces, studied as an exceptional object, then placed with all his other studies, arraigned in the equity of his attention.

Thanks to the range of that attention, Walker Evans showed himself to be a populist artist, even if he had an epicurean style. He was remarkably positioned by such dualism to give an account of the Depression zeitgeist. It comes through his work as a set of conditions that he lets speak for themselves, devoid of emphasis on either historical urgency or human misfortune. People's lives go on wherever the culture of the time—his true iconographic priority—will take them. He examines the textures and conditions of material life, without surmise about their effects on human beings. Is it a fallen culture that presented itself before his eyes or a healthy one just then suffering temporary difficulties? Evans gives too much evidence for viewers to conclude one way or the other.

The photographer himself, however, was not undecided. Even in the small body of his New York work (relative to his panorama of 1930s America), he insists, with all the authority of what has been called

a "pitiless" style but was probably more an inquisitional one, that his sampling encompasses the variables of things as they are. He visually lists or takes inventories of items, each contributing in its modest way to the characterization of an era. Yet he could only assume that attitude from a position psychologically outside the confines of the American Depression. Evans saw that culture in historical terms, though also with a dispassionate spirit. He partakes of nothing, he is interested in everything.

In Evans's 1934 formal study of truck drivers, the truck has as articulate a presence as the men, who glance at the photographer a bit warily. He regards them with their vehicle, given equal importance as an attribute of their work. The dilapidated exterior in *Waterfront Poolroom* is revealed in a nimbus of light. Torn or falling apart, signs of recreation and especially movie posters from 1930s America appear in the work of Evans and many others as upbeat presences that have aged poorly in the discomposed present. In Evans's photographs, time is a process that wearies and eventually undoes human construction. The weight of the past bestows a lovely mortality upon things that survive only as relics in an era that can no longer keep them in use.

How different Evans's agnosticism about progress is from Shahn's faith in eventual social improvement. For Shahn, the oppression of time is replaced by the more immediate toll that penury takes on human consciousness. Just the same, an impecunious state, in the long and short of cultural fortune, is a changeable affair. When time affects the work of Ben Shahn, it does so as personal memory, the burden of which is invested in a democratic society whose distribution of rights, especially for minorities, is unassured.

For example, his picture of a commercial portrait photographer's window on the Lower East Side (fig. 6) is embedded with family memories resonant of Jewish experience from his own past. The wedding pictures, the Bar Mitzvah boy, the graduate: they speak of life's little promotions. They're as unexceptionally formulaic and vernacular as they can be. But, as Shahn views them, these images leave a question hanging in the air: what happened later? Their slightly disjointed arrangement, together with the shading that dims some of them at the top, suggest that Shahn's outlook was less sanguine than that of the sitters who once grinned on cue in the studio. A viewer comes away from this tableau with an impression that the ritual hopes of family life are marooned in a disenchanted and unkempt afterward.

We need only compare Shahn's picture with Evans's *Photographer's Window of Penny Portraits, Birmingham, Alabama* (fig. 7), of the same year, 1936, to make this impression more definite. Evans frames 325 little "penny pictures" of Southerners in a grid that implies they are in a nonhierarchical system, guaranteed an automatic equality within which individuals count but are indistinguishable. The singularity of their persons is annihilated by the spectacle of the Savannah studio window as an emblem of (at least the white) American community, crystallized by Evans with a sparkle that is really decorative.

Laura Katzman compares these photographs as self-reflective pictures of pictures, and as comments on the politics of media, yet it's hard to imagine this image from Savannah and Shahn's from the Lower East Side as "thesis" pictures.[19] They were certainly not intended as summaries of ways of life or as political statements. They do no more than take modest notice of forms that arrange individuals in two kinds of groups. Nevertheless, there runs under the tidiness of the one group an assumption that everyone belongs cohesively and unproblematically in the same unit. Evans quite evidently relishes the grid as modernist order and as true Americana. (He also thought the faces were funny.) On the contrary, in Shahn's big city, gaps reveal only the forced and euphemistic quality of the gathered portraits, their lack of social centering *except* as a commercial advertisement.

In the field of visual imagery, one of the most salient traits of the 1930s was the rise of propaganda. Movies took the rhetorical lead—and the bigger budgets—with an incalculable effect upon world consciousness. But still photographs played a significant role, too, conscripted into high-minded nationalist programs that rose to prominence in inverse proportion to the decline of economic fortunes. Soviet photographs, sponsored and financed by the Stalin government, accentuated the labors of workers for the good of the state. In Hitler's Germany, individuals were pictured only as servants to the destiny of the Reich. In this hysterical ideological free fall, the accent was on pride, and on an endorsement of "achievements" or "right conduct" from which the rulers tolerated no public and, often, no private dissent.

But in U.S. photographic propaganda, such as that of the FSA, the note most often struck was sympathy. Wary of all abstractions, Americans accepted "the common man" or "we, the people" only as shorthand terms for individuals who could use some help. So long as that help was forthcoming from official agencies, the citizenry would abide the hypercentralization of Roosevelt's programs. In Europe, propaganda photographs were addressed indiscriminately to everyone; in America, they were published for the bourgeoisie, whose goodwill was necessary to sustain ameliorating programs. One has only to compare the official magazines *U.S.S.R. in Construction* and the Nazi *Signal* with the commercial *Life*, where photographs of the poor sometimes appeared, to catch the obvious difference.[20] "Sympathy" could be given on the basis of a realistic description of damaged lives, a genre topically vitalized by the onset of new documentary practices.[21]

Yet sympathy is a more complex human sentiment than pride. Those who posed for well-wishing strangers risked embarrassment; those who viewed the results, a tinge of guilt. Furthermore, an undertow of critical content is always implicit in the realism of documentary, for documentary work, from Hine's to the present, is motivated by an investigative candor, either in tension or, often, in conflict with the benevolence featured in official rhetoric. As Ben Shahn said, it is very well for photographers to have a soft heart, but they must also have a hard eye.

That eye was trained, for the most part, on agrarian zones, which more handily furnished ruined scenes than the city. Of course, the mandate of Roy Styker, head of the photographic section of the FSA, dictated this regional choice of subject. But he also had some animus toward the city, which he perceived as a threat to old-style American populist values. In this, he was not wrong. The sympathies that photographers extended to the metropolitan citizenry, chiefly New York's, took note of its cosmopolitan, and therefore —to a nativist mind—its alien makeup. American farmers needed to regain their position in order to reassert their self-sufficiency. Foreign-born city people, with their ethnic allegiances, and members of urban racial minorities, who had yet to claim their place, did not figure prominently in the New Deal.

In 1936, a photographer named John Gutmann (1905–1998) took a close-up picture of two black men walking on a New York street under elevated tracks (pl. 18). Signs, objects, shadows, and figures create a wonderfully energetic pattern. A viewer might suppose—correctly—that Gutmann had a trained eye. Even three years after his arrival in America, this German painter who had fled Nazism was still startled by our urban realities. But they were more than just visually intoxicating, they were socially exciting as well. Upon his initial disembarkation in San Francisco, Gutmann was elated by the sight of Asians, blacks, whites, Native Americans, and Mexicans shooting dice together in a scene that, as he later reflected, founded his vision of Depression America.[22]

To take this photograph, Gutmann used a medium-format camera, a Rolleiflex, that could not focus at very close range. His trade-off of some foreground blur against the finically described textures beyond is a freshening pictorial touch within a calibrated design. It also associates the rifles that are for sale in the street kiosk with the public place, and the two black men with his own personal territory. Gutmann made his living as a contracted photojournalist for European press agencies, and it was with pictures like this, of such muted yet edgy impact, that he introduced to his audience abroad what must have seemed the improbable openness of American social culture.

Another expatriate photographer, Alexander Alland (1902–1989), orchestrated the theme of New York's multiethnicity as a deliberate program. Having come from Sevastopol via Istanbul, he was no stranger to the multistrained quality of metropolitan life. Alland, a genuine cultural pluralist, was alone in having given Gypsies pictorial attention, and he made an extended study of a black Jewish congregation in Harlem, a group that enjoyed, if that is the word, double status in the book of minorities. In an illustrational mode, he often worked with a decided sweetness of tone yet with some Latina exotic dancers (pl. 19) and a crisp view of a Chinatown street he caught a skip of life on the move (pl. 20).

Gutmann and Alland were only two of the photographers who fanned out along the New York streets and into homes during the later 1930s. With a drive that was sometimes loosely organized, these men and women aimed to make visible—even to publicize—what was largely unregarded: the existence of groups not assimilated into the host American culture. To that end, the photographers tended to structure their work into projects, and occasionally into picture essays suitable for feature articles in magazines. Alexander Alland had unsuccessfully proposed a body of work on foreign-born New Yorkers to *Life*. Aaron Siskind (1903–1991), with co-workers, and monitored by Michael Carter, a black sociologist, brought out some work from *Harlem Document*, their photoreportage, in *Look* (1940).

In many such pictures, only now being rediscovered, the accent had moved from economic distress—though it obviously prevailed and was not ignored—to communal togetherness. What actually bonded people as they cooked, prayed, or worked, what festivals they celebrated, how they gossiped with neighbors and interacted in families: these were matters investigated by the phalanx of idealistic young photographers, informally networked at the Photo League. This organization, which had earlier split away from a Communist film unit, was itself a kind of community outfit. Its adherents could take courses there, see shows, attend lectures, and exhibit their work.

Those who came out of the Photo League were on the whole affirmative in mood yet activist in temper. Learning their craft as they went along, they mingled briefly with the lives of others whose cultures were very different from their own. This difference at first acted as a magnetic element in the outlook of the Photo League. Its members honored the principle that our democratic system was accountable to all its citizens, that all had equal and inalienable rights under law, no matter what their creed, origin, or color. So much the better if this notion offended that America where the Ku Klux Klan still flourished, Father Coughlin's anti-Semitic broadcasts were welcomed, and Catholics could not attain national office.

Nationalist propaganda in the Europe and United States of the 1930s fixated on cultural homogeneity, either downplaying or ignoring ethnic and tribal presences within the state. In this context, the New York photography that discloses these presences was dissident, even as it upheld a fundamental belief in American self-imagery. It says something about Alexander Alland's moral perspective that he retrieved and printed Jacob Riis's forgotten negatives, and it is revealing of Morris Engel's conscience that, on Twenty-first Street, he felt he was walking in the footsteps of Lewis Hine.[23] In these figures, new urban photography emulated its reformist precursors, but without portfolio.

Engel's *Harlem Merchant* (pl. 21), of 1937, does, in fact, recall Hine's work and is reminiscent of Shahn's. It fuses the solicitude of the one with the toughness of the other—in memorable poise. The head of the un-shaven black merchant, framed by the compartments for his cheap, disheveled merchandise, appears imprisoned within his booth. Communists thought of Harlem as a recruiting ground for revolutionary causes, but liberal photographers of the 1930s like Engel (b. 1918) regarded it much more humanely as a zone of despair, where people were up against the greatest odds in white democracy.

However, if we turn to a picture of a Harlem business by a black photographer, James Van Der Zee (1886–1983), *Manhattan Temple B.C. Lunch* (pl. 22), of 1936, the staff, posed next to the window, are at only a physical, no longer a mental, distance from the photographer. It was not on the imaginative horizon of this commercial (and vernacular) portraitist to import a dramatic evocation of "sympathy" into so familiar a setting.

Gradually, by the late 1930s, a shift occurs in the social atmosphere of photographs depicting ethnic or racial minorities in New York. The normalcy of community has replaced a nagging, everyday sense of impoverishment. No longer considered estranged or victimized, people appear in cohesive social situations —their "otherness" naturalized in the process. The familiarity of their ways takes precedence over the specificities of their different cultures, even as their cultures are affirmed as sources of strength. Ben Shahn's eavesdropping method almost implies that viewers participated in New York street life, but now a younger photographer like Walter Rosenblum (b. 1919) actually breaks through random contact and fraternizes with his subjects.

On Pitt Street, on the Lower East Side, the people were easy with this young man. The work he did there was undertaken as a student project at the Photo League, designed to examine the street as a site of quotidian transactions—in other words, city genre. But with his approach to the street's mixed usage restricted to one block, the idea of the bigness of the city fades from view. Except for the density of happenings, the environment could be a small town. The setting is construed as only a few tightly framed buildings, and they are human-scaled. Everyone seems to know one another, they talk a lot, and circulation takes its own time. At such a pokey pace, various story lines begin to suggest themselves. It's almost as if Thornton Wilder's *Our Town* were restaged on city blocks. But Rosenblum walked an actual New York street, in territory that was neither Middletown nor Gotham, a turf he couldn't help but describe with homegrown affection (pl. 23).

Something of that mood underlies Aaron Siskind's famous *Harlem Document* (1937–40), although, as the subject was more complex, so was the method more analytic. Siskind and his collaborators from the Photo League's Feature Group, which he headed, quite often failed to resist the temptations of poetry—to their credit—but their goal was really a sociological study. Like the Lower East Side, Harlem in the late 1930s was past its early optimism, although the teeming inhabitants of both neighborhoods did not hesitate to exist. Those in the ghetto of Harlem were horribly overcrowded and gouged by white landlords who knew their tenants had nowhere else to go. "I remember," said

Gordon Parks, who was raised there, "swarms of slow-moving people, moving close together up on Lenox Avenue—past the chili shacks, rib joints, funeral parlors and storefront churches—knowing one another but seldom bothering to speak. A city of blackness crammed inside a white city where, when you walked out the door, you became a stranger."[24]

Approaching that inner city with an 8-x-10-inch view camera, Siskind believed that photographers could work for better housing and civil liberties of blacks, and yet they must endow their work with a personal vision. In accord with their views from the ideological left and right, respectively, both the *Daily Worker* and *Fortune* glibly misinterpreted *Harlem Document*'s reportage. But Siskind's group refused to see Harlem residents as either heroic or dangerous; they come forward as aggrieved, resilient, dispirited, sensual, and quite frequently pious. The difference between media stereotypes and the content of this Harlem imagery is the difference between a determined projection of preconceived meaning and the observation of behavior and moods.

In this case, it was informed observation. The white, working-class photographers lived in run-down tenements, as did their subjects. The picture takers, first-generation offspring of Jewish immigrants, mingled with the children of recent black migrants from the South. Both sides knew displacement and prejudice, though obviously in different intensities. Of course, the presence of the camera implied the privileged mobility of those who used it, which may help to explain their sensitivity to the confinement of life in Harlem. Though the "document" certainly emerges as rhetorical in tone (the photographers wanted conditions changed for the better, after all), it's nuanced in feeling.

Words scrawled on the boarded-up entrance of a once-elegant Harlem apartment building: "Dange. Keeou." A kid enters through the torn slats of its first-floor window, unintimidated by the danger (fig. 8). In another scene, young boys wearing fedoras and adult topcoats gather at a tree stump, while a dolorous little girl shows her response to exclusion from their group (pl. 24). In still another photograph, a mother and her daughter sit next to each other, evidently spectators at a Harlem parade. The photographer has singled them out, even at the cost of the mother's disapproving glance (pl. 25). These images are eloquent about space: an unknown interior space that's off-limits and a social space that's charged by psychological dynamics, either between the subjects themselves or between them and the photographer. Especially in

Aaron Siskind (1903–1991), *Condemned House* from *Harlem Document*, 1938. Gelatin-silver print, 107/8 x 85/8 in. (27.5 x 21.9 cm). George Eastman House, Rochester, New York. Gift of Aaron Siskind. © Aaron Siskind Foundation

Harlem Document's view of space, images articulate the marked or unmarked, but still palpable, boundaries across which the young negotiate their lives.

In Harlem, energies still unfulfilled are viewed across a racial divide. Such perceptions were not an issue in photographs of the Lower East Side, the cradle of Jewish memory. There, a neighborhood that had seen its day was pictured with implicit lament. These two phases of concerned New York photography are also distinguished by the contrast between an earlier focus on an aging, or at least a weathered, population and a later emphasis on frustrated youth. The pages were turning in the moral outlook of these city photographers, whose imagery pleaded for more room for Harlem's inhabitants, room for health and equal opportunity, which American society, if it were just, should not deny them.

Social justice and the retention of cultural identity were not, however, the only themes that engaged photographers in those days. The romance of technology and the thrill of entertainment and fashion also added their fizz to the record of the decade. *Life* and *Look* were born in this age; in fact, the Luce press (which included *Fortune* and *Time*) dominated it. Together with Condé Nast, who ran *Vanity Fair* and *Harper's Bazaar*, these organs of publicity, news, and style went far in developing a new market for photographic imagery. They pumped up visuals to incite pleasure in looking as well as discovery through looking. And they served, not incidentally, as propaganda for America's good life. Concerning *Life*, Terry Smith has written, with maybe a little tartness: "It brought together, weekly, the fertile fictions of a nationalistic industry, a benevolent government, and an honestly striving, basically tolerant, essentially democratic people devoted to the values of community, family life, and personal independence."25 One look at a picture by Otto Hagel (1909–1973), a *Life* photographer of the time, with its flurry of confetti at the stock market, might suggest a metaphor for what happened in actuality—*Life* hit the jackpot (pl. 26). The comparable and somewhat earlier media parallels in Europe were, on the whole, more left-wing. They were endowed with far fewer commercial resources and had smaller subscriptions, so they contributed but a footnote to the centrality of the New York media in the formation of world opinion through still pictures.

If we think of the most confident and successful Amercian photographers of the 1930s, Margaret Bourke-White (1904–1971) and Edward Steichen will most likely head the list. They celebrated power in New York with breathtaking panache. That is literally the case, at their most dramatic, when they positioned single figures against the backdrop of the city, each sharing in the other's glory.

As a star photographer of industrialism for *Fortune,* Bourke-White installed herself in a glamorous studio, high up in the Chrysler Building. Here, in 1930, she pictured a leonine Sergei Eisenstein, the Soviet film director, having a shave—with skyscrapers as a magnificent, capitalist chorus (pl. 27). This piquant gag shot juxtaposes the virtuoso of modernist film montage with American moderne—the Chrysler's Deco styling. As for the city itself, it's showcased as the triumphant setting of an entrepreneurial culture, playing host to a visitor from an adversarial system.

By the early 1930s, Steichen had traveled a long way from his Pictorialist period, his administration of U.S. Army aerial photography during the war, and his abstract still lifes of the previous decade. He was now a high-paid impresario of salon portraiture and fashion illustration. In a setup for *Vogue* (pl. 28), his soignée young ladies have the city at their feet. They're top of the line in class, style, and grace. Oblique lighting brings out the best in their silky flair, yet in this night shot on a penthouse balcony, facing the city as it glitters across the river, it's as if the place needed to be enchanting in order for these goddesses to rule over it.

It took Lewis Hine to evoke the city's highest point with a genuine poetry, though also in plebian terms, in *Steelworker, Empire State Building* (pl. 29), of 1931. This was captured during the construction of the Empire State Building, a labor that the fifty-seven-year-old photographer recorded at ever-scarier heights, as he ascended the scaffolds with his worker subjects. We remember F. Scott Fitzgerald's dismay on discovering from up there that New York was only an island, not a universe. Presumably, his experience was a lesson in humility. But for Hine the universe consisted of productive work, with which his own efforts were in sympathy; wherever he found work, it gave him satisfaction.

Hine photographed the plaque listing the Empire State Craftmanship Awards, a roll call of ethnicities. It's conceivable that, in such an act, he was recalling his study of the immigrants at Ellis Island, from all over Europe, whose descendants, twenty-seven years later, were erecting the world's tallest building. His pictures show how much he felt at home up there, on the narrowest of girders and far from solid ground, with these bolt fitters and rivet tossers. The edifice itself

meant less to him than the muscular, intelligent, and mechanical effort to raise it high, realized by off-spring from the concord of nations.

In the pictures by Bourke-White and Steichen, as well as this one by Hine, a power of visual technique matches the exaltedness of the content. Their juxtaposition of near and far in the same deep focus compares with the imaginative leap that situates the individual as a protagonist against a really wide expanse of the city. A materialist like Berenice Abbott could not have imagined this duality, which has allegorical overtones. The celebrity shot, the fashion picture, and the proletarian lyric share this feature, too: they are about fun. Only in the last of these, however, is this fun expressed with joy and associated with "the common man."

The Rough and Gregarious Town

Let us contemplate the disquieting story of Arthur Fellig, a.k.a. Weegee. The origin of his professional moniker seems to have been a corruption of "Ouija," the name of the board game that supposedly foretells events, just as he supposedly foretold crimes, so as to arrive in time with his flash. Though at first he had only a local reputation in New York, he should be placed on a level with the two nationally famous Ws of his time, Orson Welles and Walter Winchell. Together, the three flourished as innovating dramatists of hard sell in theater, movies, radio, photography, and news. A feverish impulse runs from Welles's 1938 broadcast *War of the Worlds* (which terrified listeners persuaded that Martians had landed), through Winchell's telegraphed opener, "Good evening, Mr. and Mrs. America, and all the ships at sea," to Weegee's lurid book of photographs *Naked City*, of 1945. The Ws were sensationalists in their approach to their material, autocratic narcissists in personality, and prophets whose genius defined American myths of the 1940s.

Among the photographers of the period, Weegee (1899–1968) uniquely identified himself as the archetypal New York native. He took Manhattan, the heterogeneous whole of it, quite consciously as his province. He can be said to have acted as its publicist, though a curious one, since he cheerfully agreed with all those who abused the city as well as those who approved of it. Weegee was an ostentatiously plebian creature who may have been as grubby in reality as he was in his persona. As a freelance photographer of crime, accidents, and "human interest," working for tabloids like the *New York Daily News*, he had press entrée to practically any scene that caused a commotion. Or that could be made to look as if a commotion had taken place. Nothing less would do.

He was of that alleged fraternity, the New York millions, his journalist's access to every form of metropolitan life but a reflection of the insider status he claimed as an observer of multitudes. Of course, Weegee may have been no more than a bogus Everyman, but he played that role to the promotional hilt. It afforded him the rank of omniscient chronicler, supposedly without prejudice or illusion about those he pictured— preferably in great disarray. For him, tumult was the everyday vehicle of New York life, itself embroiled in a melee of indigenous dialects. Weegee would have agreed with Jackie Mason's remark, "A person who speaks good English in New York sounds like a foreigner." Blacks, Anglos, Italians, Russians, Jews, Latinos, and Chinese were all the same to Weegee: people caught in situations that he might turn into "news."

This leveling of real ethnic difference, even if for commercial reasons, gave him an advantage over photographers who might have had to surmount compunctions when moving outside their familiar environment. Between the dangers of exploitation and sentimentality, they had to walk a wavering, self-conscious line. Weegee's photographs never speak on *behalf* of minorities, but also he hardly thinks of them as living across some gap or at any cultural distance from his own station in life. His characteristic tone is curt, but also remarkably familiar, as if he were a waiter at a Jewish deli, slapping down a pastrami on rye. This was even true of his fashion shots for *Vogue*, which are endearingly inept. It was often his job to record calamities but never to commiserate with those who suffered them. When citizens are burned out of their apartments, or they're murdered, or they're injured in accidents, Weegee presents these scenes as just unlucky circumstances, not the result of conditions for which the system might have to take responsibility. He had as much range as Lewis Hine (whom he admired) in portraying the diversity of people under pressure or in trouble, though none of Hine's concern for their plight.

In the early 1940s, the New York art and photographic establishments recognized Weegee's work as imagery that amounted to a statement far more significant than scandal or disaster reportage. He soloed at the Photo League, with *Weegee: Murder Is My Business*, in 1941. The Museum of Modern Art exhibited his pictures in a show of 1943, *Action Photography*. The moment coincided with the acknowledgment that some pulp detective fiction and Hollywood noir revealed more about American life than consumers could ordinarily expect from popular genres. Movies from the 1930s about racketeers, *Scarface* (1932), say, were tales of crazy "others" gunned down by their own violence or that of law and order. But Raymond Chandler's novels *The Big Sleep* (1939) and *Farewell, My Lovely* (1940) evoked a netherworld where private eyes and small-time crooks compromised each other with twisted motives in a moral haze. Against the background of the coming "good war," authors like Chandler could show with pleasure that Americans were too innocent about their own human nature. Weegee was one of this ilk.

The soiled settings and sleazy mood of many photographs by Weegee far exceeded the requirements, and probably the interest, of any city editor; they comprise a portfolio of indiscretions that could only have been motivated by the needs of a voyeur. With an in-frared, and therefore invisible, light, he snuck a picture of a sailor pawing his unwilling girl at the movies. What gives *Lovers at the Movies* (fig. 9), of 1943, its edge is not so much the couple's behavior as Weegee's prurience—something with which bemused viewers conspire as soon as they look at the picture. Here, the nonchalance with which he crossed the line between tolerated snooping and private obsession is symptomatic of the atmosphere of license in the big city. Weegee's camera underscored the fact that breaking of taboos had become a notorious—and marketable—feature of New York life. It's a tribute to his impact that a much later Hollywood movie based on his life was titled *The Public Eye* (1992).[26]

This playing with the theme of the detective, as portrayed in a film alluding to his work, would have suited Weegee's underhanded agenda. Even as it transgresses a social boundary, the picture of the "lovers" betrays a new zealous dimension of seeing. Weegee's eye simultaneously took in the little drama of the couple and those who are oblivious to it. They look at or are inattentive to the screen, the implied, off-frame attraction that brought them there in the first place. Given the absence of the movie itself, this medley of action contributes a surprising charge to the image.

Such reshuffling of interest was in any event necessary when, as was most likely, he got to the death scene *after* the shooting. The murders of organized crime had been for a while his most lucrative staple, and it was in a spirit different from Jacob Riis's that Weegee spoke of "slum clearance"—mob homicide. Even after Prohibition had ended, in the late 1930s the mobs were still fighting for control and killing each other. When the war came, many gangsters were drafted and found themselves doing the same work in foreign lands that they did at home, only at higher risk and for less pay. With his usual subjects overseas, Weegee looked around for others, and discovered a puzzling new social space.

A vision of the city emerges in which flesh and its entanglements become the chief, unauthorized subject. The atmospheres of the circus and girlie magazines get mixed in his depiction of a ballet rehearsal (pl. 30), where it seems that emotions as well as luminous bodies are cantilevered every which way within a black void. As he flashed this scene with his usual tabloid harshness, Weegee was inviting viewers to enjoy his sense that none of it adds up, though everyone is ludicrously suspended. In this instance, as well as countless others—shots of police "coolers," drunken binges, opera soirees, patriotic rallies—the photog-

FIG. 9
Weegee (b. Arthur Fellig, 1899–1968), *Lovers at the Movies*, c. 1943.
Gelatin-silver print, 10 3/4 x 13 5/8 in. (27.3 x 34.6 cm). International
Center of Photography, New York. © Weegee/International Center
of Photography/Getty Images

rapher established his theme of New York as a human
comedy of mismatched faces and gestures. For him,
the city was like a strip show gone bananas.

Extreme spectacles involved him less, however, than
the uncontrolled reactions to which they gave rise.
Try as he might to arrange matters according to his sarcastic intent, it was the sheer random, ill-assorted,
and unaware display of consciousness that carried him
through the night. Much of what he saw and then
concentrated on, with visual smarts, was marginal to
the dire occasion. Eventually, the narrative impulse
of the reporter gave way to a new understanding that
stories themselves simply dissolved into the industrious chaos of the metropolis.

The revelation of this near pandemonium occurs
quite memorably in Weegee's photographs of the beach
at Coney Island (fig. 10; see also pl. 31). Here, the

citizenry gathers, not to some civic meeting, but as an off-work swarm of bodies, mingling every physique, age, and background, though not color. If they can be designated a mass, still this is not a united assemblage. For this one moment, to be sure, the people pose for their collective portrait; they let themselves be seen by the "public eye." Somehow, by his contact with those in the foreground, Weegee made it seem as if the whole motley crew, which ranges a half-mile back to the parachute tower, comprises his extended family. In the next instant, though, they'll be elbowing one another for a tiny patch of sand, relating only to their own companions, dissociated from the rest. At Coney Island, Weegee raised his curtain to uncover New York in the 1940s.[27]

Between the World's Fair of 1939–40 and the construction of the United Nations Building in 1949, New York reached a historic acme as a cosmopolitan center. This state of affairs reflected more than the disparate origins of its people. Rather, the metropolis became the visible capital of Allied freedom and progress, sustained in a cankered world. At its docks, millions of GIs were shipped out and later came back, fewer in number, after years of strife. New York embodied the fondest hope of internationalism and provided its own most spectacular stage for it, to the applause of a global public. Where else but in this city could Eleanor Roosevelt have promoted the lofty Universal Declaration of Human Rights? The fairground and the UN high-rise advertised a dream of peace among power blocs that in practice gave each other little quarter. How fitting that these architectural complexes were best known by their geometric—that is to say, their idealized—forms.

Times Square, however, was at the heart of the city, the real meeting place of the crowd, avid for its signs. Of the great crossroads in the early 1940s, the photographer Lou Stoumen (1917–1991) wrote: "It was where you took your date, or found one . . . where you bought your shoes, books, kazoos . . . under the Wrigley sign. . . . What better place to be alone and hungry? And when big events were happening—elections, world series baseball, important deaths . . . declarations of war and peace—it was there under the flashing news bulletins traveling around the New York Times building. . . . You knew you were perhaps a citizen of the world."[28]

The most famous photograph of the city during that time, *V-J Day*, by Alfred Eisenstaedt, depicting a sailor overwhelming a nurse, had Times Square as its

Andreas Feininger (1906–1999), *West 42nd Street*, 1940.
Gelatin-silver print. © Collection The New-York Historical Society,
New York

background. But when Ruth Orkin (1921–1985) shot
V-E celebrations earlier that year (pl. 32), with TV cameras (!) overlooking the crowd, she conveyed the real
power of the square as a world amphitheater at a
penultimate moment.

If Berenice Abbott had described New York's upward
look in a low period, Andreas Feininger (1906–1999)
expressed its pulse in the thriving decade that followed.
The son of a well-known German painter, Lyonel
Feininger, he arrived here in 1939 and found work as
a *Life* photographer. He often equipped himself with
telephoto lenses, which had become highly developed
for military use, and took a systematic approach to
the city, articulated in his methodical itinerary: services,
transport, occupations, neighborhoods, media, and
so on. His attitude toward New York is that of an appre-
ciative outsider, and he diligently examined how it
works (not the same as Lewis Hine's question: who
actually does the work?).

Feininger's *Noon Rush Hour on Fifth Avenue*
(pl. 33), of 1949, makes that already congested scene
appear to be even more jammed, as he flattens the
receding perspective of the street with his long focal
lens. Rather than lack of space, it seems to have
been the process of circulation—almost as if people
were corpuscles flowing in an artery—that interested
him. He achieved similar effects in prospects looking
down on the great concourses and roadways with which
Robert Moses was girding the city. Across from New
Jersey or Queens, or on the Staten Island ferry, Feininger endowed the skyline with an Oz-like grandeur.
It's a citadel of energy, yet also a magisterial vision,
floating on water.

On the street, as a pedestrian, he studied the texture of businesses, always with an explanatory intent.
Where do people go? What is available for them to
buy? In order to depict these purposeful attractions with
scruple, the photographer does not vary his serene,
attentive responses.

In comparison with this almost diagrammatic
stance, Fritz Neugass (1899–1979), in his epigrammatic
view of Thirty-fourth Street (pl. 34), captured shop
signs along with the metropolitan crowd as a pattern
of reflections and juxtaposed spaces. Neugass perceived disparate features as a new unity come together
all at once: the crowd upside down in a ceiling mirror, the contrast between interior and exterior, above
all, exchanges between strata of dark and light. For
an instant, the human forces and the constructed
presences of the street come together and sing the
city's song.

In contrast, Feininger gave his complete attention to each of his subjects, one at a time, delivered through crisp outlines and the richest gamut of black and white. The wares, products, and blandishments of metropolitan commerce are clogged and stacked for immediate purchase and use. New York, as he judges it, is a warehouse of supply and demand, constantly replenished. What's startling and funny about Feininger's picture of a raunchy Times Square movie theater, with "sexy" posters (fig. 11), is his view of it as just one more output of entrepreneurial spectacle.

Feininger and Weegee were very different personalities who nevertheless had in common an idea of New York as a man's town, a place where men slaked their appetites and produced the goods. Weegee often differentiated social milieux: he mocked the cultural pretensions of the upper class, showed his affection for blacks, and identified with the drunks at Sammy's on the Bowery. For his part, Feininger performed as a dignified booster who had much in common with the Byron Company. The classes are again just human strata; folkloric bits add their charm, while the city overall swaggers as it manifests its power. Where would memory, or its regrets, fit into this scheme of things? Or, for that matter, aspiration? New York was not changing, as Berenice Abbott supposed in the 1930s: it had already changed. In the form given to us by Feininger, it appears to us as an immense, solidified *now*.

Without question, his work owed its strength to its certitudes. Weegee's willingness to play fast and loose or do tricks raises interesting doubts about his emotional coherence. With Feininger, though, we know where we stand—always in the best place to grasp the whole of the thing presented. The appropriate viewer of a Weegee photograph is his momentary alter ego; the ideal viewer of one of Feininger's images is an individual interchangeable with any other citizen.

In photo classes, Feininger's imagery was esteemed for its modernism. In fact, he had evolved a contemporary way of seeing Manhattan without participating in any of its avant-garde sensibilities. Here was where the Surrealist André Breton resided; where Willem de Kooning and Jackson Pollock were risking pictorial legibility in an Expressionist form that internalized the war's violence; and where Weegee portrayed the city as a local cauldron of its own violence, described with flippancy. Feininger's Manhattan, in contrast, appears chaste, dynamic, brawny, and in no danger whatsoever. During and just after a world crisis, these were winning attributes. Though the legacy of Andreas Feininger had nowhere to go except into

cliché, he put the finishing touches to New York as an indelible icon at its historical zenith.

Yet the buoyant energy that infused most New York photographers of the 1940s took another course, memorable in its own right, a concern with the smaller joys and sorrows of life in the metropolis. With the Photo League entering its most ebullient phase, what counted most was a dialogue between setting and faces. Arnold Eagle (1910–1992), Sol Libsohn (1914–2001), George Gilbert (b. 1922), Arthur Leipzig (b. 1918), Sid Grossman (1913–1955), Rebecca Lepkoff (b. 1916), and Morris Huberland (b. 1909) aligned themselves in a humanist style that was remarkable for its spontaneity and warmth of feeling. As for Morris Engel and Walter Rosenblum, after their military service, they resumed their careers in photography with similar goals. One outlet for their work was the lively *PM's Weekly*, with its pointed political cartoons and a sympathetic photo editor, Ralph Steiner.

In backyards, where children played; at outdoor meetings, while New Yorkers listened to some speaker; even on the subways and the elevated trains, as people read newspapers or were lost in their thoughts, photographers bore witness, getting traction with how it was. Some of these subjects had already been broached in leaner years. Rebecca Lepkoff, for example, shows an elderly woman on a littered street, passing a synagogue: "Cong. Anshei Sholem Kadonower" (pl. 35). Next to this locked place of worship are faded posters for a film starring Dana Andrews and Joan Crawford. But for the film, the sadness of this image could have come right out of the 1930s. Now the pictures more characteristic of the 1940s are increasingly energetic in their arrangement than those of the previous decade, and they're perceptually quicker, despite the continued use of the big Speed Graphic press cameras demanded by news media.

Gradually, it dawns on a viewer that the subjects of the photographs were as invigorated by a new atmosphere as those with the cameras. Physical conditions were not so good that they couldn't be vastly improved, but "conditions" presently took second place to the issue of New York *psychology*, viewed on its own terms. Photographers saw or inadvertently noted that a nationwide effort to strengthen the country, flushed with resolve, was inciting some new and vivid reactions within the democratic environment. Americans, engaged in a world struggle of unclear outcome, began to realize that they had untapped emotional and productive resources. Between irksome new shortages and rationed domestic materials, and the hapless 1930s inability to buy them, there was a gladdened difference that wrote itself on people's faces. Only a few years before, in the Depression, a popular song asked, "Brother, can you spare a dime?" But during the war, people were hearing "Rosie, the Riveter." The war years were an era when a once-riven populace instinctively closed social ranks, though blacks and Jews in the armed forces were having a very different experience. The outside threat was grave, but so was an inner confidence. As the city that most visibly embodied such confidence, New York, for once, drew the fondest ratings from the rest of the country.

But confidence should not be equated with complacence. In point of fact, if one scans the photographic record, the inhabitants of the city would seem to have had mixed responses to their situation. Their varying spirits flickered across their most expressive faces. They could be severe and determined, but also gregarious, weary, or at a loss. An easier circulation returns to scenes of daily life that had once been pictured as tense, even in friendliness. Those on the street are implicitly more approachable than ever before. Photographers maintained their high alert, but they could put their voyeuristic impulses on hold. Within these affable circumstances, New Yorkers emerge as seasoned and flavorsome characters, people we don't forget.

What we see, in a portfolio of faces, is a reworking of the group portrait in a civic context. The groups tend to be small, and the photographers close the physical range between themselves and their subjects. Morris Huberland's *Outdoor Meeting* (pl. 36), of c. 1940, and Walter Rosenblum's *Block Party, New York East Side* (pl. 37), of 1942, pack a few, heavy, highly individuated figures within a tight frame. They are attending outdoor public meetings. Given the political orientation of both photographers, the events were likely to have been left-wing, but the severe atmosphere of Rosenblum's photograph contrasts with the prickly mood in the picture by Huberland. In one as in the other, though, we have the sense of coming upon a defended perimeter of serious people, convened in high purpose. Men are absent from such tableaux: these are the plain, dowdy, everyday women of New York, who face burdens and are not to be trifled with.

At a political rally in Madison Square Park, George Gilbert focuses on a sign: "All Out with FDR for Victory in '42" (pl. 38). Sunlight from behind casts his shadow on the placard, while the marchers squint or shade their eyes with a kind of happy pain. And

what marchers! A powerful matron, a snaggletoothed man, a snide-looking intellectual, all of them express enthusiasm at something they hear. In fact, the rally was called to urge Roosevelt to start a second European front, in aid of Stalin.[29] Though it was intended as a family portrait of fellow reds, happenstance gave this picture a wonderfully abrasive content, worthy of Honoré Daumier.

In contrast to such togetherness, Sol Libsohn in *Hester Street* (fig. 12; see also pl. 39) somewhat earlier caught a splay of attention, a ricochet of glances, from a cluster of people that belies any idea that they may be construed as a group. Still, how can we interpret their statuesque presences, caught in momentary stances, as other than an ensemble, modulated by degrees of introspection? An irritated passing man at lower right snaps that mood and makes the picture. We realize that each figure within its personal space is averted from the others, with an ingenuity that is truly urban.

The observation of space, indeed, goes far to underline the psychological qualities of loose gatherings. Sometimes they're just inert, with subjects depicted as merely lined up in anonymous sequence, their only goal to get somewhere else. During the 1940s and 1950s, for example, a subgenre of group portraiture dealt with subway passengers. In no other public place of the big city is self-absorbed behavior more socialized than in the train. Immobilized by the restricted space, unsorted strangers who literally rub shoulders contrive not to look either about them or at one another.

Arnold Eagle nevertheless framed their self-containment as a theme with variations (pl. 40): two men deep in newspapers (one with a headline about Nazis) flank a sad older lady, drawn into herself. It seems a stretch to call this a group portrait, because the passenger bench is circumstantially shared by noninvolved people. They have no collective motivation, nor are they posing. Just the same, since the sailor and the worker are personifications of the war effort, the image amounts to more than a random city scene.

Between 1938 and 1941, Walker Evans took many subway pictures, under difficult circumstances with a concealed camera, which was against the law. Unable to frame his images on the spot, he later cropped, then gridded, his several studies of working- and middle-class passengers, in preparation for a book that he never published. Evans conceived the work as an inventory of common people "in a dream 'location' for any portrait photographer weary of the studio and

of the horrors of vanity."[30] Across the aisle, people lapse into ennui or distraction, although more generally they seem just "out to lunch." Yet the accumulated semivacancy of their expressions—"naked repose," as Evans put it—builds into an eloquent study of dilated time in city life. It is possible, too, that this intelligent photographer had other issues to consider. Much later (1962), Evans reflected, "You don't see among them [the subway passengers], the face of a judge or a senator or a bank president. What you do see is at once sobering, startling, and obvious: these are the ladies and gentlemen of the jury" (pl. 41).[31]

The spectrum of New York faces depicted by the Photo League in the 1940s is a heartfelt roll call of citizens in the democratic republic. The fact that subjects are plain in appearance and engaged in the most ordinary pursuits seems only to emphasize their common purpose, rare in the history of New York photographs. For example, what inner strength gives the bocce players photographed by Morris Huberland their powerful stance? They're Olympians of space, formally attired, with laundry drying on lines for a backdrop. Bocce is a sport for older men with clever wrists and good eyesight, but instead of being about their game, the picture tells of their fraternity in an Italian tradition and their command of their own ground.

Compare Huberland's Italian Americans (pl. 42) with Arthur Leipzig's *Coney Island—Steeplechase* (pl. 43), of 1952, at a Coney Island arcade. Both photographs convey a lovely rapport between figures and urban detail that speak of city dreams. Coney Island's hurdy-gurdy of lights induces a vertigo of which the charming young women seem unaware, yet the sparkle in their eyes reflects the carbonated atmosphere of this hyper-American scene. For photographers who wanted to suggest that New York presented an appropriate environment for its ethnic groups as well as for its cozier citizens, the city graciously obliged.

Sometimes, the place is merely sketched in, and only the faces do the talking. Sid Grossman was on good terms with loquacious New York. In classes, he upheld the worth of visceral commitment to the perception of the human moment; as a photographer on the street, he tried to live up to his word as a teacher. By the mid-1940s, after his return from the army, he had left behind the phase of his work devoted to high-caliber social documentation—in Harlem, Chelsea, and the Ozark states. Much of his unpublished New York street photography is tentative in its address, as if he had to relearn what civilians were like, at a moment when his Communism stood in the way of his hunger for expression. At first, he took note of details of dress and casual interaction, as people lolled about; the work is concerned with getting the feel of a scene. A sense of New York colloquial manners informs a picture he did of guys sitting around on a summer day (pl. 44). All except one of them look at the photographer with mild amusement, but that one cadaverous, shrunken figure, with his ill-fitting clothes, is mentally in another space.

Then Sid Grossman went to Coney Island. The bathers on its beach had been treated by photographers forty and fifty years before as sporting figures of a decorous era. In the 1930s, photographs by Reginald Marsh and Morris Engel depicted Coney Island with good humor as a jamboree of beauty contests or family life. Thereafter, we have Weegee, who turned the spectacle into a crowd scene, ludicrous and erotic in equal measure. Weegee kept his distance while others lost their heads, but Grossman shortened distance, so radically that we feel that he becomes an actor in what he showed.

In *Coney Island* (pl. 45), of 1947–48, his Latin twenty-somethings go wild with glee on their towels or blankets. Whatever it took, he got right in there with them, amid their hilarious convulsions and their eager limbs. At this point-blank range, courtship reveals itself as a goofy and marvelous shambles. One sometimes can't figure out who is with whom, or who touches whom in such a turmoil of overlapped intimacies, cut at the frame so arbitrarily that it deprives subjects of essential body parts and viewers of their balance.

With his maximum contrasts of light and dark and his fondness for sharp edges, Weegee gave precise forms to mayhem. Grossman, in contrast, behaved as an Expressionist, immersed in modulated tones. In night scenes at the San Gennaro festival in Little Italy (pl. 46), of 1948, he profited from the blur of lights and figures, recorded on slow film, to evoke both his own excited performance and that of the crowd. More than that, he intuited that a picture was built on its fidelity to ephemeral perception, with all its tremors, not on how precisely things were described. New York street photographers had not thought that way before, and it presaged all kinds of new openings for them.

At the Photo League itself, Grossman was a divisive personality. Party-liners expected this radical to invest himself in polemical imagery, although such an agenda no longer concerned him. In addition, for much of the membership, he was intimidatingly subjective and blind to the history of the medium. The rank and file pictured most of their subjects with kindness—except policemen and Republicans—but they were overloaded with conflicting stylistic choices, which proved schismatic when it came to aesthetic positions. A roster of speakers during those years included Paul Strand, Ansel Adams, W. Eugene Smith, and the critic Elizabeth McCausland, Berenice Abbott's friend. Lewis Hine had been a much-loved visitor there before his death in 1940. The quasi-Abstractionist Minor White wrote for its publication, *Photo Notes*, in 1950, the year before the League folded, its support drained away in response to its presence on the attorney general's list of subversive organizations.

George Gilbert took a revealing picture at the League in 1946. It shows Jakob Deschin, photography critic for the *New York Times*, with a member, Angela

Calomiris, who later informed against the League for the FBI. On the wall are two small posters: one says, "That child in Russia needs your aid"; the other asks readers to give to the USO (United Service Organization, an outfit befriending military personnel on pass or leave).[32] The attorney general could not have been more obtuse than to suppose that these photographers, who believed in good causes, were members of a subversive cell.

Looking back, we can see that crosscurrents— which mixed different political and aesthetic impulses—infused the scene with a certain tension, favorable to photography. Beyond the Photo League, they were reinforced by other visual resources and outlets for the medium, clustered in New York. There were, to begin, *Life, Fortune, Look, Collier's, Vogue, Coronet,* and *PM's Weekly*, active clients in the world of magazines and press. Steichen, director of the photography department at the Museum of Modern Art from 1947 to 1962, featured promising photographers in group shows. Alexey Brodovitch ran a workshop under the sponsorship of the New School for Social Research that was something of a think tank for new talent as well as a scouting pool for *Harper's Bazaar*. In the 1940s, the likes of Louis Faurer, Lisette Model, Richard Avedon, and Ted Croner attended the workshop. Certain connections between fashion and street photography were exemplified by Avedon—following the lead of the Hungarian Martin Munkácsi, a photographer of particularly athletic models. Robert Capa, another Hungarian, the most celebrated foreign (photo) correspondent of his time, co-founded Magnum, the paramount photo agency of the century, in 1947, with Henri Cartier-Bresson, Chim, and George Rodger. Magnum was an intensely energetic, war-seasoned, and self-aware group that provided visual news yet kept its copyrights. The demand for pictures of all categories had risen, in New York, to an unimaginable volume.

In the heady trade-off between editorial or commercial and personal work, there emerged a consciousness of the reciprocal influence each had upon the other. Noir film style also played a role in this process, both influencing and affected by still photography. These were champagne days in image culture. Gjon Mili (1904–1984) pictured the smoky café entertainment of New York—such as the Stork Club or 21— with artful manner and a B-movie's glamorous production values (pl. 47). Other photographers viewed this dynamic professional scene as a mandate to take risks. They broadened their subject matter, embold-

ened their style, and showed a liking for abrupt and ambiguous content.

When he was away from jobs for Brodovitch, art director at *Harper's Bazaar*, Ted Croner (b. 1922) considered New York with a visual ruggedness that verged on the brutal. On Fifty-ninth Street, he took a pungent photograph of two figures: a Clark Gable–like tough, cigarette in mouth, and a black man who looks at him. Signs provide reading matter: "Police Dept" "The Outlaw—Jane Russell" (pl. 48). Croner used texts in this picture and another, in which a marquee advertises a film, *Home of the Brave*, as markers indicating an environment pressurized by a high level of testosterone. Elsewhere, he shows us passersby, seen, like buildings, from far below, and appearing only as amorphous dark shapes that chafe each other in the cold (pl. 49). Croner displaces any account or even intimation of sociality by means of broad gestural sweeps that are only vaguely reconstituted as mismatched and spectral figures, without faces though heavy in purpose.

As the 1940s wore on, photographers overlaid the League's tradition of the informal group portrait with a renewed involvement in action on the street. The togetherness of people still lingered as a motif— or maybe as an ideal—but it could no longer be projected onto faces with the conviction of earlier years. In the latter part of the decade, we will not find the equivalent of the 1941 portrait by Lou Bernstein (b. 1911) of a black husband and wife, who display their connubial bond with a sly pride, even as they withhold from the onlooker a knowledge they alone can share (pl. 50). Instead, faces now tended to be glimpsed as only one among many elements in situations that had their own rhythms and discords. This is to speak not of Weegee's "industrious chaos" but of a more porous view of New York life, which breezes with lyrical intent. The timing of the picture's exposure played a more critical role, for purposes that were now consciously artistic.

Once again, an example was furnished by a visitor, in this case, one already known and much discussed by his New York colleagues. Henri Cartier-Bresson's street style is manifested in counterpoints of disparate incidents presented as an integrated field. His grasp of that field is at work in *New York* (pl. 51), of 1946, an image of a crowd greeting arrivals from a ship. In that moment, high-intensity grief and excitement act as foils in a wave of human distraction. Homecoming is a composite of delayed union and remembered absence, precipitated in the rustle of bodies.

Someone's arm flies up, someone else's arm, that of a weeping man, sinks down, like beautiful flanges. Emotionally, we don't know where to settle or with whom the artist identifies, and we suspect that he wants it that way.

Helen Levitt (b. 1913) is a most independent New York photographer; her work moved out from its early debt to Shahn's, which she respected, and to that of Evans and Cartier-Bresson, whom she knew. Levitt is best known for her book *A Way of Seeing*, prepared in 1946 but not published until 1965. In its vignettes from Harlem, Yorkville, and Lower East Side streets, an initial impression of playfulness—on the part of both subjects and photographer—later shifts indefinably in tone toward a certain melancholy.

The pictures remain sunny, and the urchins in them, as well as their elders, appear to be having a normal good time, more or less. Nowhere does Levitt allow the slightest hint of a home-front metropolis, inflected by alarms from abroad. Her street people, on the contrary, often seem to be involved with each other in their own immediate territory. Beyond, there stretches an urban elsewhere, if not exactly an alien zone. Levitt evokes a sense of a sociality that huddles in, leaving the rest of the place nondescript and unconcerned. Her foregrounds are usually busily occupied, but, because the busyness is isolated, we begin to feel that something about the city is recalcitrant, avoided, and unnourishing.

This noticeable, though not intrusive, shortfall of rapport between the city and its citizens puzzles us in imagery caught up with movement. Levitt made her living as a film editor, and she did cinematography for two films, *The Quiet One* and *In the Street*, the latter a short essay that depicts the perpetual motion of characters who run around and jump up or skitter like mad. Their apparent frenzy is accelerated by the most staccato editing, which might have been prompted by Levitt's enthusiasm for early Soviet cinema. Instead of workers, however, her subjects are largely children, either black or Puerto Rican.[33]

Children's tightly knit behavior constantly speaks of early social communion, while at the same time it provides kinetic opportunities for the camera. This may be one reason why Levitt concentrated on them. Another is suggested by Colin Westerbeck, who notes that Levitt was a shy person, for whom kids were unintimidating subjects. He writes: "Street photographers who specialize in children produce too many pictures that are cute, like photographers who specialize in cats. To be any good, the pictures have to tran-

scend their subject. We never take novels about children seriously unless we can take them as allegories of an adult world. . . . Levitt's pictures give the impression that she doesn't particularly like children."[34] If this favorable judgment is correct, then Levitt was a lone, contrarian woman in a tradition of male photographers who empathized with children very much.

Hine considered children in their identity as workers, prematurely aged and burdened, toiling in exploitive conditions. He implied that boys on the street were far from home or family, and he showed them diminished in adult space; when they were in groups, he presented them as protectively banded together. In either case, children were unconnected to the larger society and therefore in a threatened state.

With the photography of Aaron Siskind, Arnold Eagle, Morris Engel, and Arthur Leipzig from the 1930s and 1940s, juveniles come into their own as full-fledged people. Looking at all these small creatures, a viewer might reasonably conclude that the entire population of New York was underage, for, in such a milieu, an adolescent would count as a senior citizen. Seemingly unaware of larger travails in the world beyond their own, the children nevertheless reflect some echo of it, as they play in forts improvised from crates (Siskind) or at war games, as miniature soldiers (Leipzig). Eagle depicted a little boy, his sneaker strings untied, and his protective older sister, with a *tendresse* that preserves their sibling charm (pl. 52). In 1947, Morris Engel followed a shoeshine boy on his professional rounds, framing the boy in a mirror when a cop addressed him. This photograph (pl. 53, from an extended essay) wonderfully summarizes themes that run through the engagement of New York photographers with their spaces: the presence of movies, an interracial mix of pedestrians, an off-balance view, and the expanded group of the street. Though the kid is the picture's hero, he's almost lost in a scenario that has many subplots and counterpointed figures.

Levitt turned this tradition into something more mysterious. It is probably true that she was able to resist the lovability of kids, as Westerbeck suggests, and it is certainly the case that she refused to simplify them. Their games can be aboriginal and their playgrounds may sometimes be wastelands, but in their masquerades and even in their clownery—their pose as desperadoes in their own territory—they come across as unknowable souls. Levitt was taken by their gamin hide-and-seek on the front stoops and on the steps of their brownstones. She was probably in her own search, too, tracking their onetime presence by their graffiti, yet discovering her exclusion from their ritual and arcane interplay. One of her most enigmatic images is of a hand pointing from a curtained window—a sign that might be indicating either "Clear out!" or "That way" (pl. 54).

Levitt's "way" proved, in the end, to be dialectical. When mothers appear with their offspring (pl. 55), the scene is quite grouchy but still choreographed with fluent contrasts of forms and feelings. A hitherto unpublished image of black children dancing is like a pavane, at once grave and lyrical, witnessed in a privileged moment (pl. 56). The photographer long maintained an interest in the manners and gestures with which even the youngest of her subjects care for one another. Always low-keyed and ostensibly tossed-off, the musicality of her work compares faces with storefronts, and the warm culture of minorities with the insensate background of the city. This aspect of her vision is as apparent today as it was when James Agee stressed it in his essay for her book. Another, much later writer, Ben Lifson, suggests the delicacy of her scruples: "Levitt's style respects it all and tactfully keeps its distance, neither permitting an emotion to overwhelm the world of a picture nor the world's loveliness or shabbiness to trivialize an emotion."[35] Levitt's visual poetics may very well have been reinforced by her moral lucidity.

As they accumulated, the array of different forces that played into the visualization of 1940s New York became more competitive and fractious. With the advent of Cold War anti-Communism and the early McCarthy, old-style social engagement became dangerous and lost its popularity, whatever the sentiments of disaffected radicals. At the same time, the idea of the metropolis as a place to celebrate lost its innocence and began to fade. The solidarity forged by wartime dread was over, to be followed by a fierce peacetime scramble for opening markets and new profits. For photographers, this was an unstable prospect. In the past fifteen years, many of them had worked for the WPA or had menial jobs in their industry; a few had photography assignments in the armed services, others were freelancers for newspapers. Now their options changed, in an opportunistic environment that held promise in what appeared to be an engrossing commercial sector.

To many of them, the career rewards of the immediate future were either unappetizing or only too seductive, leading them, in any case, away from the energy with which they had once borne witness to the city. Siskind and Grossman withdrew into modes of photographic abstraction and Expressionism, emulating painting styles with marginal success. Weegee went to Hollywood, anxious to sell his notoriety. Far from its source, his flair quickly petered out. In his autobiography, Weegee relates a story that speaks of his bewilderment in the coils of the American fame machine.

At some point on a New York street in the early 1940s, he accosts a lonely old man wearing a black cape. "You Stieglitz? I'm Weegee. You may have read about me in the magazines." They go to An American Place (the old man's quarters), where Weegee hears Stieglitz say that he is exhausted, sick, a self-declared failure, and an abandoned hero. He also learns that Stieglitz "never compromised with his photography for money or to please an editor"—that is, Weegee's normal course of action. It is a colloquy between an eminence of the receding generations of cultivated German Jews and a protagonist of the triumphant wave of Russian successors. In the end, Stieglitz slumps over in pain. "I waited till he recovered then left quietly . . . wondering if that elusive fame I was after was worth while."[36]

To a few, like Ted Croner or Louis Faurer, who had made their living by other means, squeezing in private moments for their art, that fame would nevertheless remain the only worldly reward of a vision pursued without financial recompense. There could be no question that an artistic consciousness had percolated through some photography, guided originally by a documentary aim. Helen Levitt can surely be said to exhibit an artistic temperament, no less than a doctor displays medical tendencies. But how, if at all, were such temperaments to adapt to or be reconciled with the conceptual leadership of new painting and sculpture? Most of the photographers in New York were still more or less loyalists to a descriptive tradition. Into the gap entered the fashion industry, which decisively shook the scene's pictorial variants into an unlikely new cocktail.

If *Harper's Bazaar* had done nothing more to further the cause of American photography than to give Lisette Model (1906–1983) a few breaks, it would have been enough. In 1941, Alexey Brodovitch sent this Austrian émigré, who had arrived in 1938 from France, out on assignment to Coney Island, from which she came back with pictures of very fat American bathers. As one of them illustrated the pages of a magazine devoted to eulogizing the slimmest of figures, the success of this work requires a little explanation.

To begin, one might recall the liaison between American and French fashion in the 1930s, followed by the availability of top-rank foreign talent displaced to Manhattan by the war and looking for work. *Harper's Bazaar* would derive intellectual prestige from the provision of such work, at a moment when the magazine was expanding its coverage of celebrities, theater, and culture generally. Brodovitch took that expansion further by sponsoring what was, from his perspective, unsettling imagery that cast an acute, downward look into American class structure. He gambled that publicity dividends would arise from the contrast between the magazine's appeal to privilege and its views of the reality below—gloss, played up by gross.

To later eyes, however, the earthiness and vitality of Model's bathers compare very well with the forgettable sniffishness of *Harper's Bazaar*'s mannequins. Model's advantages were not only her obviously greater feeling for humanity but the graphic strength of her formal instinct. With the work of this photographer—who had studied music with Arnold Schoenberg and who was friendly with Fernand Léger and Piet Mondrian—editors got far more than they had bargained for.

PM's Weekly's Ralph Steiner may have had a more accurate take on Model when, in 1941, he published her street portraits of vacationers in Nice, work from the early 1930s. He was unaware that they had already come out in the French magazine *Regards*, an organ of the European antifascist left, published under the auspices of André Gide, André Malraux, and Ilya Ehrenburg.[37] Steiner decided that the portraits themselves—gamy depictions of wealthy people in idle postures—were illustrations of a kind of moral low life. He brought them out under the simplistic (to say the least) title "Why France Fell."

Model's art is definitely antibourgeois: her judgments indict the middle class's smugness as well as its selfishness. For example, she depicted a man in profile, seated on the sidewalk, his hat out for coins (pl. 57). Coming toward him, and toward the photographer, is a horde of pedestrians. Model associates herself with the lone man by her amazing street-level proximity in the immediate foreground, a device that also truncates the passersby from the waist down, so as to underline their existence as an uncaring, brainless mass. Locking in horizontal shadows from the right, the frame intensifies the contrast between the man's stoic, powerful face and the crowd's blurred momentum. A viewer would not be wrong to accept this picture as a comment on alienated social relations, but at the same time the robust concision of the tableau serves to electrify her statement well above the level of a moral commonplace.

Model had great compositional skills. She placed bulky presences in taut spaces, as if each had no further business than to be destined for the other. When she applied this resource consistently to pictures of very different subjects, they acquired a grandeur of design, no matter how tacky the locale. New York itself did not inspire her photographic style, which had matured in Europe, but the city did give Model an enlarged stage for her encounters with social phenomena. Since she was prone to viewing them as theatrical events, the word "stage" is appropriate. Weegee, too, had a sense of theater, but it was centrifugal, whereas Model's was centripetal, a drawing in toward the center. So accentuated is this centering that her pictures almost have the density of still lifes, even when movement is explicit in the scene. Yet Model cropped her photographs, to avoid symmetries. A staggered yet powerful rhythm marks her studies of New York feet in motion. They come close to abstraction in their cadence of shape and interval while also expressing the inexorable crunch of the street.

When she peered into store or restaurant windows, however, Lisette Model accomplished something even more original. Glass is a compromised surface: transparent yet also reflective, it picks up echoes of objects from behind the viewer and veils some that are before her. We find such visual disjunction in many photographs by this petite woman, who used it to meditate on solitude in New York. The man in a Delancey Street restaurant (pl. 58) becomes a figure estranged in a play of light and shadows projected from multiple sources. He's a kind of *untermensch* hemmed in by a real interior, yet randomly camouflaged by a spectral urbanscape. In this photograph, the setting itself gets into the act as a reflected overlay on the man at the right.

Delancey Street, on the Lower East Side, a neighborhood filled with crypto-Europeans, reminded Model of Paris. Such a memory may be at work in the apparitional qualities of *Reflection, New York* and other photographs she took of city windows, where near and far had their counterparts in present and past. During her European youth, Model had a long spell of psychotherapy; in New York, she was a displaced person living by her wits in a precarious field. Whatever they may reveal about the perceptual aspects of New York streets, the windows also tell of the photographer's self-reflection. All those scurrying feet in her sidewalk pictures imply, perhaps, the impetus of a crowd that she could never understand, while all those ambiguous nuances associated with glass windows may speak of those individual experiences that can never be retrieved. Almost as if she had to row against these wayward currents, Model developed a style that was simultaneously punchy in layout yet undecidable in content.

The art of Lisette Model signals a break in what might be called the psychological evolution of New York photography. It's manifested in her attitude toward the citizenry, so often interpreted as a misanthropic stance. She was unquestionably equipped with satirical impulses—as was Weegee. Both could give a caricaturist's wicked attention to the human face. One look at Model's picture of the cheaply jeweled and plumed denizens of Asti's restaurant (pl. 59) is enough to show us how easily she could turn them into fools. This hostility runs through a number of brilliant, well-received pictures she took of vulgar, avaricious, and narcissistic behavior in chic New York nightspots. But when Model turned her gaze toward the destitute, she squeezed lemon juice on a few of them, too. And this, in some quarters, would be hard to forgive.

Just the same, a case for Model as an antihumanist photographer is hard to establish. It was human inwardness that concerned her and the lack of it that she attacked. This distinction would never have occurred to Weegee, the comedian. Model's art veers toward the tragic. Where he was a gymnast of disparagement, almost asking you not to take him seriously, she employed a selective malice. It is quite true that she took advantage of people—including poor ones—who could not imagine the unflattering guise in which she would portray them, but her photographs suggest that vacuous behavior, as much as a *spiritual state*, is not confined to just one class.

Model was the first socially conscious photographer of New York to operate beyond the gravitational field of Lewis Hine, whose faith in progress and in the camaraderie of work had had its day. Model came from a ravaged Europe in which the ideal of social justice was temporarily obliterated, but she saw that American democracy did little to acculturate human deviance, or to help the destitute. Hers was less a dispirited or fatalist view than fascinated recognition: she depicted misfits, dropouts, and poseurs as charismatic, irrepressibly flawed beings in a cruel environment.

In her private teaching, which exerted an influence deep and wide, Model emphasized that the greatest failing of photographic practice was indifference. When she approached human debility or an oddness that could be sinister, it was as a fully engaged artist. In contrast, anecdotal or even reportorial photographers were likely to be disengaged, for it was the story that mattered to them, not their feeling. Where others might judge her beggars to be afflicted loners, she saw them as "strong personalities" with whom she identified, because her life either had been or could be like theirs.[38]

At the time, editors and colleagues regarded Lisette Model as a forward-looking artist by virtue of her pictorial strength, but it was her effrontery that counted more, and proved to be the most modern thing about her. She redefined the documentary mode, introducing motives that could be questioned. Weegee and Model are like bookends to the chapter of photography in 1940s New York. In their work, the stressed optimism of the Photo League, where they were both respected, took on a darker shading. Weegee went on to a kind of fame, if not fortune; Model was skeptical of fame and experienced steady indigence. Yet, in a slightly delayed action, she inspired a significant following. Without the insights of both these photographers into the unsavory aspects of American society, whether ordained by culture or conditioned by the city, it would be impossible to imagine the candor of the work that was to come.

The Indispensable Target

As a metropolis that enjoyed extraordinary fame in the history of twentieth-century photography, New York had a rival—and a glorious one, at that. Paris was the sister capital of modern times. The international genre of street photography is unthinkable without the push initially given it in Paris: what New York photographers learned from Atget and Cartier-Bresson was incalculable. When the work of younger Parisians like Robert Doisneau and Édouard Boubat was shown in Manhattan, shortly after World War II, it, too, was greeted sympathetically, even as it revealed a very different urban culture. The difference between the Parisian and the New York accounts of city manners is quite interesting, but the contrast between their political visions is provocative.

After Paris was liberated from the Germans in 1944, images expressed the joy of release, without implying any new foundation for the city's culture. True to their backgrounds, the photographers exhibited liberal sympathies and a populist spirit, within a lyric mode. It was natural enough for them to look back, but as they did so, they purged or modified certain of their traditional motifs. For one thing, love was no longer an act that had to be bought and sold: couples engage in it freely along the *quais*. For another, fascinating transvestites bow out of the picture, to be supplanted by humorous eccentrics. Concierges make their appearances, with their overweight cats. Accordionists still wander about, but rather than in bars, they're seen accompanying the street dances of the 14th of July. Such is the frequency of these dances in the pictorial corpus that they become an element in the iconography of Paris, a ritual of nationalism identified with the sweetness of life.

From Paris in the late 1940s, in fact, come some of the most touching pictures in the history of the medium, depicting the uplift of faces amid drear industrial suburbs. Doisneau was their poet. Ten years later, his neorealist style, and that of many witty colleagues, would be glazed by a more illustrational intent. The exponents of Parisian photography—Doisneau, Ronis, Boubat, René Jacques, Izis—appear to us as genre artists of a certain age, with memories.

Though the Parisians were preserving their tribal customs, as such images assert, France was going through unsettling and arduous times. In the *après-guerre*, the French experienced unrest caused by the purge of collaborators (*l'épuration*)—a literal trial of French moral consciousnness—the rise of existential philosophy, a hardening of Communist activism, the need to rebuild a destroyed infrastructure, and the dismembering of their colonial empire, first in Vietnam, then in Algeria. Given this background, a minor industry of picture books, curated to celebrate traditional Paris, has to be understood as a wistful reading of the historical moment. In their restorative and healing pages, the charm of the capital prevailed, *despite* everything.[39]

If Parisian photographers in the 1950s preserved an amorous relationship with their city, their New York opposite numbers nursed a quarrelsome rapport with Manhattan. Regardless of ferocious ideological divisions among its people, Paris was seen as a network of consonant societies, each of them unquestionably Gallic. As they were not perceived as French, Parisians of color or those with marked ethnicity didn't fit in, and consequently were not photographed.[40] By contrast, their New York counterparts continued to draw the camera's attention. Though citizens by law, the assimilation of these New Yorkers into the social weave was uneven and problematic, and photographers tended to regard the unresolved status of hyphenated Americans as a very photogenic phenomenon. The urgency of much New York photography was heightened by the sense that it was *cognizant* of everything.

Between the ethnic or racial cultures of New York, in staggered renewal, and the metropolitan host culture, unable to identify itself except through its wealth and consumerism, a huge gap opened. New York, during the 1950s, revealed social chasms that fissured the nation's self-satisfaction. Like many intellectuals, photographers may have been critical of our imperium, yet they tended to study its mood rather than to analyze or protest its policy. They were situated in a metropolis that claimed a central position in the world, even though it could not integrate its communities. New York in the 1950s lacked "soul," a quality Paris had in abundance. Our photographers could be utterly riveted by their circumstances while not feeling in the least resident within them.

A remarkable picture of 1954 by Leonard Freed (b. 1929) may be taken as a pointer to this state of affairs (pl. 60). Wall Street and its life rise up above the photographer's vantage in a subway stairwell. The prospect is at once a scene of local pedestrian traffic and a portrait of the city as a mighty construction. These forces are so successfully welded that the striding, weighty figures are likened to the buildings themselves. A high aerial walkway connects verticals that flank the passage of men who loom inordinately in their own space. From another perspective, they might

have been taken as quotidian, unassuming citizens, but in Freed's picture, shot from below, the elements, dark against the light, combine to evoke a power that is oppressive. Forty years before, Paul Strand had shown Wall Street workers as pitiable ants (pl. 11); now, they seem to have internalized their institutional culture and have the power to crush us.

These business types strangely resemble the celebrants of an Italian-American religious procession on Mulberry Street in 1952, seen in *San Gennaro Festival* (pl. 61), photographed by Dan Weiner (1919–1959). As he stands in the crowd, his camera a trifle elevated over heads, Weiner catches a surge of males who appear simultaneously quite pugnacious, with their cigars, and reverential. In this scene, medals sported on chests coexist with a polychrome saint, while a band member toots a trumpet next to a United States flag. Freed's picture contains such a flag, also. Although these images depict two very different scenarios, the Stars and Stripes has a normal, yet questioned place in both. In a small, monocultural town, the flag might look like a natural adornment to obviously American proceedings; here, in 1950s New York, it's depicted as rhetorical legitimization by skeptics with an attitude.

This was an era in which photographers portrayed New Yorkers as either having taken aggressive charge of a particular space or being out of tune with it. It is remarkable how often the people of the city—if it is understood as a common zone—could be made to look other than indigenous. Photographers like Freed and Weiner, to be sure, are preoccupied with the territorial imperative of subcultures, which they regard with some hostility, editorializing the tension they feel in the teeth of happenings whose spirit they won't or can't share. That tension is manifested in their physical point of view, which is peripheral, and also in their way of characterizing the activity of groups as a mesmeric, yet sinister pageant. There is something automaton-like about this collective behavior, a surrender of freedom as an accomplished fact. Lisette Model had earlier opened up this spatial psychology; now, it gained momentum.

Certain previous ideas about New York were transformed by its visualization in the 1950s. Where once they had sought social connectedness with the crowd, photographers began to demonstrate their external relation to scenes that were staked out by others. Partly this was a question of a certain self-consciousness that observers—in this instance, Jewish—registered as individuals within a mass. Though some of their predecessors had seen that mass—or constituents thereof—as a vital organism, younger photographers tended to conceive of it as a conformist throng. Their own identity, however, brought with it new uncertainties, a sense of disaffiliation, which more and more became the subject of their contact with New York. The city, under these circumstances, became a source of dismal allure, and also of a faint odium.

Both these tones are evident in Weiner's picture of Marlene Dietrich, Truman Capote, and Harold Arlen at El Morocco in 1955 (pl. 62). Here are stars apparently at home in chic surroundings that the photographer describes as raucous and glitzy. You can almost lose the famous faces amid the competitive zebra-skin banquettes, the heavy napery, the bouquets, the pseudo-palms, and an irrelevant diner. As a paparazzo photograph, it's low grade, but as social comment, this picture shines. Notice the crablike hands of the principals. In Alexander MacKendrick's near-contemporary movie *Sweet Smell of Success* (1957), a similar restaurant is portrayed as a conspiratorial den where gossip, scandal, and puffery are bought with favors or cold cash. Other photographers—William Klein and Garry Winogrand—were to sport with such plummy scenes, reminiscent of Model's. Weiner is not openly derisive of the setting, like Weegee, but he lets show his indifference to its "glamour." It's as if he were asking viewers to agree with him that El Morocco's customers were welcome to their space.

In photographs of Paris, social space looks fluid and communal; there might sometimes be disjunction, and, of course, a photographer's voyeurism, but little hint of trespass. In New York, photographers have often tagged space with psychological markers, suggesting that the viewer and the subject, though physically near each other, are estranged in separate cultural areas. When Leonard Freed depicts two yeshiva boys behind a brownstone entrance door just then being opened by someone's hand (pl. 63), we can't help thinking of a division in space that might be described as "theirs" and "ours." This time, the photographer acts as a viewer trying to see initiates of a tribe protected in their dark cavity. Though Freed himself is Jewish, he framed his urban zone and their secluded turf as two spaces that barely communicate. With the titans of *Wall Street*, his tone implies a certain malignance; here, on the same level with his subjects, he insinuates a note of melancholy separation.

On the surface and in commercial media, however, everything in the United States seemed quite rosy. Robert Moses's New York crossways had enabled a mobile population to commute to the city from their dream houses in trim suburbs. The times were flush and credit was good. Relations between the sexes were publicly (and necessarily) wholesome. The birthrate was up, and people could hardly fail to have noticed that the United States was a superpower, the rest of the world nominally available for their nation-state to mold according to enlightened democratic principles. Social-science techniques were newly applied to daily living: though Freud was popular, Doctor Spock ruled. What could anyone do to shake the equanimity of a people whose master of ceremonies was Ed Sullivan? Yet, a key book of the period, William H. Whyte Jr.'s *Organization Man* (1956), suggested that there was a repressive, dehumanizing undertow in all this sociality. Another book, David Riesman's *Lonely Crowd* (1950), actually schematized it.

Riesman analyzed three basic types of behavior: other-directed, inner-directed, and autonomous. The last was represented by a figure that rose to fame in America during the Cold War—the rebel. Milton Berle may have opened American comedy of the 1950s and Lenny Bruce, the foul-mouthed, may have finished it, but no one embodied the type of the rebel more successfully than the inarticulate and vulnerable characters played by James Dean. Without doubt, the most famous photograph of 1950s New York is Dennis Stock's picture of Dean bedraggled and utterly alone in a rainy Times Square. This fragile misfit was portrayed as suffering at the hands of an obtuse society, and the young, so-called silent generation loved him for it. For their part, a number of sensitized photographers also perceived the agora of New York as a theater of sadness, even when crowded. They weren't rebels or political dissidents, nor were they celebrity shooters like Stock who used Broadway as a prop in a biographical essay. It was just that they knew an adversarial place when they saw one, and it was Manhattan.

Part of their outlook may have been conditioned by material constraints. Louis Faurer, Garry Winogrand, Saul Leiter, Robert Frank, and Leon Levinstein were all employed in commercial or editorial jobs that sapped energy from their powerful sense of vocation. The values in their main line of work and in their chief pursuit (for which they were exquisitely qualified) happened to be very much at odds. When they moonlighted on the streets, these photographers projected some of their yearning and their disappointment. In theory, the street represents the arena of freedom; in practice, the street is visualized as a prosperous zone occupied by enervated, drifting, and forlorn beings.

Louis Faurer (1916–2001) had a meditative instinct that he superimposed upon an anxious view of New York in shadowed perspectives, where fluorescence appears to give only an ineffectual and tinny light. Along Broadway, he photographed pedestrians with umbrellas spread under the glow of a marquee advertising Stanley Kramer's *On the Beach* (1959), a film about the end of the world brought about by nuclear war. The movie's title, which suggests summer, and the chill metropolitan scene go elegiacally together. Indeed, with a certain fancifulness, Faurer's mood brought elegy right into ordinary traffic. He achieved a quite inexplicable effect of pity and of sorrow through tremulous atmosphere and hesitant gestures or expressions. One night on a street, two deaf-mutes are in silent converse, but it's as if a stream of distant, out-of-focus light blobs has become the spoken words they cannot exchange with each other (pl. 64).

What Faurer did with the equivocations of half-light on reflective surfaces had not been seen before. Lisette Model and Ted Croner had certainly intimated the tonal possibilities, but Faurer, working at the same time, took them further. He was capable of evoking figures as dark profiles that skitter and dissolve as reflections on glass, or that repeat themselves in different sizes. A viewer is easily confused by this maze of echoed shapes framed in bus windows and the staircases that lead up to elevated train stations. One of Faurer's best-known photographs is a double exposure of a huddled-in boy at a street accident, which mutates into a scene of formally dressed figures at a hotel entrance.

This artist also did not hesitate to draw on collage as a model for gathering simultaneous views of a city that confounds our gaze with its elusive and weightless presences. Whether at short or long range, Faurer could melt disparate solids, making it appear that the eye is losing its grip on the urban space. His glimpse of Manhattan reflected in the glass doors of the Staten Island ferry (possibly as it sails away from the city) turns the skyline into such a phantasm that its existence might be doubted (pl. 65). Only slightly more substantial, but still not well materialized, the dark shadows of the photographer and another passenger anchor the frame. In a Faurer image, things and people do move, but as if in a floating world.

Such an unmoored state confers on New York a gratuitous aura of disempowerment. Though citizens are afoot, they pause or at most step lightly into what looks like a gaudy void. Faurer has two preferred subjects: the vending beggar and Times Square. If we

ask what a beggar's experience of metropolitan space might be like, Faurer supplies a disquieting answer. Articles of only token value—paper flowers or pencils—are presented for sale but are really solicitations for alms. The meager potential of this transaction stands in for the other, indefinite exchanges that are possible in the city; they, too, have only a meager potential, and the pathos of it becomes Faurer's real theme. Times Square acts as a metaphor for the same fruitless and unresponsive space represented by the beggar. Amusements may smile or twinkle, they even occasionally seem to mock with a spirit that has a bit of the carnival in it (pl. 66), but mostly, like traffic lights on a misty evening, they're remote and spectral. The plaza is a place for tourists, slightly agog. No one belongs there; no one owns it. For a walker of the city, fluidity of movement achieves about as much, in the end, as the despondent stasis of a loner. Faurer perceived all this, not as a critic of consumerism, but with an air of regret.

Saul Leiter (b. 1923), who supported himself as a fashion photographer, came to similar if more introspective conclusions about New York's atmosphere. His characteristic note is diaristic. With a tautness and thrust more pronounced than Faurer's, he worked the mode of the photographic vignette, reducing context yet implying hubbub. This approach courted surprise, his own no less than the viewer's. In many such instances, what is framed through the lens and what the photographer might have seen, or remember having seen, were at some variance. Leiter's willingness to risk incoherence, still uncommon in the early 1950s, was nevertheless matched by his sense of design. The presence of Lisette Model might account for some of this approach, but we also have to remember the impact of Cartier-Bresson's 1952 book *The Decisive Moment*, originally titled *Images à la sauvette*—images on the run or the sly.

Colin Westerbeck wrote of Cartier-Bresson: "The image is balanced precisely halfway between a meticulous composition and a knee-jerk reaction. The two elements are contradictory yet mutually dependent."[41] Saul Leiter, who knew the Frenchman's work from his 1947 show at the Museum of Modern Art, was a virtuoso of these contradictions. He shot through the window of a restaurant, catching what at first seems only a broth of grays but what at second glance turns into the back of a top-coated man. A third glance reveals a lonesome coffee mug that sprouts a spoon handle (pl. 67). The dark shadow of the photographer, by chance, as it seems, highlights the man's indistinct, whitish profile. This scene is composed of nothing, yet Leiter makes it eventful. In its ephemeral composure, we glimpse the jigsaw of impressions that elsewhere and almost always the city scatters through an unremembered process.

Only a still photograph can pluck sense from these active forms, but only an eye that is innocent will register their rare and indifferent beauty. Leiter's eye was innocent, for it could grasp the primordial in its accidental impact; his mind, however, was geared by a sophisticated estrangement. With rush and blur, the photographer shows the bewilderment of a child or the apparent anguish written into the mask of an old woman. Here is an enhancement of life that does not exactly give viewers a cause to cheer.

Even an incident as innocuous as a man looking into a barbershop has a troubled appearance (pl. 68). A reflection of his profile, cut at the eye and visible only to the photographer, glares back admonishingly at this window-shopper. Leiter's use of color—the red, white, and blue of the barbershop pole, the red of the Coca-Cola sign—reinforces the belligerence of this vignette. With his pioneering use of color as pattern and as fragrance, Leiter jams the urbanscape with new, thermal information. Ambiguous grays are one thing; warms and cools, filtered into this illusory world, are another. For the disturbance of this work wells up in a kineticism that teases with an alarm that is not quite delivered, and a loveliness that has an edge. If you ask how any of this could have been noticed, you might wonder, also, if it could even have happened.

What kind of a city, during the Eisenhower years, do these few photographs propose? Manhattan appears to be a place transfigured by two kinds of subjectivities, both of which depict people in clannish control of their space or dispossessed within it. In any case, a malaise hovers at the city's corners and on its thoroughfares. Something is definitely "off" with the metropolis; life there seems coerced or arrhythmic, but we can't point to any physical cause. The shabbiness of the Depression explained the low-grade angst of 1930s New Yorkers; two decades later, they're seen possibly in better circumstances, but not more contented. Or, rather, is it that some photographers are subtly reproaching them for their well-being? To understand this strange state, it might help to think of the population as the object of the photographers' spleen, an attitude, according to the Random House dictionary, composed of "melancholy," "cold mirth," or "peevish temper." In a splenetic mood, photographers noted

that while business was normally carried on, civility was somehow misplaced. This spectacle was determined as a kind of psychic disturbance in the relationship of citizens to the street.

William Klein (b. 1928), an expatriate New Yorker who returned to the city from Paris for eight months in 1954, was enchanted by this anomaly, no matter how it displayed itself. On the GI Bill, he had studied with Fernand Léger, and later photographed his own abstract paintings, reversible panels that were pivoted on poles. The ideas (if not the art) of Léger—a socialist painter of monumental constructions who urged his students to study the streets—infused Klein's up-to-the-minute avant-garde involvement with blur and gesture. As if these manifold imperatives were not enough, he was also deeply engaged with typography and graphic design. Alexander Liberman, art director at *Vogue*, saw Klein's abstractions in Paris and asked him to work as a graphic designer for the magazine. Klein also thought he would like to do a "photographic diary" of the city, and Liberman encouraged him with the thought of publishing extracts from it in *Vogue*.

From the scorching photographs he took of his hometown, Klein organized a book that was little recognized by colleagues and scorned by American publishers at the time. Klein's *Life Is Good and Good for You in New York: Trance Witness Revels* was published in France in 1956. Robert Frank's *Americans* also had to wait for a French publisher (1958). Both these projects, pointedly critical of American society, got raves in Paris, where the political environment of anticapitalist intellectuals, more than photographic taste, probably accounted for this hospitable reception.

Simone de Beauvoir, who first came to New York a couple of years before Klein's visit home, was astonished but also alienated by what she saw. Very soon, she discovered that "beneath the multicolored paper wrappers, all the chocolates taste of peanuts, all the best sellers tell the same story. Here are a thousand opportunities open to choice: but they are all the same. Americans can enjoy their freedom without ever noticing that they [sic] are not true conditions of freedom. On posters, what displays of shining white teeth before Coca-Cola, Lucky Strikes and dishes of Quaker Oats: a smile like lockjaw." Yet, she concludes, "Americans do not submit passively to the propaganda of smiles; in an atmosphere in which optimism is obligatory they gladly become cordial, trusting and generous; a man's pleasant manner is less suspect the less interested

he personally is in the success of the system; he is
more hoaxed than hoaxer."[42]

Although Klein knew New York better than Beauvoir, he, too, was seeing it as an outsider. At the same
time, he was also an insider who loved New York for
what it was. How else to interpret his shot of three
dapper and silly peanut figures, with their vending
machines, beneath portraits of the company's dignified founders (fig. 13)? They could almost have provided a sardonic illustration to Beauvoir's journal. Such
tableaux offered occasions for a laughter of which
Paris had a much shorter supply.

Hoax or hype—Klein couldn't get enough of either.
In his work, the deconstructionist meets the absurdist head-on, and the picture wins. He never met an advertisement he didn't like. As a battleship is designed
as a gun platform, he considered New York as a vast
sign platform. That's why he could photograph buildings by themselves, without people, yet make them
speak. He used billboards, plastered with faces, as sub-
titles and sound track for a whole culture. Wherever
he went, there was physiognomy, animate or not. As

FIG. 14
Rolf Tietgens (1911–1984), *Times Square U.S.A.*, 1952.
Gelatin-silver print. Courtesy Keith de Lellis Gallery, New York

for the ideology of American freedom, his photographs certainly don't support it, but they do affirm his freedom to make sport of it. New York was the indispensable target.

Klein's insight into American media displays a more inclusive consciousness than Andreas Feininger's and Weegee's. The first thought only of business power; the second employed media as sarcastic footnotes, as in the scene of a dead body in the foreground, and a marquee announcing "Joy of Living" in the background (pl. 69). Klein knew Weegee's work and shared its wiseacre attitude, but in Klein's imagery, the hucksterism of prices and promises doesn't just make cameo appearances, it really bloats urban space. He implies that New Yorkers live vicariously through their mediascape, even that they're functions of it. There is no background that is not also a foreground, no message of everyday import that is not also uppercase and usually extreme. Thus, his close-up photograph of a newsstand, with its shrill, staggered tabloid headlines: "Gun . . . Gu . . . Gu . . . Gunma" (pl. 70). A viewer comes away with the impression that all this is like baby talk—goo-goo—portrayed by an artist who has seen Futurist painting.

We don't know whether to perceive the effect of work by Lou Faurer and Saul Leiter as raw or refined: their aesthetic operates midway between brusqueness and restraint, achieving images that are a perfect, poised amalgam of both. With Klein, though, we have no doubt of the aggressive gesture with which he sucker punched street life—when people seemed to react in a like spirit, he claimed that he was only making a kind of self-portrait. Still, he was not the first to depict Times Square, for instance, as a pugilistic zone. A German immigrant, Rolf Tietgens (1911–1984), did a wonderful portfolio of work here, in 1952 (fig. 14). Every one of Klein's blowsy perceptions about the square is already anticipated by Tietgens, minus the vitriol; all Klein's uproar is there, too, but without his psychological provocation. In the 1995 edition of his *New York*, Klein noted, "I would provoke subjects but so would they provoke me. Being photographed was considered to be, somehow, a riot and one acted accordingly."[43]

This note of mutual provocation defuses the animosity in his overall picture of the metropolis. How often can a viewer think that a real blow will be delivered in the interaction between photographer and subject? It is all play-acting that announces itself as part of a charade, New York sass that gives as good as it gets. Klein's world, in this respect, is far removed from that of J. D. Salinger's *Catcher in the Rye*, whose adolescent rebel, Holden Caulfield, imagined that all of adult society was unutterably "phony." In contrast, *Life Is Good and Good for You in New York* uncovers a hypocrisy that would have been more convincing as bad faith if it had been not been pictured with such high spirits. A riot is an extremely disorderly situation and, yet, if understood as slang, can be a funny happening, a joke.

It's as if the photographer snapped his fingers and a preposterous image culture came alive on both sides of the camera, each party wise to the other. Any cap pistol pointed by a little boy is a surrogate camera, and vice versa. These people, young and old, assume themselves equal to any competition. The fans at Ebbets Field root for their team yet can easily be imagined doing the same for the Pax Americana (pl. 71). Although they didn't exactly pose for their collective portrait, they knew themselves to be in one, at a particular moment, and somehow Klein gives that confrontational moment a historical cast. Compared to Sid Grossman's group portraits and Weegee's crowds at Coney Island, Klein offers us the American public as spectators at a coliseum. "If you weren't looking for work, black, or getting shot in Korea," wrote John Chancellor, "it was a very nice time."[44] Weegee presented himself as intruding into the frenzy of human nature. William Klein had Weegee's impolitic drive, but he also behaved as a man of politics, so it was natural for him to offer us a barbed view of a nice time.

When it came to the ethnic peoples of New York and blacks, those same, rather anarchist politics were at work. Klein upheld minority cultures as founts of spontaneity to which he was viscerally, and also intellectually, attuned—his photographic form and their live-wire antics act as alter egos. (Klein's use of irradiated light, coarse grain, and dissolved contour was self-consciously undisciplined.) Simone de Beauvoir was attracted to Harlem, too, but across a divide and in the manner of a French philosophe. The photographer's affinity with people of color, however, was enhanced by his placement *between* cultures. His much later films on Eldridge Cleaver, Muhammad Ali, and Little Richard were French movies about black American heroes with idiosyncrasies. At the same time, these movies can be seen as belonging to a heritage of attention paid by New York Jewish photographers to black Americans.

Gordon Parks, by contrast, was a black New York photographer with an established career in a white world. When Parks photographed a religious soapbox speaker in Harlem, listeners were looking elsewhere:

it's an energetic picture that has an ambiguous content (pl. 72). Klein's snap of a black kid slipping over an iron park fence has athletic verve, but the child's face is questioning, and there's a sleeper on a bench, what Klein has called a "home for the homeless" (pl. 73). Klein's New York is, in the end, an effusive and vulgar billboard that exists only as a home for the homeless.

Whether they came from abroad, as Lisette Model and Robert Frank did, were expatriates, like William Klein, or arrived from other American towns, like Lou Faurer and Saul Leiter, many photographers found New York disorienting. For them, the city lacked hospitality, but it was their place; they could not accommodate themselves to the metropolis any more than they could dismiss it. To exist at that period in New York was to live in the megacapital of a superpower during the nuclear era. At the same time as they bore toward the city the most sincere ill feelings, photographers recognized it as the site where the action was. So conflicted was their investment in Manhattan that it both muted their complaints and darkened their pleasure. At the midpoint of the decade—1955, the year that Sid Grossman died—an event took place that lifted their medium to unprecedented public acclaim and should have placed them in the most favorable light. Instead, one of the offhand consequences of Edward Steichen's exhibition, *The Family of Man*, was to shunt them, and much of what they stood for, to the side.

Insofar as it related to developments in New York photography, that show at the Museum of Modern Art was a paradoxical phenomenon. Steichen had encouraged and exhibited a number of the most serious workers in the field; Helen Gee, the owner of the Limelight Gallery, a Greenwich Village showcase for new photography, wrote that if any neglected talents happened to be around, Steichen "unburied them." Robert Frank, who had assisted him as an interpreter in Europe, was one of them; Leon Levinstein was another who benefited from the museum's good graces. Roy DeCarava was represented in *The Family of Man*, and so were Lisette Model and Garry Winogrand. In the MoMA context, however, their accent on the predicaments of living was submerged in a tide of images chosen to show the heroism of human endurance, while their emphasis on the loner estranged was discounted by a rhetoric of togetherness. In Steichen's book, there was no room for their uncertainty, their candor, or the toughness of their form.

When organizing an official statement about the community of world peoples, Steichen had little

Leon Levinstein (1910–1988), *Untitled*, c. 1955. Gelatin-silver print, 11 1/8 x 13 7/8 in. (28.3 x 35.2 cm). © Stuart E. Karu, courtesy Howard Greenberg Gallery, New York

tolerance, it seemed, for the interesting neuroses he advanced at other times in the cause of photography as art. In contrast, his plan for this occasion was to advertise the medium as a quasi-corporate one that reported on the parallel struggles and achievements of functioning societies. To that end, he presented his photographers as being on a common, journalistic mission, an understanding that distorted the intent of New York's more individualistic photographers (though Robert Frank was grateful for being included and professed a liking for the show). For them, the effective glance was self-reflexive, skeptical of its social surroundings, attributable to the person who looks. For the museum, the photographic image was required to be momentous and inspirational, especially when the subjects faced daunting odds or were in humble circumstances. At the same time as some photos were blown up to poster and even wall size, there was no shortage of modest images, such as a smiling Peruvian flute player, repeated throughout the show, and Gene Smith's end piece, *The Walk to Paradise Garden*, two cute tots pressed into the service of requisite uplift.

The visual style of *The Family of Man* was informed by *Life*. A disproportionate number of the photographers came from the magazine; they suffused the show with *Life*'s characteristic graphic compositions and illustrative goals. The way they were deployed in the theatrical portrayal of doings in far-flung locales does not concern us here, but the nature of Steichen's globalism does. It could not help but lend institutional support to a commercial organ's political ideology. Although it projected a metaphor of world unity by presenting the recognizable family patterns of the most diverse cultures, Steichen's program did not actually observe those cultures. Still less did it reflect the texture of life in New York, a microcosm of world cultures not always congenial to one another. Visitors to the show were encouraged to believe that, though its subjects often did not look like "us," they behaved like "us." The "us" in question had won the war, enjoyed the benefits of material wealth as well as a democratic society, and at least nominally respected civil rights. In the words of Eric Sandeen, Steichen "assumed that . . . everyone would want to become like us: his was an American vision of a one-world order."[45] Rockefeller money underwrote the world tour of this self-congratulatory vision.

In an era of McCarthyite blacklisting, racial discrimination in Little Rock, Arkansas, and CIA-financed coups in Guatemala and Iran, some Americans could be excused for not subscribing to this "one-world order." Those New York photographers who tacitly criticized that order might be described as pragmatic observers of their environment, but in fact, they exhibited a tendency to escape from it through styles that were increasingly subjective and introverted.

Steichen had stirred the pictorial pot, using many international ingredients, and came out with an ingenious version of bourgeois U.S. social realism. The evolution of certain photographers in New York, however, must be seen as a collateral offshoot of modernism. Quite often, their work was powered by an antimaterialist impulse—in reaction to both the consumerist environment and the physicality of photographic description. To that principle they added a schematism of incident, even a certain flattening of planes, and an accent on private, sometimes almost ineffable experience. The black photographer Roy DeCarava gave to that experience a moody inwardness, removed from the outside world of white America. Leon Levinstein (1910–1988) endowed it with ecstatic, though sometimes morbid, undertones.

Their imagery conveys highly emotional content with great economy of means. These two photographers typically get close to their subjects, within low-spoken conversational range, such that we might wonder that no one seems guarded or even aware of their presence. DeCarava may have achieved his apparent invisibility through permission based on a kind of fraternal trust; with Levinstein, it was a function of stealth (fig. 15). The one artist realized effects of composure and meditation even in active scenes; the other forced his dynamic view even on people at rest. Both grasped an essential pattern energized by blocky forms, but DeCarava's photographs risk losing it in his characteristic deep shadow, whereas Levinstein's hyperbolically dramatize it by sharp, almost Manichean contrasts. Even so, they both have stakes in a pictorial atmosphere that lives on the tension between narrative in the present and memory of the past.

DeCarava took upon himself a mission: to be a spokesman for the black community of Harlem and its culture. In his application for a Guggenheim Fellowship, awarded in 1952, he wrote: "I want to photograph Harlem through the Negro people . . . at work, at play, in the streets, talking, kidding, laughing. . . . I want to show the strength, the wisdom, the dignity of the Negro people. Not the famous and the well known, but the unknown and the unnamed, thus revealing the roots from which springs the greatness of all human

beings. . . . I want a creative expression, the kind of penetrating insight and understanding of Negroes which I believe only a Negro photographer can interpret."[46]

Although no contemporary white photographers were making similar statements, DeCarava's affirmative rhetoric reminds us of Steichen's philosophy, later developed for *The Family of Man*. In fact, Steichen sponsored DeCarava's Guggenheim application. At the same time, though DeCarava touched on a universalist theme—"the roots from which springs the greatness of all human beings"—he insisted that he would picture a reality that "only a Negro photographer can interpret." In terms of cultural politics, he was staking an exclusionary claim: the prior right that a member of a group assumes in the representation of that group. No one—not Hine, Siskind, or the Photo League—had done that before. Nor had any of them forsaken the documentary, the outsider's approach, for a purely subjective expression in portraying American blacks.

On behalf of his people, DeCarava evokes a special world of internal states that are revealed only through his lens. The lovers he shows, the kids, neighbors, musicians, and workers display a togetherness that seems inviolate. It is the most radiant element in an otherwise penumbral space. The light functions like plaintive jazz, a state of grace that reinforces the communion of his subjects in their isolation. This is the "dignity" to which he referred in his grant proposal. Though the blacks he portrayed lack goods and material resources, their familial bonds provide a heritage of great wealth. Again, this judgment parallels beliefs like Steichen's, except in its painful extra implication: that the fellowship of black Americans is unique, sharable only among their own, and that the society of Harlem is necessarily a ghetto, segregated as it is from urban white culture.

In contrast to DeCarava's tonalist nocturnes without flash, Leon Levinstein's sculptural, day-lit scenes grate upon the eye with little nuance. He provides a striking exception, though, in a photograph of a shop window with reflections that half obscure yet half reveal bitter-looking men, together with a more recalcitrant figure in his own space (pl. 74). They suffer their momentary group portrait with an ill humor that is softened by clouds mirrored in the window and even a glimpse of a tree within the shop. While Levinstein liked astringent, weathered faces, and wound-up bodies, DeCarava purveyed a melancholy akin to Edward Hopper's, possibly structured by memories of images by Edward Weston. On the other hand,

Levinstein comes out of Shahn, via Grossman and Model. These genealogies put one in mind of a difference between American and a quasi-European solitude, as interpreted in New York.

Loneliness, as depicted by Hopper, is a constant state, embodied by characters in airless but harshly luminous interiors. The artist contemplates human beings in the guise of generalized, affectless figures, suspended in work or domestic surroundings to which they don't relate—if anything, the light in a Hopper room seems to drain his subjects of their volition. DeCarava, on the contrary, appears to think that people acquire force as they seek light.[47] He may have related somewhere to a Hopperesque raw model, yet, with a mood that can only be called spiritual, he infuses into it an evident social circulation. DeCarava endows his subjects with a gentle and pacific tone that implies their inner strength, but he also leaves the impression that this strength is under duress, that the people of Harlem remain wounded and unfulfilled because they are under siege from the culture at large.

Levinstein sees in ethnic New Yorkers, and those discriminated against by racism, a spasmodic consciousness of exclusion, out of which anger might well up. It can be ugly; often he makes it look defiant. His subjects may be on edge with each other, and they're at odds with the city. A mother holding her baby looks as if she were witnessing an atrocity (pl. 75). This photographer does not hesitate to show us urban casualties, unresigned and scowling; he comes upon them in such close quarters that we are astonished to realize that we are not psychologically among them. His view is unbearably candid, but he works at the same time only as a witness to the scenario of isolation, rather than as a confidant, like DeCarava. Levinstein photographs a young black woman with a cigar, peering anxiously around a corner (pl. 76). It would be easy to imagine her on high alert to a possibility that might bode ill, a possibility that the city offers with careless frequency.

Among these poets of estrangement, Levinstein is, oddly, the most optimistic. It is true that even when he wants to put things in the best light, the sky is overcast. But his energy is thrilling; it livens the friction that is often his subject. In fact, the very instability of the social relations he pictures suggests a war of nerves in which no party has a determined advantage. These photographers depicted people who, though at large in the city, did not expect to be treated sympathetically by it. By the mid-1960s, when he took the photograph of the woman with the cigar, suspicious in a hostile city, his urgent style was nevertheless out of date. So, too, was DeCarava's.

Many New York photographers of the 1960s and afterward tended to perceive metropolitan cultures with a downward look. People of ethnic, racial, or sexual "difference" were visited by an inquisitive camera, as if they were metaphorically penned into reservations. DeCarava wanted to disarm his white viewers with a benevolent vision of Harlem yet to remind them, subtly, of the continued pressure their world imposed on his. For Levinstein, social relations were too vehement to be sorted out. Though divergent, these arguments branded their proponents as humanists from another age, invested in the have-nots of urban life. As for the city itself, its public space, its civil territory, it receded to a role on the sidelines of photographic drama. Although it continued to be the site, it ceased to be the main subject of a brilliant photographic tradition. The city subsisted as the implied background of a number of private observations, even as, or perhaps because, its center did not hold.

Lights, Color, Action!

One warm and hazy day on Park Avenue, a man and a woman were sitting in their top-down convertible, when a photographer snapped them from behind, catching them slightly aware but still off guard. Only the third passenger in the car, a monkey, gazed back fully alert to the intruder. This little creature bared its teeth and looks really mad (pl. 77).

It might have been just a random incident, except that the photographer in question, Garry Winogrand (1928–1984), took another picture of a simian subject, eight years later, in 1967, at the Central Park Zoo. This time, in a crowd, he gets close to a well-dressed black man and white woman to whom chimpanzees sweetly cling. On this brisk, sunny occasion, the animals have to be kept warm, a fact deduced from their parkas and pants. Viewers may be excused their puzzlement at the oddness of this group conducting itself as if on a normal family outing. It is all quite decorous, yet unseemly.

Starting roughly with the 1960s, Manhattan photographers, with increasing frequency, notice presences that are enough outside the usual traffic as to suggest bogeys on a radar screen. We might be alarmed, perplexed, or titillated by such sights, but we do not easily forget them. New York, in fact, continues to supply large numbers of ill-fitting citizens, from a generous reserve. It's just that during the Vietnam War years, they're usually embraced with a spirit that has nothing to do with solicitude.

For many of those years, an enormous, heavily bearded blind man, known only as Moondog, stationed himself at Midtown corners. Clad in felt robes, wearing headgear with horns, accompanied by a staff-spear that Moses would have envied, Moondog stood immobile in the privacy of his unguessable world. With his opaque dignity, he put to shame the religious cranks of Times Square and the winos of Skid Row. In 1963, Mary Ellen Mark (b. 1940) photographed six Santa Clauses, vaguely like Moondog but ridiculous, one reading the *Daily News*, in a mission cafeteria (fig. 16). Conceivably, these Christmas season temps could have been winos themselves. If so, they produce an effect of "too-muchness," at which a viewer doesn't know whether to laugh or cry. Moondog was an avant-garde composer, well regarded in Europe; these anonymous men in charity costume suggest a Halloween gone amiss.

Long before, in the 1930s, photographers had sallied forth on activist campaigns, drawing attention to the plight of derelicts, ghetto dwellers, and other unfortunates who had slipped through the cracks of

societal concern. Images of the distressed were meant to arouse the will to rehabilitate them through city legislation. Now, people like these, low on the food chain, and others sometimes very unlike them— but always curious—were photographed for aesthetic reasons. This shift in attitude, though gradual, gathered unmistakable strength from the 1960s through the 1980s.

It was not mere eccentricity that attracted the picture maker. "Curious" subjects, rather, were defined more broadly by their often unknowing incongruity of display in the civic space, their presumption that they blend in, against odds that are conspicuous to viewers. The presentation of self had somehow backfired and had come to seem disfavored. Surely, this can and does happen to members of any social class, at any moment. The camera, a mechanical contrivance, can make a person of whatever means look peculiar or unpresentable in a split second.

In the hands of a paparazzo, the contrivance might well be used to indict vanity and to take down the famous a peg or two. This leveling effect is carried out with an obvious tone of resentment (which the public secretly enjoys) and, sometimes, derision. No one can judge with confidence that New York photographers, in pursuing their aesthetic goals, were exempt from class prejudice or personal disparagement. But what chiefly motivated them does not seem to be an impulse so trite as animus. Rather, they saw a psychic world between or aside from the protocols of conventional social exchange: relationships among those who did not appear to fit together, faces that expressed other than what a situation called for, behavior or dress that could not be explained. Photographers were drawn to such incongruence as felines are to catnip. One is hard put to say of the resultant pictures that they showed deformity any more than nobility— only that their subjects inspired wonder. The photographers fastened on those with imperfect control of their images or who simply did not know they were strange. Except for documentary purposes, Moondog was not photographed, very probably because he was aware only too well of the marvelous figure he cut.

This agenda of fascination developed some preferred topics. In the 1960s, Richard Avedon photographed in an insane asylum. Peter Hujar looked into a house for retarded children. Diane Arbus, a most brilliant student of Lisette Model, visited nudist camps, carnival sideshows, ballroom dances, muscle-man contests, and old-age homes. Winogrand went to the zoo and shot pro–Vietnam War hard hats at demonstrations. Leon Levinstein haunted the circus and Coney Island and did not neglect the prostitutes around Times Square. Mary Ellen Mark pictured transvestites (pl. 78). This list can be extended into the 1970s and 1980s with Larry Clark's boy hookers, Robert Mapplethorpe's black-leather crowd, Nan Goldin's East Village bohemians, and Eugene Richards's pushers and addicts.

Some of these photographers operated as general practitioners in urban malaise, others as specialists. Of course, as they were attracted to exotica and weirdness rather than dysfunction per se, they abstained from judging their subjects. Aside from Bruce Davidson (b. 1933), whose important work on East One-hundredth Street belongs to an earlier, social-documentary tradition, they cultivated subject matter at a slant to the pictorial history of the city. Little interest had previously been aroused by odd lifestyles, regalia, cults, fetishism, and cross-dressing—in other words, fringe scenes that did not advance ideas about metropolitan life in general. What we're given, instead, are niches and enclaves of in-group conduct, suddenly made visible. Nan Goldin's approach to her circle of junkies, in fact, is positively communitarian.

With pictures featuring such subjects, it would seem to follow that their makers had an oppositional view

of bourgeois mores. Arbus et al. portrayed homosexuality, for instance, well before society was able to come to terms with it. (The battering of gays by police at the Stonewall Inn in 1969 proved this rather conclusively.) For all those in the hinterland who regarded New York as a fleshpot turned sour or run amok, Arbus provided supporting evidence, vivid beyond belief. Yet her tone was hardly admonishing or approving, as if to judge human behavior. Rather, she made clear that, wherever she looked, she was mesmerized by unnerving presence.

For the classic street photographers Garry Winogrand and Leon Levinstein, to be sure, all venues were potential zones of opportunity, in the wide-open emotional panorama of New York. A far younger man, Bruce Gilden (b. 1946), met Levinstein at Coney Island, and learned from him. Gilden's hyperbolic effects are often achieved by fill-flash, shot from below, topped off by the distortions of a wide-angle lens (pl. 79). To this day, he walks the city, wrenching from it a cascade of faces that appear to express bitterness, or a nameless dread. New York, he seems to say, with a tenacity almost comic, is no place to be, unless you're paranoid.

Aside from their gamy subjects, these photographers also evolved a generic form, distinctive of the time. The style of the 1950s had been, on the whole, rather smudgy: in bad weather and low light, New York looked like a busy, indistinct wilderness of neon signs and glass reflections, fretted with querulous faces. Thereafter, an unequivocally hard-edged description enters into and takes over the frame. This explicitness is often linear and quite detailed: serviceably realist, yet without making a fuss about realism. With its Expressionist contrasts, flash is often used by Winogrand, Arbus, and Larry Fink at parties. Though their pictures recall Weegee's Dionysia, their harsh luminism is, in fact, much colder. It puts us in mind of a type of observer with an appetite for control, one who isolates figures in space with such precision that their gestures and carrying-on may be appreciated all the more readily as flawed social artifacts.

What took place in New York photography of the past thirty years is inconceivable without its earlier, historical context, most certainly the heritage of engagement with minority cultures, the melancholy view, and political dissidence. Younger photographers knew of Lisette Model, and some had heard of William Klein. The new school stood on photographic ceremony no more than its prototypes. But the days of the immersed, self-reflexive picture maker were gone. One must also say that even the days of introspection were gone. Louis Faurer and Saul Leiter still extended themselves or, perhaps better, projected upon their fellow citizens a certain wounded demeanor. Diane Arbus mooted that empathy in tableaux that refrigerated all social relations. (A model might have been the impassive and clinical August Sander, the great German portraitist of the interregnum, whose work she acknowledged as influencing her own.) Though her pictures frequently intrigue by the wily consent she must have obtained from her sitters, a viewer is never encouraged to ask anything about the personality behind the camera. That potential of meaning is blanked out by the transparent sensationalism of the "find."

The commanding photographers of this period act as if their material is so pungent it speaks for itself. Whatever their contest of wills, the acerbic spirit of the seer wins out over—or deceives—the seen. When Mary Ellen Mark depicts a young boy at a Vietnam War parade, exhibiting a pennant reading, "If your [heart] is not in the U.S.A. Get your [ass] out now" (fig. 17), or when Garry Winogrand snaps a tigerish Governor Rockefeller at a political victory celebration (pl. 80), the bad vibes are just one more element of a spectacle recommended mainly for its bizarre overtones. Avedon's celebrity sitters were at his unkind disposal, but he titled the book in which some of them appear *Nothing Personal* (1964). That same impersonality of approach startled observers of earlier pop art, which was ironically unreflective about the power of mass media. Of course, the pop artists' refusal to editorialize about the displacement of commercial icons into a gallery environment carried a provocative power of its own.

It's appropriate to have mixed feelings about the moral stance of much New York photography of the 1960s and 1970s. Ambivalence, in fact, is a legitimate response to photographic aesthetics ridden with inner conflict. To people acculturated to the absurdist fiction of Terry Southern and Joseph Heller, or the poker-faced decadence of Andy Warhol, the steeliness and grotesquerie of Diane Arbus's images appeared as a parallel shock. But fiction and painting are not arts comparable to photography, where the relations between subject and object take place in the real world. If you snap pictures in a madhouse, for instance, you must exploit inmates (even those enjoying your attention) who cannot react to your presence with any social understanding. Quite often—too often—the outlook of the photographic campaign is quasi-anthropological, which

implies condescension. However, when you're out on the streets, and at your own risk, among people in possession of their wits, power relations are more equitable. We often have the impression that "power" (the power of looking) is placed at the service of the subject, who is then shown to exercise another power —the power of presence and fascination. This exchange, whether it was by mutual consent or not, sometimes produced an effect for which Diane Arbus had her own word: "Terrific."

In remarks gathered in the famous Aperture monograph on her work, Arbus discloses aspects of her process. "There's this woman making a face. I really mean it's terrific. I don't mean I wish I looked like that. I don't mean I wish my children looked like that. . . . But I mean that's amazingly, undeniably something." And "somebody else's tragedy is not the same as your own. . . . There are certain nicenesses that I think you have to get out of. . . . We're nicer to each other than the intervention of the camera is going to make us." Of nudist camps, she said, "It's a little bit like walking into an hallucination without being quite sure whose it is. . . . The first man I saw was mowing his lawn." Finally: "I used to have a theory about photographing. It was a sense of getting in between two actions, or in between action and repose. . . . It was just an expression I didn't see or wouldn't have seen. One of the excitements of strobe at one time was that you were essentially blind at the moment you took the picture."[48]

In these lucid thoughts, what stands out is "hallucination," the potential reward for transgressing blindly, and without niceness, into astonishing worlds. Her *Jewish Giant at Home with His Parents* must stand as a trophy of hallucination. In war photography, the worker accepts physical risk as a hazard of the job; Arbus knowingly accepted some moral risk as a consequence of her obsession. She sometimes spoke of the experience, especially when she engaged sexually with her subjects, as a feeling akin to loss of self. Patricia Bosworth writes, "It seemed as if merging with her subjects, both 'straights' and 'freaks,' was a way of giving herself to them after they revealed themselves to her camera."[49]

For his part, when he was asked why he photographed, Winogrand said, "I get totally out of myself. It's the closest I come to not existing, I think, which is the best—which to me is attractive."[50] John Szarkowski, the then director of the photography department at the Museum of Modern Art, recalls that Winogrand, like many, was terrified of the Cuban Missile Crisis

of 1962, that it came to him that he was "nothing—
powerless, insignificant . . . and that knowledge, he
said, liberated him."[51] Walker Evans believed that the
ego of the artist must be uninvolved in the observing act. These younger photographers, in contrast, need
to feel that their egos are obliterated as they search
their way in the dark. Evans's instinct was maybe a gesture of pride, while their notion acted, perhaps, as
a therapeutic rationale. Long before psychoanalysis, Dr.
Johnson expressed a kindred thought: "I live in the
crowds of jollity, not so much to enjoy company as to
shun myself."

In the Gotham of the 1960s and 1970s, the almost
feverish jollity of the times masked a fear of solitude. It was an era that saw a spectacular rise in urban
crime, a breakdown of communal values, the falter-
ing of the nuclear family, domestic conflict over the
Vietnam War, and the burning of the South Bronx.
Young mods danced to all hours at the Dom, as the
Camelot White House held stylish court. Andy Warhol
displayed his *Ten Most Wanted Criminals* serigraphs,
and IBM announced the coming of the computer age
at the 1964 New York World's Fair. That same year,
a young woman, Kitty Genovese, was loudly stabbed to
death for thirty minutes in Kew Gardens, Queens,

while neighbors turned a deaf ear. In 1968, a black school board in the Ocean Hill–Brownsville section of Brooklyn fired fourteen white teachers, an act that prompted the mostly Jewish Teachers' Federation to go on a strike that envenomed relations between liberal Jews and blacks. As the party time of the 1960s skidded out of control, the high-octane disaffection of the New Left came to the fore.

New York photographers did not participate in the barefoot doctrines of the counterculture; they were too urban for that, and too middle class. Also, they were positioned uncomfortably between two activist generations. The old, Marxist left had discredited itself in the eyes of the New Left, with its blanket emphasis on overturning the system (this, during President Lyndon Johnson's War on Poverty and civil rights legislation). The photographers of the 1960s and 1970s were part of that system, but on different levels alienated within it. Their choice of "extreme" subjects had something to do with their uneasiness in a culture that, after all, was having a nervous breakdown. If the direction they took was allied with any intellectual figure then creating an insurrectionary buzz, it was with the psychiatrist R. D. Laing, who taught that mental disturbance was "normal" in a culture that had rationalized an immoral war.

About the introduction of odd "new people" in the work of Klein, Frank, Davidson, and Winogrand—a group incomplete without Model and Arbus—Marshall Berman wrote that the photographers give us "no choice about whether we want them to be part of our New York. . . . They make us part of their New York."[52] The use of the possessive pronoun "their" is significant. To whom does this place, once again, belong? When the focus was on blacks and Latinos, the implied answer would be: "These are New Yorkers [that is, full-fledged Americans], too." Now, with the presentation of subjects declassed because of their sexual preference and psychic or physical vulnerability, the answer is: "This is America, period." Any judgment of this sort has to be less pleasant, but it is also presented as more realistic than the earlier hopes of social justice and inclusionist ethics, the legacy of New Deal liberalism. In these photographs, the old civic issue of racial or ethnic differences, still unassimilated, takes second place to the more painful recognition that a society such as New York's is everywhere composed of flawed human beings—they are us, and we are not yet naturalized to our condition.

What makes Bruce Davidson's *East 100th Street* (published in 1970) so interesting is the perhaps

involuntary stand it takes between the older and this newer, humbling point of view. This Magnum photographer had earlier depicted the Freedom Riders and the protest march from Selma to Montgomery, Alabama. When, between 1966 and 1968, he went to the "worst block" (his words) in the city, he photographed the black people in their homes as well as on the streets, their gatherings, their family life, their decayed tenements, above all, their loneliness. "Like the TV repairman or organ grinder," he wrote, "I appeared and became part of the street life."[53]

The visual nostalgia of Davidson's project is betrayed a little by his reference to an organ-grinder, not a figure to be seen in Harlem of the 1960s, but one who does appear in the work of the Parisian Eugène Atget. As for TV—ubiquitous in all American homes by the mid-1960s—it acts as a counterpoint to a little girl at a window, seen vaguely through a floral embroidered curtain (pl. 81). Just as there are many poetic images like this, scattered throughout Davidson's book, others jolt by their rawness, the sense they give of life lived in extreme privation. The emotional temperature keeps on switching, with pictures at the colder range impressing us with what, at the time, was their contemporary spirit.

More than a dozen years later, Davidson began to photograph New York subways for a new project. This was a classic metropolitan subject, treated by Walker Evans, Lee Sievan, Arthur Leipzig, and Arnold Eagle in times past. Davidson has a vivid sense of New York history, particularly as it was experienced by post-Holocaust Jews. He had photographed in a cafeteria on the Lower East Side and had hoped to make a film based on Isaac Bashevis Singer's novel *Enemies, A Love Story*. At rush hours, Davidson saw the "packed cars of the subway as cattle cars, filled with people doomed to a terrible fate, each face staring or withdrawn with the fear of an unknown destiny." Horrifically fanciful as that was, the photographer took some very real precautions when he went underground, including a police pass, coins for beggars, and a whistle "for summoning help."[54]

On endless transits, he took a mass of hot, grating, funky pictures, in a slow Kodachrome and weak flash that transformed the subway into an infernal prison (pl. 82). Maria Morris Hambourg writes of the subways during Evans's time as already grimy and sordid affairs, yet they were prim compared to Davidson's.[55] He sees their polychrome graffiti not only as universal defacement but as a kind of hieroglyphics. And he conceives himself as a wanderer with safari jacket, perilously asking for consent to take pictures, or stealing them, in a heart of darkness. Sweet moments appear as a surprise but provide little relief in this collective ordeal. Later, the subway cars were cleaned or replaced, and some of the graffiti sprayers, who had left their mark and impolitely voiced their despair, were taken on by galleries, where their art enjoyed a brief vogue.

Ernst Haas tried out color and Saul Leiter possessed it, with real sophistication, as early as the 1950s. But the aesthetic of color in New York photography comes into its own only in the mid-1970s. Joel Meyerowitz, whose style was aligned with Winogrand's, restored chroma to a Fifth Avenue hitherto seen only in black and white. It was left to Helen Levitt, though, to explore the beat and nuance of color as a lyric phenomenon. The pinks, blonds, cobalts, and russets in one of her 1972 scenes of children seem as choreographed as the gestures of the kids themselves (pl. 83). These figures play in a shadowed area luminous with halftones where modulations transform a mean street into an enchanted spectacle.

The discovery that New York indeed exists in color coincided with an apparent rise in the fortunes of photography in the cultural establishment. By the mid-1970s, dealers, collectors, museum curators, professors, and critics were belatedly realizing that the photographic image was the primary means of visual communication in the twentieth century. In the 1950s, a print, even by an acknowledged master photographer, would not have fetched more than fifty dollars. Now, by dint of its own substantial history, and thanks to John Szarkowski's enlightened support for both vernacular and Modernist photography at the Museum of Modern Art, the medium came under intense, excited scrutiny in the American press as well as the academy. Within the space of only a few months, both *Newsweek* and *Artforum* devoted special issues to photography. How, asked academics, were groups represented by outsiders, and what were the uses of photography as an instrument of corporate or government power? What was the relation of the image to the event pictured? The undeniable function of photographs within the media, and yet their problematic artistic qualities, made them a slippery, and for that reason irresistible, subject for new study.

It turned out that photographic studies took two divergent directions. One examined photographic images from the viewpoint of formalist aesthetics. The other was more attuned with 1970s developments such as the advent of identity politics, the women's movement, multiculturalism, and the appropriation of commercial media—above all photographic media—by artists in the gallery world. Barbara Kruger and Cindy Sherman, who exaggerated the set-up character of film stills, are exemplary scavengers of photographic genres. As their tendency came to dominate attention in art circles, it brought with it a new emphasis on the fictionality or (to put it in the moral terms favored at the time) the unreliability of photographic witness. In the end, the idealism of form lost out to deconstructive critique as a guide for image interpretation. To those who were uncomfortable with the transcriptional character of photography, it was reassuring to learn that the medium, to its core, was not to be trusted. Political critique all too easily translated the fragmentary record and limited perspectives of the medium into an essential mendacity.

Photographic color was as a matter of course associated with hype. The galleries' photo-artists had no trouble turning the luscious palette of commercial photography into something lurid or murky. This denatured and parodistic color established a distance that separated the artists from their sources, not for expressive so much as for polemical reasons. Bruce Davidson, adept in the use of glamorous color for corporate reports, employed in *Subway* hypersaturated, abrasive chroma that negates distance for the sake of his personal account.

Nan Goldin (b. 1953) also used color in her involvement with the "glamorous" charades of the gay world in which she traveled. Because her work with transvestites and cross-dressers is diaristic in mode, her style is graphic in aim. Most often she shoots indoors, where artificial light from many sources creates a familiar dissonance. Goldin's work with color slides focused on male glitter, plumage, and costume—their sluttish and camp folderol (pl. 84). More relaxed than Model's and Arbus's, this work installs her as a heroine of consciousness in the problematics of gender. (In fact, she insists that she has found a "third gender," neither male nor female.) In a textbook on abnormal psychology, she once looked up information about women who fall in love with drag queens and discovered that "we were so perverse as to be unclassifiable."[56] Perverse or not, Goldin is, and has been, a realist artist who observes transsexual social display as a normal phenomenon, and with a true affection.

In her *Ballad of Sexual Dependency*, a work of more than ten years cast in the genre of a family album (successively performed as a slide show),

Goldin set forth her friendships, and the friendships of her friends, many of whom fell away or died, often of AIDS. In the preface to the 1986 book of this title, she wrote that her subjects experience the need "to live fully and for the moment . . . a need to push limits. There is among us an ability to listen and to empathize that surpasses the normal definition of friendship." And then: "The people and locales in my pictures are particular, specific, but I feel the concerns I'm dealing with are universal . . . it's about the nature of relationships."[57] (During those same years, significantly, Jules Feiffer's mordant cartoons took up that same theme in the *Village Voice.*)

What distinguishes Goldin's relationships from most others in this exhibition is that she is an insider to what she sees. All social and psychological barriers come down in the astonishing—sometimes X-rated—intimacy of her pictures. Roy DeCarava also transmits a sense of intimacy within his social environment, but he never allows us to see the effect of these relationships upon his subjects. His lovers may tenderly embrace, but hers clutch each other, sometimes with a carnal desperation that belies the longevity of their union. Goldin can show a woman crying, next to a smiling man (pl. 85), and she has depicted herself after having been beaten by her boyfriend. Women sometimes get the worst of it in their affairs, but they are true friends to one another, a bond that radiates throughout much of the *Ballad*. And besides, what is there to substitute for our human relationships? For Goldin, they often take place in apartment bedrooms or bathrooms, but she also tries to convey their interactions in public places—named bars, gay shows, and punk clubs.

To think of Goldin's sociology as rooted exclusively in New York is to miss the point of her "diary," and it's also not accurate, since she gives us, in addition to a New York, a London, a Berlin, and a Tokyo confidential. By the 1980s, Manhattan could no longer be said to hold exclusive title among world cities to artistic innovation, or even urban grandeur. Meanwhile, most young photographers who had come to art world notice had entered a conceptual phase that had nothing to do with the act of witness, let alone a concern with the life of their city. The immemorial New York of legend was retired without notice and not even on half-pension.

Jane Livingston's book *The New York School* (1992), the first comprehensive study of Manhattan-oriented photographs, ends its survey with the year 1963. That cutoff date is far too early to account for a number of vital figures who contributed to the pictorial characterization of the city. But it may be a marker to suggest the gradual trailing away of consensus about the centrality of New York as a topic in photographic practice. The erstwhile and now shopworn iconicity of Manhattan was replaced by scenes of ever more local or even private import, which no longer represented any thinking about the city as a whole. Nevertheless, a generation born mostly in the 1940s still responds to New York as a comedy of manners, and still enjoys its capers and its mysteries. At first sight, you might take them as scenes from any large city, until you detect their Gotham sense of humor.

Larry Fink (b. 1941), who easily betrays his lineage back to Weegee, via his teacher Lisette Model, may be the last member of the "New York School." The satire he brings to fashion soirees and coming-out balls is combined with an unheard-of suavity of light. His use of an off-camera flash orchestrates chiaroscuro from odd points, as if to suggest multiple relationships in a created darkness. Like Goldin, he's swept up by glamour, though without being seduced by it. The finery and gentility of the occasion, on the contrary, act as a foil for his skill in producing a voluptuous image. But this image will never make the society page. There's too much to look at, and something incidental, like a fern or a hand, gets deliberately in the way. Fink manages to suggest that a party at the Metropolitan Museum is a crypto-jungle, where elegant people have subliminal trysts. Among models at a retro-style fashion cocktail (complete with cigarette holders), George Plimpton, dean of WASP highlife, espies the field-jacketed photographer, and is not pleased (pl. 86); nor is a woman at the Frick, who is comically alarmed (pl. 87). The comedy of these, and other pictures by Fink, lies in a certain mystery. What could there have been, in all that persiflage and exhibitionist beauty, that did not want to be seen?

Though in earlier days—the 1980s—Fink had been a tendentious observer, he is presently a cunning artificer, leaving clues to a story that is never resolved. He just goes right ahead and suspends doubts about his real subject in a portentous atmosphere. Maneuvers such as these clearly fall outside the category of reportage, documentary, and most other genres. Their conventions and their putative audiences are irrelevant to a new type of photographer who acts as a ferret with a special taste for the inexplicable. No longer a polis, the city is regarded as a hunting ground for small incident that may, at any moment, speak of the cruelty, the ludicrousness, or the impromptu wacki-

FIG. 18
Jeff Mermelstein (b. 1957), *Untitled, New York City*, 1996.
Fujicolor crystal archive, 16 x 20 in. (30.5 x 40.6 cm).
© Jeff Mermelstein, courtesy of the artist

ness of life. It takes the most responsive intuition, the
most acute eye—and, no doubt also, a great deal of
luck—to impress the consistency of this view upon
the beholder.

What is a viewer to make of an isolated work shoe,
smoking on the sidewalk (pl. 88)? Such an article ordinarily doesn't do that sort of thing. Nor are we prepared for the apparition of a blond Nereid, covered
only by three lettuce leaves, on Fifth Avenue (fig.
18). The vegetables and her hair rhyme with each other,
not so the green luminosity of her face, cast by a
television lamp, compared to the light of day. Without
their local color, the pedestrian yet sometimes off-
beat hues of New York, these scenes would lack sub-
stance. It is important for the photographer, Jeff
Mermelstein (b. 1957), to insist that such bizarre situations happen and that we could have found them
ourselves. A pigeon sports a bloody beak. On an unnamed street, four unrelated people simultaneously
feel the need to check their wallets or their apparel. (In-

Jeff Jacobson (b. 1946), *Untitled*, 2000. 35mm Kodachrome original transparency, digital epson print, 30 x 20 in. (76.2 x 40.6 cm).
© Jeff Jacobson, courtesy of the artist

congruity can be discovered through redundancy, as well as exception.) Someone is walking a large iguana, someone else has a book in his mouth. The photographer's mode of encounter is extremely abrupt, at waist or even ground level, and his timing is split second in an off-balance world. King of a pile of *New York Times* at a newsstand, a Chihuahua confronts all comers (pl. 89). Mermelstein's title for the book in which these images appear, published in 2000, is *Sidewalk*.

A slightness and randomness of expressive vignette have been, of course, the meat of street photography throughout its modern history. But latter-day practitioners in New York found that it was the spawning ground of a made-to-order Surrealism. Consider Jeff Jacobson's masked man in a sweat suit, with bunny ears, talking to a woman dressed as a nun, but with fishnet pantyhose over her exposed behind. They are an unlikely pair, waiting for the PATH train (fig. 19). We have heard of found objects; there are also lost contexts. Jacobson's book *My Fellow Americans* (1991) reveals him as a virtuoso of strobe, shaken camera, and long exposures. He employed these non-naturalist techniques to ferret out an underlying disturbance crackling in the spirit of Americans across the continent. For Manhattan, though, Jacobson (b. 1946) dispensed with that style in order to emphasize the concreteness of hallucination.

Halloweeners from New Jersey are one thing, but window dressers seeming to struggle against befurred, headless black mannequins with Day-Glo green hands are quite another (pl. 90). The one moment tells an amusing anecdote; the other intimates something almost sinister. On contact with this street scene, of a type that is not, after all, uncommon, the photographer must have shot impulsively—and blindly. But to a contemplative viewer, the tableau offers unauthorized, plummy, and irrational overtones. A black man and a white man, both working class, roughly handle feminine figures clothed in hyperluxurious and ultra-erotic garments. Meanwhile, the figures appear to react with histrionics, as if somehow irked by male assault. All the hot cultural buttons of sex, class, and race are insouciantly pushed in Jacobson's picture. Weegee would have appreciated this, though he lacked Jacobson's irony. Arbus might have liked it, too, though she was never as elegant and offhand. But the animism of the display is a new element that injects an uncanniness into these ludicrous and urgent gestures.

Jacobson performs as a scrambler of messages and territories. Ill-sorted motives provide alibis for some undreamed-of meaning, or are in an untoward place. A viewer does not take in one passage before it suggests or is contradicted by another. So the shadow of a raised leg looks as if it were about to stomp the picture of a nude couple, wrapped in the Stars and Stripes, on a phone booth, while the shadow itself makes visible a reflection of a car headlight that looks like a reptile's eye (pl. 91). Simple as design, this image presents a delusional space. It is tempting to say that there never was a more New York picture, a more apt expression of the city's transgressive and slap-happy theatrics. In language and social exchange, we usually find what Neil Postman calls "appropriate semantic environments." As an example, however, of one who speaks *inappropriately* in context, Postman supposes a batter who steps up to the plate, turns to the umpire, and says, "Father, I have sinned."[58] Jacobson's "sins," in this respect, are delicious.

The ferret respects and is opened up to urban reality by not having conceived too much of it ahead of time. That is why the recent work in this exhibition may look familiar but feels different from imagery based on received notions of New York. It's a looser, almost preconscious way of looking, alert to embryonic signs and happy confusions. We recognize this pictorial situation by a release of wild energy in the frame that may take any vector, by a flood of coincidence, miraculous timing, or quirky detail. We would not have sighted the id of the city but for fresh eyes, able to make concise emblems from sheer extravagance. Mary Ellen Mark's kick-boxer sends nearby characters askew on the boardwalk of Coney Island (pl. 92). At the same time, he is listening to a tiny radio strapped to his arm. Ralph Gibson (b. 1939) gives us a still life of worn, orange-brown work shoes set off in a brick and wood environment, all painted in oversaturated blue (pl. 93). The white edge of a cut-out male figure streaks down, like a lightning bolt, toward one of the shoes. In its homeless textures, signs, and blocky colors and forms, New York, for Gibson, is an abstraction that can be put into a tight corner. He calls the retrospective book, from which the shoe picture is one plate, *Deus Ex Machina* (1999).

These wonderful, obviously capriciously seen moments advise us that the city can take leave of its senses. But they are, by their nature, glimpses that do not speak of the idiosyncratic togetherness that New York announced to the twentieth century. Even when the younger photographers turn to that community with sympathy, the city still does not reveal the order it had before. Coney Island has never been as tropical, for instance, as it is in the eyes of the colorist Alex

Webb (b. 1952). The radiation of heat at Luna Park came naturally to this Magnum photojournalist more accustomed to work in equatorial regions (pl. 94). He's alert to the pinks, browns, yellows, greens, and reds scattered in competition with the juggler signs in the circuslike surround. Almost lost in the visual bustle are his main characters, a young woman who fails to get the attention of her young man. As for Midtown skyscrapers (pl. 95), Webb composes them with an even more complex density, as they're entangled in the semiquavers of glass reflections. Once again, heat radiates through this phantasmagoria of misplaced signs and figures, topped by the ghostly logo of the Stardust Dine-o-mat. Had Louis Faurer collaborated with Andreas Feininger, they could not have realized a finer poetry.

Sylvia Plachy (b. 1943) does something equally reminiscent in her evocation of a crowd at Times Square (pl. 96). In this fabled place, once the site of great events, she conveys the excitement of jammed faces amid fluttering confetti, but not a mood of celebration. Everyone has the air of being in a masquerade, without costumes. Plachy was for many years the author of a weekly "unguided tour" of New York for the *Village Voice* (one chosen image per issue), and, at equal length, she ardently supported her fellow Hungarian, André Kertész. In the background of her aesthetics, a historian would detect the fragrance of his lyricism. But she displays her own delicacy in a panoramic image of a meat market, in which the lovely phosphorous hues are nicely out of keeping with what must have been quite smelly work (pl. 97).

At the end of the century, what kind of civic place did New Yorkers suppose their city to be? It had certainly recovered from its nervous breakdown of the 1960s. Twenty years later, the hippies and yippies of that period had been replaced by a new class, the yuppies. In the film made from Bret Easton Ellis's 1991 novel, *American Psycho*, young Wall Street sharks viciously one-up each other about the style of their business cards. Headphones had made their appearance, and now, cell phones. Everywhere, gyms sprouted for the sake of happy treaders on their mills, working off calories ingested in overpriced and noisy restaurants. Times Square had become Disneyfied, as distinct from dignified. Mayor Rudy Giuliani took credit for lowering the crime rate, but at the cost of infuriating minorities, profiled and brutalized by the NYPD.

One New Yorker said, "Let's talk about the other New York: the New York where most New Yorkers live. . . . We must do much better for so many more in our city. . . . It's time to end the era of the clenched fists, the closed doors, and the locked gates—of harsh rhetoric and mean-spirited policies that divide police and communities."[59] The voice was that of Fernando Ferrer, Bronx borough president, opening his campaign (at the time this was written) to be the first New York mayor of Puerto Rican descent.

In the long course of its history in New York, photography had given heed to the ethnic and racial minorities, of all boroughs, on whose behalf Ferrer was speaking. They had so increased in number during the past twenty-five years, which witnessed the belly-up of the welfare system, that the city easily retained its cardinal status as a polyglot center. Some groups have fared better than others. Bruce Davidson, for instance, shows gays, unmolested and comfortably ensconced—some even entwined—on the grass in Central Park (pl. 98). Public consciousness of their civic rights has advanced, somewhat, since the days of Arbus. But at least one photographer remains faithful to all those newer arrivals of every color and language; faithful, also, and necessarily, to the morality that Lewis Hine pictured in 1905.

Among others, Mel Rosenthal (b. 1948) photographs Cambodians, Hmongs, Muslims, Russians, Hondurans, half at a loss, half delighted to be in Queens or Brooklyn. They are living that same dream that brought in millions from abroad before them. Their lot, in these first years, is no better than that of their predecessors. But a change has come over the outlook of these strangers, recorded by Rosenthal's immigrant photography. It is perfectly acceptable for them to stand out and maintain their traditions, which many of them evidently and proudly wish to preserve. Rosenthal's vantage is straight, illustrational, and at their service. Not for one moment will he turn them into something "terrific," as Arbus did with her unusual subjects. When the Bronx was burning in the 1970s, the Bronx that had been his childhood home, Rosenthal returned to the ruin and photographed its inhabitants. Many of them smile, whether because of a precious happy moment or because of their trust in the photographer. On Bathgate Avenue, one summer, some quite ratty old mattresses had been thrown on the street. In the background, water jets effusively from a hydrant, just like the hydrants that cool off Helen Levitt's kids in 1940s Harlem. Rosenthal takes a picture of all this at the moment a black teenager somersaults over that horrible bedding. We don't see his face and, therefore, perceive his spirit. But the point is that he's suspended—in a picture where he will never fall (pl. 99).

Jewish Sensibility
and the Photography of New York

The description of New York photography in this book has been guided by two questions: how have photographers reacted to their city, and how has the city, at successive historical moments, affected their reactions? There can be no doubt that these two queries frame a subject-object dialogue that resulted in a unique phrasing of Manhattan images over much of the twentieth century. We think of that phrasing as a collective enterprise, eventually shaped into an intelligible tradition. The historical literature gives us biographical, stylistic, media, and even some political readings of accomplishments in this image bank. Still, one of the most evident features of New York photography has so far not been addressed by writers: the fact that, in every account, the great majority of the photographers concerned were or are Jews.[60]

In truth, we're largely dealing with a picture archive of an American city visualized by Jews, to which a few distinguished Gentiles have contributed. The latter include the Byrons, Lewis Hine, Edward Steichen, Karl Struss, Alvin Langdon Coburn, James Van der Zee, Berenice Abbott, George Grosz, Walker Evans, Gordon Parks, Andreas Feininger, Rolf Tietgens, Roy DeCarava, Ralph Gibson, and Alex Webb. By the end of the 1930s, the first nine had done their most noted work on New York; the photographs of the remaining six are scattered through a much lengthier period. Though they were involved with many other subjects, and thin on the urban ground, still—with the exception of Hine, who was central—their vivid engagement with the city marks an *alternative* tradition in the gallery of New York images.

In the modern visual arts, a quantitative imbalance so heavily weighted in favor of Jews reveals an anomalous situation. But can their ethnic background be singled out as a perceptible influence upon the content of their work? And what insight, anyway, might be gained by a distinction between Gentile and Jewish visual "traits," supposing that they were even identifiable? The answers to these questions would appear problematic and remote, but for the fact that reflection on the imagery itself brings them into tempting range. In their social viewpoints, expressive patterns, and choice of subjects, photographs of New York, as a whole, do noticeably fall on either side of a divide to which no one has given a name. Viewers encounter this divide so often that it can't be incidental —quite the contrary, it's fundamental. Photographers on both sides worked and work with a common devotion to the city, yet project it through very different assumptions. To ascertain the scope of New York photography, it's necessary to see it as composed of two repertoires, one larger than the other.

When I first considered these issues, I fancied that I could detect a kind of psychological presence, a specifically Jewish cluster of values and proclivities infusing a pictorial atmosphere that is tangible enough, yet elusive. As it happened, the sense of a general "atmosphere" took shape only when I recognized the part that instincts play in the construction by Jewish photographers of a personalized space. Rather than as a place that awaits them for documentary report, they present the city as formed instant by instant out of their impulsive responses. It is their improvised exchange with their subjects, not a kit of fixed and essential attributes, that distinguishes their work. Instead of having accepted their bearings as an obviously accomplished fact, Jewish photographers appear to be making, even negotiating, their way. For them, New York is not so much a place to be described as a setting that poses a question: what is the relatedness of seer and seen, as influenced by the social orders represented by the city? Each has a fluid and unforeseen vantage that can be decided. The photograph pictures that decision, on terms determined by its maker. An atmosphere, to be sure, can only be alluded to, but a specific social and psychological relationship, resolved in space, is a thing built, and can be analyzed. That analysis, overall, is woven throughout the pages of this book. Here I want to highlight its key points.

The patriarch of early New York photography was Alfred Stieglitz, a Jew alone among Gentiles. Since he insisted that art communicates across boundaries (which, of course, it does), ethnocentrism was contrary to his beliefs. Could there, nevertheless, have been some residue of Jewish identity that affected his work? Roughly twenty years ago, I asked two men who had known Stieglitz if, in their presence, he had ever let slip any reference to his Jewish descent. At first, the photography historian Beaumont Newhall and the stage director Harold Clurman drew long blanks, then some old memories stirred. Newhall recalled that Stieglitz once spoke of his father as "frustrated" by being refused membership in the restricted Jockey Club. Clurman dredged up a more theatrical vignette. In the 1920s, he and Malcolm Cowley, a critic, once made an unannounced visit to Stieglitz at Lake George. They came upon him at 4:00 A.M., "the hour of the wolf," not only fully awake but raging and distraught at having been abandoned, shortly before, by Georgia O'Keeffe. After at last calming the older man, an embarrassed Clurman recalled hearing Stieglitz mutter, "That's what comes from being with a shiksa."

As an affirmation of Jewish consciousness, these were, of course, negligible disclosures. They indicate only that Stieglitz was human enough to be pained by a reminder of his difference—the heritage his highly assimilated and wealthy family had put behind. I learned little more about the inroads of such heritage when I asked Walter Rosenblum, whose father was an Orthodox Jew, and Morris Engel if they thought Judaism had in any way touched their work as photographers. At most, they admitted to an attitude of caring for others, a solicitude that came to them as if through familial example and memory. Since they practice a nondenominational aesthetics, however, these humanists would hear nothing more of a "Jewish question." It smacked too much of the narrow constraints of their upbringing, on one hand, while, on the other, they felt it would misrepresent the content of their work.

Any opinion that might be advanced about a hypothetical Jewish sensibility, at least from its source, seemed likely to come dead on arrival. Recently, and with only a few words, William Klein changed all that. He told Anthony Lane in the *New Yorker*: "I think there are two kinds of photography—Jewish photography and goyish photography. If you look at modern photography, you find, on the one hand, the Weegees, the Diane Arbuses, the Robert Franks—funky photographs. And then you have the people who go out in the woods. Ansel Adams, Weston. It's like black and white jazz."[61]

How striking to hear on what terms Klein divides the field. Rightly confident that some distinction can be made, he associates his side with an urban consciousness, the other side with a pastoral one, Jews with an authentic blues-based jazz, Gentiles with a jazz style. (Although a more apt equivalent would be the sound of American romantic symphonists such as Howard Hanson or Samuel Barber.) The linkage between Jews and blacks, in fact, tells of more than a musical metaphor. Any student of photographic history knows how frequently blacks appear as subjects in photographs taken by Jews, but Klein's statement points to something beyond iconography: a would-be cultural liaison with blacks, a Jewish identification with another people who have had experiences and memories to be "blue" about.

Nevertheless, Klein was speaking on behalf of a cultural privilege he asserted through downward mobility. In the Eisenhower era, America's bourgeoisie held central place, and middlebrow culture was firmly in control, rigidifying the already imperial political situation with parochialism and complacency. Klein, the European-trained modernist, emphasized his social critique by associating Jews with the folkways of a repressed minority. It had not been the same for Shahn, Siskind, and other photographer dissidents of the 1930s. Cultural politics, for them, had not yet become personal in the way they would for Klein. As photographers who exposed Depression hardship, they tried to hold the political establishment to account, while a liberal, though weakened, middle class gave what support it could. By the end of the 1930s, Jewish intellectuals, headquartered by the *Partisan Review*, were going through a political metamorphosis that would run from Stalinism to Trotskyism to anti–Cold War liberalism, and finally, for some of them, to pro–Cold War conservatism. One faction upheld literary high culture of the twentieth century; another, by the late 1950s, was interpreting American vernacular culture with a view toward reformulating intellectual identity on native ground. If these political and cultural trajectories were indeed a search for identity, it was one with which Jews were familiar.

An identity crisis is often construed as a totem of modernism, but Jewish photographers in New York had a tortured relationship to that internationalist belief system. Stieglitz's refinement was an early installment in the "universalism" of a modernist credo; Strand's later portraiture of plain, yet noble Everymen subscribed to it, too. But this ecumenical modernism grew weaker in the activist performance of the Photo League, which was dedicated to the cause of particular minorities. The apparently rancorous debates within the League in the late 1940s pivoted on the question of politics versus aesthetics, with the latter— during the era of the blacklists—a more than occasional victor. Sid Grossman and Aaron Siskind, as we saw, had already turned away from the depiction of social problems to embrace photographic versions of idioms in new painting. (Franz Kline's art comes to mind.) By the 1950s, Weegee imagined that his Picassoid distortions and cartoonish trick photographs of celebrities represented his "real" art.

Some photographers diverted their visual styles because they were motivated by a need to penetrate behind the apparently inexpressive—polite—facade of straight description. Leon Levinstein, for example, imposed a ferociously subjective design on interpersonal street relations, a kind of violation of anyone's nominal privacy in anger, misery, and pleasure. Levinstein achieved a miraculous balance between willful-

ness of style and intimacy of contact. With him, and the others I mentioned above, perception of the world was transformed by focusing on the perceiving self.

By the 1950s, if they had troubled to look around them in the culture of photographic modernism, some of these Jewish photographers might have noticed that it was possessed by their lapsed coreligionists yet did not feel like home. I intuit this *unheimlich* feeling as a resonance of their continual movement, their cranky attempts to always reposition themselves, first toward their subjects, then toward each other. These photographers characteristically give the impression of betting on quixotic discoveries, of wanting to get to some beyond, of being always in transit yet never arriving. Robert Frank's collage development after *The Americans* (1958)—a monumental work that was already a most peripatetic affair—reveals his feckless search to keep an edge. Garry Winogrand went on long and promiscuous shooting jags, not sure if at any moment he had connected with anything. Bruce Davidson studied Brooklyn street gangs and blacks on East One-hundredth Street, not without anxiety. Diane Arbus plunged into hitherto avoided worlds of social manias, sexual display, and subcultural lifestyles, thirsting for shivers.

We do not observe any such restless, voracious behavior among Gentile photographers. Though only a small ethnic minority surrounded by Jewish colleagues, they radiate a sense of proprietary nonchalance when they picture the city. New York is where it happens to be, and they are where they are, in a fixed, calm relationship to it. As Andreas Feininger moved around, switching motifs, he photographed always with the same intonation of unproblematic scrutiny. Although he was a recent immigrant, he had already "arrived" and been incorporated. Even Roy DeCarava, who maintains good credentials as an outsider to white New York, has a steady emotional compass that keeps him on course, guided by a quiet hubris. (His work displays great structural but no social tension— his main subject, after all, being Harlem.) Running through all their imagery is a personal reticence blended into an aura of entitlement. The greater number of their subjects hold their place, gauged by these photographers in what is understood as common territory.

It may be that Jews behave differently because of their lovers' quarrel with assimilation—not a social assimilation, as earlier, but a cultural one. In the matter of the "Jewish" novel, for instance, it makes a difference whether characters speak in Yiddish-inflected tones or standard English. Saul Bellow's career, writes

John Murray Cuddihy, "could either remain within the conventions of the modernist novel—and thus be forced to do a cultural nose job on its Jewish characters, 'assimilating' them—or break out of the WASP modernist novel, reverting, for example, to the picaresque form with its looser 'admissions' criteria."[62]

Jewish photographers of New York in this exhibition, unlike their counterparts in fiction, never had to face Bellow's dilemma, because WASP cultural sensibility—and influence—in their area was marginal. That may help to explain why, excepting a few small passages in work by Shahn, Eagle, Huberland, and Davidson, they did not depict other Jews. It was never so much a question of affirming the presence of the tribe as it was of disseminating what amounted to its ethos. Even the most famous American photojournalist of midcentury, W. Eugene Smith, built upon a Jewish tradition and dramatized its concerns for the biggest of big media—*Life*.

At this point, what I characterized before as a subject-object dialogue must also be seen in the light of the distinctive traditional sensibilities that give it form. The Jewish take on the urban spectacle, as represented by the photographs here, implies jumpy schedules for relating to the United States. Jews hold that democracy neither depreciates nor neutralizes ethnic or "racial" cultures—including their own—but, rather, keeps them in living, often problematic suspension. In contrast, the normative view takes for granted that, since our unifying institutions have long been in place, the process of Americanization has already been accomplished. Democracy is a civic good in which our social classes line up in a reasonably fixed arrangement, deserving of no special comment. For many Jewish photographers, though, American class structure remains permeable and volatile, in a state of creation.

Compare, for example, Walker Evans's *Girl in Fulton Street, New York* (fig. 20) with Lou Stoumen's *Sitting in Front of the Strand, Times Square* (fig. 21; see also pl. 100). Evans focuses on a cloche-hatted young woman with an acutely sharp demeanor, seen against a confusion of male passersby, reflections, a crane, and cast-iron facades. Stoumen catches a man, also young, who at that moment has a soulful look, amid the hucksterism of Times Square signs. Both photographers are drawn to a single figure within a city setting that is embellished with competing signals. Evans is interested in the disorder of the incident but frames it with slightly skewed horizontals and verticals that hold the stabbing diagonals. His concern

is with a perception of apparent chaos that is contained
by his discovered structure. Stoumen is at construc-
tive work, too, but in this case he constructs a dramatic narrative about being by oneself in the city. The
man's hands are folded, and his figure is cast into the
darkness of the theater facade behind him. Finally,
another man seems to notice (and by noticing, points
to) the introspection of the main character. Evans
emphasizes the phenomenal complexities afforded by
the glimpse; Stoumen, its emotional possibilities
. . . the contrast between a sign that reads "City For
Conquest" and that other sign—a person engulfed
in an unrelated environment.

Evans's woman is proposed, simply, as a member of
the urban habitat; he and his subject are as much
at sea within it, or as much in possession of it, as anyone else. For Stoumen, the perspective works, on the
contrary, to invoke psychic distinctions. His subject is
a *solitary* in Times Square, the world's busiest crossroads. Here is a wistful stranger with whom the photographer connects. The crossroads is undoubtedly
a grand place, but it is not "theirs."

Both these pictures exemplify themes we have seen
before. Whether the public space of the city is in-
herently sharable, and therefore no big deal, or whether
there exist partitions, invisible yet strongly felt: such
an issue is revolved in an important sector of New York
photography. A photographer's instinctive reaction
to the sociality of metropolitan space is determined
essentially through the placement of figures, but
faces also signify. When Berenice Abbott depicted the
Fifth Avenue crowd, or Rudy Burckhardt Madison
Square Park, it was not people they photographed, just
population—and though physically on the move,
this mass is psychologically inert.

In his subway portraits, however, Walker Evans
highlighted individuals, but with an equal strength; he
treated them as units of population (pl. 41). They're
doggedly singular, in small or large detail, at the same
time as they make up, soul by soul, the aggregate of
who we are. The transparency of that thought endows
the subway riders with utmost, quotidian beauty. Limited space constrains their bodies, but, though close
at hand, Evans does not involve himself with feelings
about them as people. His enigmatic circumspection
on this score contrasts with Sol Libsohn's hypercon-
clusive (though unpremeditated) picture of people gathered on tenement stairs (fig. 12; see also pl. 39). Separated only by inches, each of them is cocooned in his
or her own consciousness. With Evans, the space is
psychologically neutral; with Libsohn, it looks charged

as if with negative protons. These Lower East Side people appear interchangeable in their mutual, but surely circumstantial, antipathy. A viewer is tempted to feel that they have nothing communal to do with each other. For them, as it seems, there exists only private space.

To whom, then, does the vastness of New York "belong"? For all those who know they're merely fellow users of the street, along with everyone else, the question is somewhat ridiculous. But suppose you were Alfred Kazin, whose *Walker in the City* (1951) is the classic tale of Jewish fear of, and wonder at, the New York street. Recalling his experience as a stammering child in Brooklyn, he wrote: "It troubled me that I could speak in the fullness of my own voice only when I was alone on the streets, walking about."[63] His generation came of age on the street, and found that the experience of modern life in the city so contrasted with his upbringing in a Diaspora home as to mark a difference between two worlds. Like him, the Jewish photographers of New York spread themselves throughout the city's neighborhoods. Many of them, too, had been acclimated to the bewildering streets where strangers and opportunities thronged, but they remembered that others had not left, or were unable to leave, the world of their upbringing. These citizens could not be said, as yet, to "belong."

I think Helen Levitt's art is more than a little concerned with this issue of belonging. Look at her picture of a few black men hanging out at a mailbox (fig. 22). Their associated body language, allowing an over-the-shoulder glance toward her, betrays the distance between an in-group and an observing stranger. Levitt has isolated her figures along the left margin of the frame, on an empty, sunny street; it would be hard to assert, on the basis of this picture, that, beyond their neighborhood, they have stakes in the metropolis—that undefined "somewhere" from which this fellow user of the street, Helen Levitt, has come upon them. If their territory does not extend into "her" region, the photographer has certainly intervened into theirs, but with no consequence other than to encourage them to show their cool.

To belong with others, even, or especially, in a small space, implies a local solidarity; to share a city space, unthreatened by your fellow citizens, is to diffuse solidarity, not eliminate it. Evans's subway riders share their small space, but they belong there merely because a seat is available to them. The subway resembles a hotel or a restaurant, in one sense, for it's the impersonal site of recurrent vacancies and re-

populations. People leaving a theater are also leaving a common purpose, soon to dissolve; people who travel in packs maintain their purpose. They stand apart from the impersonal surrounding by their conspicuous—and maybe protective—unity. Festivals and ethnic parades, on the contrary, mix the act of sharing and the condition of belonging so as to declare a joint impetus in a civic or religious occasion. Yet Leonard Freed's image of Wall Street (pl. 60) and Dan Weiner's of the San Gennaro festival (pl. 61) revert to the simile of pack behavior, removed from civic culture. By contrast, Sid Grossman literally immerses himself in the San Gennaro celebration, excited by it, not at all as a public event, but as a personal affair.

I can easily imagine it being said that cities are well known to affect strollers with a mood of kinship here, a feeling of hostility there . . . and what of it? We dip into city streets as into shifting coalescences of diverse forces on multiple, simultaneous errands that unweave and reconstitute themselves through waves of loose attraction. But rarely have such urban phenomena been particularized as acutely as they have in photographs of New York. If at first we catch sight only of "business," or of New Yorkers just being there, we nevertheless come away with the thought that some psychological role has been attributed to them, with an intensity that ranges from the ineffable to the rhetorical.

With its prodigious density, New York has long become the catchment area for these roles, at work in the evocation of a democratic system, recognized as uneasy with itself. As they asked that it provide acceptance for all, many Jewish photographers have often been disappointed with it. For them, solidarity is a created and always liquid condition, reversible as a tide, not a solid state to be taken for granted. That may be why children of many backgrounds are so often monitored by New York Jewish photography: at play and work, they're being inducted into that system, and pictures of them subtly describe the process.

I mentioned at the beginning of this book that we find two principal frameworks for the problem of depicting New York. One of them comprehends "the visible citadel of power," and the other contemplates "the disjointed patchwork of neighborhoods." In just one image, William Klein improbably fused both these topics (fig. 23). On the Staten Island ferry, under a cloudy sky, his boat passengers are simply out of it, neither interacting with one another nor cognizant of the great skyline, which is reduced to a disregarded

William Klein (b. 1928), *On the Staten Island Ferry*, 1950s.
Gelatin-silver print. © William Klein, courtesy Howard Greenberg
Gallery, New York

Andreas Feininger (1906–1999), *On the Staten Island Ferry
Approaching Downtown Manhattan*, 1940. Gelatin-silver print,
12¹⁵⁄₁₆ x 10¹⁵⁄₁₆ in. (32.7 x 27.6 cm). © Collection The New-York
Historical Society, New York

footnote on the horizon. They constitute a "disjointed neighborhood" at close, human range. For Andreas Feininger, in contrast, Lower Manhattan shines forth its gleaming light on a sunny day, witnessed by a group of expectant passengers as if it were a democratic epiphany (fig. 24; see also pl. 101). They stand at attention, their alert bodies a compositional prelude to the upright, climactic towers. Feininger's glorious picture concerns itself with the act of looking, and the desire that comes with the look, to be welcomed by the thing seen. The photographer looks with them, as well: passengers and photographer share their space, and they exhibit their solidarity, at the same time. Soon, everyone will land, and the pleasure of that landing already suffuses the image. As for Klein, arrival is a matter of indifference; he gives us a dispirited scenario with his characteristic enthusiasm and tang.

Considered as pictorial antitheses that represent the same metropolitan subject, these two images hardly seem capable of improvement. Feininger's ceremonious affirmation rings clear without the need to show faces; Klein's skepticism says it all by means of unsorted faces and one back. The city might be seen as a symbolic whole, but not the spirit of those who live in it or return to it. Both images depict an archetype of New York iconography, but Klein's treats it familiarly—that is, with a form of address that lacks deference. To view familiarly, in this sense, doesn't necessarily imply rejection or some disfavor, only an unwillingness to stand on ceremony.

In earlier days, photographers softened the abruptness of their content with an attitude of deference. That mixture is what makes Morris Engel's *Harlem Merchant* a characteristic statement of its time. A kind of intrusive sympathy runs through 1930s social photographs of New York. Lou Faurer and Saul Leiter continued that lead, yet lent it notes of pity and introspection. In the 1940s, however, Weegee deflected the commiserating dynamic of that tradition into something colder. Private moments of the neglected and aggrieved ceased to be object lessons in political morality, and became fair game on the daily, human round. Weegee was *familiar* with misfortune, in the sense I describe above. Others who followed ratcheted up the intimacy of his familiar view, each very differently: Model, Klein, Arbus, Levinstein, Mary Ellen Mark, Winogrand, Davidson, Nan Goldin, Eugene Richards (a rare Gentile), and Bruce Gilden.

The realism—or, one should say, the realpolitik—of their trend prompted them to make new, tough distinctions between sharing and solidarity, purpose and the failure of purpose. Familiarity was both an asset that brought these photographers unprecedentedly close to street behavior and a form of knowledge with which to decode it. What they saw was an array of peoples existing within the weakening gravitational pull of their ethnic and sexual cultures, but still at hazard in the common culture, which had not proven that it could sustain them. In other words, most New Yorkers carried on, *normatively*, in a mode of displacement. We may walk the street apparently in one physical current, yet also at psychological angles to each other. It was as if these photographers of Jewish origin were able to comprehend a minority status that permeates the whole city as a generic condition. They set the terms of discourse, blending into it a tone of activism and melancholy that was recognizable, yet ambivalent and skittish. If theirs was an outsider's perspective to New York experience, we sense that perspective not as an obstacle but as an inherent part of the experience they offered. They grasped— not always consciously, not always continuously— what made that view relevant to its era. In the end, they built up a visual record of New York, acclaimed by a twentieth-century public, unaware that these pictures comprise an argument among Jews and with their world.

Notes

1 Phillip Lopate, ed., *Writing New York: A Literary Anthology* (New York: Library of America, 1998), xviii.

2 Quoted in Peter Simmons, *Gotham Comes of Age: New York Through the Lens of the Byron Company, 1892–1942*, exh. cat. (New York: Museum of the City of New York; San Francisco: Pomegranate, 1999), 10.

3 Peter Bacon Hales, *Silver Cities: The Photography of American Urbanization, 1839–1915* (Philadelphia: Temple University Press, 1984), 280.

4 Peter Conrad, *The Art of the City: Views and Versions of New York* (New York: Oxford University Press, 1984), 74.

5 Quoted in Michael Weaver, *Alvin Langdon Coburn: Symbolist Photographer, 1882–1966* (New York: Aperture, 1986), 38.

6 Lewis Mumford, *The City in History: Its Origins, Its Transformations, and Its Prospects* (New York: Harcourt, Brace, and World, 1961), 530.

7 Michael Walzer, *On Toleration* (New Haven and London: Yale University Press, 1997), 10–11.

8 Alan Trachtenberg, *Reading American Photographs: Images as History: Matthew Brady to Walker Evans* (New York: Hill and Wang, 1989), 192.

9 Georg Simmel, "The Metropolis and Mental Life," in *The Sociology of Georg Simmel*, ed. and trans. Kurt H. Wolff (New York: Free Press, 1964), 409.

10 In Fritz Lang's celebrated film *Metropolis*, of 1927, dronelike workers provide an inadvertent echo of the intent that Strand realizes in this photograph.

11 Quoted in Gail Levin and Judith Tick, *Aaron Copland's America: A Cultural Perspective* (New York: Watson-Guptill, 2000), 36.

12 Michael G. Sundell, *Berenice Abbott: Documentary Photography of the 1930s*, exh. cat. (Cleveland: New Gallery of Contemporary Art, 1980), 7.

13 In his Dada period, Grosz often likened the human head to a football or a globe, an obvious dig at the bourgeoisie.

14 Deborah Martin Kao, Laura Katzman, and Jenna Webster, *Ben Shahn's New York: The Photography of Modern Times*, exh. cat. (Cambridge, Mass.: Fogg Art Museum, Harvard University Art Museums; New Haven and London: Yale University Press, 2000), 20.

15 Quoted in the documentary *Arguing the World* (1997), directed and produced by Joseph Dorman.

16 Kao, Katzman, and Webster, *Ben Shahn's New York*, 16.

17 Jerry L. Thompson, *Walker Evans at Work* (New York: Harper and Row, 1982), 44.

18 Belinda Rathbone, *Walker Evans: A Biography* (Boston: Houghton Mifflin, 1995), 91–92. Evans made sure to express his ire, visually, when on assignment for *Fortune* to photograph a Communist summer camp. He made the people there look particularly ugly.

19 Kao, Katzman, and Webster, *Ben Shahn's New York*, 12.

20 Leah Bendavid-Val, *Propaganda and Dreams: Photographing the 1930s in the U.S.S.R. and the U.S.* (Zurich: Editions Stemmle, 1999), 47.

21 William Stott, *Documentary Expression and Thirties America* (New York: Oxford University Press, 1973), 5–73.

22 Remarks by Gutmann quoted in Max Kozloff, *The Restless Decade: John Gutmann's Photographs of the Thirties* (New York: Abrams, 1984), 9.

23 *Morris Engel: Early Work*, with interview by Julia Van Haaften (New York: Ruth Orkin Photo Archive, 1999), 4.

24 Quoted in Aaron Siskind, *Harlem Document: Photographs, 1932–1940*, ed. Ann Banks (Providence, R.I.: Matrix, 1981), 4.

25 Terry Smith, *Making the Modern: Industry, Art, and Design in America* (Chicago: University of Chicago Press, 1993), 341.

26 *The Public Eye*, directed by John Franklin, 1992.

27 Another, historical reading of this photograph is possible: "In mood and in subject [Weegee's] subject *Coney Island, July 5th, 1942*, taken a month after the Americans had won big at Midway, was inconceivable anywhere else in the world. Despite our travails, all of us, including Weegee, were winners who never gave the prospect of defeat a second thought. Being the decisive force in the world's conflicts was very well, but what these motley, completely unheroic people needed to do was to get to the water and cool off." Quoted in Max Kozloff, "Mass Hysteria: The Photographs of Weegee," *Artforum* 36, no. 7 (March 1998): 81.

28 Lou Stoumen, *Times Square: Forty-five Years of Photography* (New York: Aperture, 1985), 158.

29 George Gilbert, interviewed by the author, May 9, 2001.

30 Walker Evans, *Walker Evans at Work*, with essay by Jerry L. Thompson (New York: Harper and Row, 1982), 160.

31 Ibid.

32 The photograph is reproduced in Lili Corbus Bezner, *Photography and Politics in America: From the New Deal into the Cold War* (Baltimore: Johns Hopkins University Press, 1999), 63.

33 Ric Burns cites the 1940s as a period when new waves of Puerto Ricans streamed into New York. See Ric Burns, James Sanders, and Lisa Ades, *New York: An Illustrated History* (New York: Knopf, 1999), 490.

34 Colin Westerbeck and Joel Meyerowitz, *Bystander: A History of Street Photography* (Boston: Bulfinch, 1994), 264.

35 Ben Lifson, "The Raw and the Half-Baked," *Village Voice*, May 26, 1980.

36 Weegee, *Weegee: An Autobiography* (New York: Da Capo, 1975), 233–35.

37 Ann Thomas, *Lisette Model*, exh. cat. (Ottawa: National Gallery of Canada, 1990), 50.

38 Ibid., 30.

39 See Marie de Thézy, *La Photographie humaniste, 1930–1960: Histoire d'un mouvement en France* (Paris: Contrejour, 1992), for a valuable treatment of Parisian photography as a humanist school, esp. 38–39 for the relation of images to texts.

40 Tony Judt, *Past Imperfect: French Intellectuals, 1944–1956* (Berkeley: University of California Press, 1992). See, in particular, his remarks on the legacy of "nineteenth-century republicans who first deployed . . . the idea that France stood for something, proselytizing an ideal of civic virtue and implicitly denying any potential or actual differences or divergences within the nation itself" (240).

41 Westerbeck and Meyerowitz, *Bystander*, 155.

42 Simone de Beauvoir, *America Day by Day*, trans. Patrick Dudley (New York: Grove, 1953), 28–29.

43 William Klein, *New York, 1954–55* (Manchester: Dewi Lewis, 1995), 8.

44 Eve Arnold et al., *The Fifties: Photographs of America*, intro. by John Chancellor (New York: Pantheon, 1985), n.p.

45 Eric Sandeen, *Picturing an Exhibition: The Family of Man and 1950s America* (Albuquerque: University of New Mexico Press, 1995), 70.

46 Quoted in Peter Galassi, *Roy DeCarava: A Retrospective*, with an essay by Sherry Turner DeCarava (New York: Museum of Modern Art, 1996), 19.

47 Ibid., 51.

48 Diane Arbus, *Diane Arbus* (New York: Aperture and Museum of Modern Art, 1972), n.p.

49 Patricia Bosworth, *Diane Arbus: A Biography* (New York: Knopf, 1984), 291.

50 John Szarkowski, *Winogrand: Figments from the Real World* (New York: Museum of Modern Art, 1988), 34.

51 Ibid., 20.

52 Marshall Berman, "The Lonely Crowd: New York After the War," in Burns, Sanders, and Ades, *New York: An Illustrated History*, 538.

53 Bruce Davidson, *Bruce Davidson* (New York: Pantheon; Paris: Centre national de la photographie, 1986), n.p.

54 Bruce Davidson, *Subway* (New York: Aperture, 1986), n.p.

55 Maria Morris Hambourg, Jeff Rosenheim, Douglas Eklund, and Mia Fineman, *Walker Evans*, exh. cat. (New York: Metropolitan Museum of Art, 2000), 109–10.

56 Nan Goldin, *The Other Side*, ed. David Armstrong and Walter Keller, exh. cat. (New York and Berlin: Scalo; Berlin: D.A.A.D. Artists-in-Residence Programme, 1993), 5.

57 Nan Goldin, *The Ballad of Sexual Dependency*, ed. Marvin Heiferman, Mark Holborn, and Suzanne Fletcher (New York: Aperture, 1986), 7.

58 Neil Postman, *Crazy Talk, Stupid Talk* (New York: Delta, 1976), 10–11.

59 Quoted in Adam Nagourney, "Entering Race, Ferrer Focuses on Giuliani," *New York Times*, June 28, 2001.

60 See, however, discussion of Judaic origin among New York photographers in A. D. Coleman, "No Pictures: Some Thoughts on Jews in Photography," *Photo Review* 23, no. 1 (Winter 2000): 1–6, and George Gilbert, *The Illustrated Worldwide Who's Who of Jews in Photography* (Riverdale, N.Y.: George Gilbert, 1996).

61 Anthony Lane, "The Shutterbug," *New Yorker*, May 21, 2001, 80.

62 John Murray Cuddihy, *The Ordeal of Civility: Freud, Marx, Lévi-Strauss, and the Jewish Struggle with Modernity* (New York: Basic Books, 1974), 218–19.

63 Alfred Kazin, *A Walker in the City* (New York: Harcourt Brace, 1951), 24.

PLATES

1

BYRON COMPANY (1892–1942)

Indians and Their Teepees on the Roof of the Hotel McAlpin, 1913
Gelatin-silver print, 10 1/2 x 13 3/16 in. (26.7 x 33.7 cm).
Museum of the City of New York, Byron Collection, 93.1.1.4468

2

BYRON COMPANY (1892–1942)

Hester Street, 1898
Gelatin-silver print, 14 x 19 in. (35.6 x 48.3 cm).
Museum of the City of New York, Byron Collection, 93.1.1.18122

3

KARL STRUSS (1886–1981)

Trolley, Horse-drawn Vehicle & El., N.Y.C., 1911
Platinum print, 3³/₁₆ x 4¹/₈ in. (7.9 x 10.5 cm).
© Amon Carter Museum, Fort Worth, Texas, P1983.23.3

4

KARL STRUSS (1886–1981)

Back of Public Library, 1912
Platinum print, 4¼ x 3¾ in. (10.8 x 9.5 cm).
© Amon Carter Museum, Fort Worth, Texas, P1983.23.2

5

ALFRED STIEGLITZ (1864–1946)

The City of Ambition, 1910, printed c. 1913
Photogravure, 13¼ x 10¼ in. (33.8 x 26 cm).
The Metropolitan Museum of Art, New York, Alfred Stieglitz
Collection, 1949 (49.55.19)

6

The Tunnel Builders, 1908
Photogravure, 7⅝ x 6⅛ in. (19.4 x 15.7 cm).
George Eastman House, Rochester, New York

7

ANONYMOUS

The Lower East Side, 1900
Photochrome process print, 12¹/₂ x 16¹/₂ in. (31.8 x 41.9 cm).
Collection of Lisa Ades, New York

8

LEWIS HINE (1874–1940)

Climbing into America, 1905
Gelatin-silver print, 6$^1/_2$ x 4$^5/_8$ in. (16.6 x 11.9 cm).
George Eastman House, Rochester, New York

9

LEWIS HINE (1874–1940)

Mendicants, New York City, 1910
Gelatin-silver print, 7 x 5 in. (17.8 x 12.7 cm).
National Archives, Still Pictures Branch, College Park, Maryland

10

11

12

PAUL STRAND (1890–1976)

Portrait, Five Points Square, New York, 1916
Platinum print, 12 3/8 x 7 1/2 in. (31.4 x 19.1 cm).
Museum of Fine Arts, Boston. Sophie Friedman Fund, 1997.776.
© 1990 Aperture Foundation, Inc., Paul Strand Archive

13

SAMUEL H. GOTTSCHO (1875–1971)

Times Square at Forty-fourth Street, 1932
Gelatin-silver print, 16 x 20 in. (40.6 x 50.8 cm). Museum of the
City of New York. Gift of Samuel H. Gottscho, 34.102.10

14

BERENICE ABBOTT (1898–1991)

Lyric Theater; Third Avenue Between 12th and 13th Street from
Changing New York, 1936
Gelatin-silver print, 8 x 10 in. (20.3 x 25.4 cm). Photography
Collection, Miriam and Ira D. Wallach Division of Art, Prints &
Photographs, The New York Public Library. Astor, Lenox and Tilden
Foundations. © Berenice Abbott/Commerce Graphics Ltd., Inc.

GEORGE GROSZ (1893–1959)

A Face in the Crowd from *First Landing,* 1932
Gelatin-silver print, 5 1/4 x 7 13/16 in. (13.3 x 19.7 cm).
Kimmel Cohn Photography Arts, New York.
© Estate of George Grosz/Licensed by VAGA, New York

16

BEN SHAHN (1898–1969)

Untitled (New York General Post Office, Eighth Avenue and Thirty-third Street, New York City), 1932–35
Vintage gelatin-silver print, 6¼ x 9⅛ in. (15.9 x 23.2 cm).
© Bernarda Bryson Shahn, courtesy Howard Greenberg Gallery, New York

17

BEN SHAHN (1898–1969)

Untitled (Seward Park, New York City), 1932–35
Gelatin-silver print, 6¼ x 9½ in. (15.8 x 24 cm).
Fogg Art Museum, Harvard University Art Museums,
Cambridge, Massachusetts. Gift of Bernarda Bryson Shahn.
© President and Fellows of Harvard College

18

JOHN GUTMANN (1905–1998)

Guns for Sale, 1936
Gelatin-silver print, 7⅝ x 6⅞ in. (19.3 x 17.5 cm).
The Metropolitan Museum of Art, New York. Gift of the artist,
2000 (2000.651.4). © 1998 Center for Creative Photography,
Arizona Board of Regents

19

ALEXANDER ALLAND (1902–1989)

Untitled, c. 1938
Vintage gelatin-silver print, 9³/₄ x 7⁷/₈ in. (24.8 x 20 cm).
© Howard Greenberg, courtesy Howard Greenberg Gallery,
New York

20

ALEXANDER ALLAND (1902–1989)

Chinatown, 1938
Vintage gelatin-silver print, 14 x 11 in. (35.6 x 27.9 cm).
© Howard Greenberg, courtesy Howard Greenberg Gallery,
New York

21

MORRIS ENGEL (B. 1918)

Harlem Merchant, 1937
Gelatin-silver print, 11 x 14 in. (27.9 x 35.6 cm).
© Morris Engel, courtesy Howard Greenberg Gallery, New York

22

JAMES VAN DER ZEE (1886–1983)

Manhattan Temple B.C. Lunch, 1936
Gelatin-silver print, 12⅛ x 10½ in. (30.8 x 26.7 cm).
The Metropolitan Museum of Art, New York.
Gift of The James Van Der Zee Institute, 1970 (1970.539.53).
© Donna Mussenden Van Der Zee

23

WALTER ROSENBLUM (B. 1919)

Group in Front of Fence, 1938
Gelatin-silver print, 11 x 14 in. (27.9 x 35.6 cm).
© Walter Rosenblum, courtesy of the artist

AARON SISKIND (1903–1991)

The Wishing Tree from *Harlem Document*, 1937
Gelatin-silver print, 11 x 14 in. (27.9 x 35.6 cm).
The Jewish Museum, New York. Museum purchase; Lillian Gordon
Bequest, 2000-58. © Aaron Siskind Foundation

25

26

OTTO HAGEL (1909–1973)

New York Stock Exchange, 1938
Gelatin-silver print, 12 1/2 x 10 3/8 in. (34.2 x 26.4 cm).
© 1998 Center for Creative Photography, The University of
Arizona Foundation

MARGARET BOURKE-WHITE (1904–1971)

Untitled (Sergei Eisenstein Having a Shave on the Terrace of Margaret Bourke-White's Studio), 1930
Gelatin-silver print, 13³/₈ x 9¹/₂ in. (34 x 24.1 cm). Margaret Bourke-White Papers, Syracuse University Library, Department of Special Collections. © Estate of Margaret Bourke-White

28

EDWARD STEICHEN (1879–1973)

In a New York Penthouse, 1931
Vintage gelatin-silver print, 9 1/2 x 7 1/2 in. (24.1 x 19.1 cm).
Howard Greenberg Gallery, New York. Reprinted with permission
of Joanna T. Steichen

29

WEEGEE (B. ARTHUR FELLIG, 1899–1968)

Ballet Rehearsal, c. 1940s
Gelatin-silver print, 14 x 11 in. (35.6 x 27.9 cm). International
Center of Photography, New York. © Weegee/International Center
of Photography/Getty Images

31

WEEGEE (B. ARTHUR FELLIG, 1899–1968)

Crowd at Coney Island, temperature 89 degrees . . .
They came early and stayed late, July 22, 1940
Gelatin-silver print, 11 x 14 in. (27.9 x 35.6 cm).
International Center of Photography, New York. Gift of Wilma
Wilcox, 1993. © Weegee/International Center of Photography/
Getty Images

32

RUTH ORKIN (1921–1985)

Times Square, V-E Day, NYC, 1945
Gelatin-silver print, 16 x 20 in. (40.6 x 50.8 cm).
© Ruth Orkin/Courtesy Estate of Ruth Orkin

33

34

FRITZ NEUGASS (1899–1979)

Untitled, 1940s
Gelatin-silver print, 6 3/8 x 4 5/8 in. (16.2 x 11.7 cm).
Keith de Lellis Gallery, New York

35

REBECCA LEPKOFF (B. 1916)

Henry Street, Manhattan, 1946–47
Vintage gelatin-silver print, 12 1/8 x 10 1/2 in. (30.8 x 26.7 cm).
© Rebecca Lepkoff, courtesy Howard Greenberg Gallery, New York

36

MORRIS HUBERLAND (B. 1909)

Outdoor Meeting, c. 1940
Gelatin-silver print, 7¹/₂ x 7¹/₂ in. (19.1 x 19.1 cm).
The New-York Historical Society, New York. © Morris
Huberland/Licensed by VAGA, New York

37

WALTER ROSENBLUM (B. 1919)

Block Party, New York East Side, 1942
Gelatin-silver print, 7 3/8 x 9 3/8 in. (18.7 x 23.8 cm).
The Museum of Modern Art, New York.
Extended loan from the photographer. © Walter Rosenblum

GEORGE GILBERT (B. 1922)

Untitled from *American Faces*, 1942
Gelatin-silver print, 14 x 11 in. (35.6 x 27.9 cm).
© George Gilbert, courtesy of the artist

39

SOL LIBSOHN (1914–2001)

Hester Street, c. 1938
Gelatin-silver print, 10 x 9⅞ in. (25.4 x 25.1 cm).
© Estate of Sol Libsohn, courtesy Howard Greenberg
Gallery, New York

40

ARNOLD EAGLE (1910–1992)

On the Elevated—Sailor, Newspaper, 1941
Vintage gelatin-silver print, 10¼ x 12¼ in. (26 x 31.1 cm).
© Dorothy Eagle, courtesy Howard Greenberg Gallery, New York

41

WALKER EVANS (1903–1975)

Untitled (Subway Passengers), 1938
Gelatin-silver print, 3¹³/₁₆ x 5¹/₄ in. (9.6 x 13.3 cm).
Collection of The Museum of Modern Art, New York. Purchase.
© Walker Evans Archive, The Metropolitan Museum of Art,
New York

42

43

44

SID GROSSMAN (1915–1955)

New York, 1947
Vintage gelatin-silver print, 7³/₄ x 8¹/₈ in. (19.7 x 20.6 cm).
© Miriam Grossman-Cohen, courtesy Howard Greenberg Gallery,
New York

45

SID GROSSMAN (1915–1955)

Coney Island, 1947–48
Vintage gelatin-silver print, 8 1/4 x 7 1/2 in. (21 x 19.1 cm).
© Miriam Grossman-Cohen, courtesy Howard Greenberg Gallery,
New York

46

SID GROSSMAN (1915–1955)

Mulberry Street, 1948
Vintage gelatin-silver print, 13 3/16 x 10 1/2 in. (33.5 x 26.7 cm).
The Jewish Museum, New York. Museum purchase;
Lillian Gordon Bequest, 2000-78. © Miriam Grossman-Cohen,
courtesy Howard Greenberg Gallery, New York

47

GJON MILI (1904–1984)

Café Society, New York, 1943–47
Gelatin-silver print, 19 3/4 x 15 5/16 in. (50.1 x 38.8 cm).
The Museum of Modern Art, New York. Purchase.
© Gjon Mili/TimePix

48

TED CRONER (B. 1922)

Untitled, c. 1947
Vintage gelatin-silver print, 14 x 11 in. (35.6 x 27.9 cm).
© Ted Croner, courtesy Howard Greenberg Gallery, New York

49

TED CRONER (B. 1922)

Untitled, c. 1947
Vintage gelatin-silver print, 11 7/8 x 10 1/2 in. (30.2 x 26.7 cm).
© Ted Croner, courtesy Howard Greenberg Gallery, New York

50

LOU BERNSTEIN (B. 1911)

Landlord and His Wife, New York City (Man and Wife), 1941
Gelatin-silver print, 13 15/16 x 10 15/16 in. (35.4 x 27.8 cm).
The Museum of Fine Arts, Houston. Gift of Wolf Associates,
82.546.1. © Irwin Bernstein/Arlene Steinberg

51

HENRI CARTIER-BRESSON (B. 1908)

New York, 1946
Gelatin-silver print, 20 x 16 in. (50.8 x 40.6 cm).
© Henri Cartier-Bresson/Magnum Photos, Inc., New York

52

ARNOLD EAGLE (1910–1992)

New York, 1937
Gelatin-silver print, 14 x 11 in. (35.6 x 27.9 cm).
© Dorothy Eagle, courtesy Howard Greenberg Gallery, New York

53

MORRIS ENGEL (B. 1918)

Shoeshine Boy with Cop, 1947
Vintage gelatin-silver print, mounted on masonite, 13¹/₄ x 10¹/₄ in.
(33.7 x 26 cm). The Jewish Museum, New York. Museum purchase,
Photography Acquisitions Committee Fund, 2000-63.
© Morris Engel

HELEN LEVITT (B. 1913)

Untitled (Finger Pointing in Window), c. 1938
Gelatin-silver print, 4³/₄ x 7¹³/₁₆ in. (12.1 x 19.9 cm).
The Metropolitan Museum of Art, New York. Purchase, The Horace
W. Goldsmith Foundation Gift, 1991 (1991.1146). © Helen Levitt

55

56

HELEN LEVITT (B. 1913)

New York, c. 1940
Gelatin-silver print, 11 x 14 in. (27.9 x 35.6 cm). The Jewish
Museum, New York. Museum purchase; Lillian Gordon Bequest,
2000-56. © Helen Levitt

57

58

59

LISETTE MODEL (1906–1983)

Asti's, New York, 1946
Gelatin-silver print, 13 3/8 x 10 13/16 in. (34 x 27.4 cm).
The J. Paul Getty Museum, Los Angeles. © The Lisette Model
Foundation, Inc.

60

LEONARD FREED (B. 1929)

New York, 1954
Gelatin-silver print, 20 x 16 in. (50.8 x 40.6 cm).
© Leonard Freed/Magnum Photos, Inc., New York

61

62

DAN WEINER (1919–1959)

Harold Arlen (Partly Hidden), Marlene Dietrich, and Truman
Capote at El Morocco, 1955
Gelatin-silver print, 11 x 14 in. (27.9 x 35.6 cm).
Collection of Sandra Weiner. © Estate of Dan Weiner

63

LEONARD FREED (B. 1929)

New York, USA from *The Dance of the Pious*, 1954
Gelatin-silver print, 10¹/₄ x 6⁷/₈ in. (26 x 17.5 cm).
The Jewish Museum, New York. Museum purchase with funds
provided by Mimi and Barry J. Alperin, 2000-73.
© Leonard Freed/Magnum Photos, Inc., New York

64

LOUIS FAURER (1916–2001)

New York City, 1950
Gelatin-silver print, 11³/8 x 7⁷/8 in. (28.9 x 18.7 cm).
Addison Gallery of American Art, Phillips Academy, Andover,
Massachusetts. Gift of Deborah Bell. © Estate of Louis
Faurer/Licensed by VAGA, New York

65

66

LOUIS FAURER (1916–2001)

New York City, 1950
Gelatin-silver print, 16 x 20 in. (40.6 x 50.8 cm).
Collection of Deborah Bell, New York.
© Estate of Louis Faurer/Licensed by VAGA, New York

67

SAUL LEITER (B. 1923)

New York, 1950s
Gelatin-silver print, 14 x 11 in. (35.6 x 27.9 cm).
© Saul Leiter, courtesy Howard Greenberg Gallery, New York

SAUL LEITER (B. 1923)

Barbershop 75¢, 1950s
Fujicolor crystal archive, 14 x 11 in. (35.6 x 27.9 cm).
© Saul Leiter, courtesy Howard Greenberg Gallery, New York

69

WEEGEE (B. ARTHUR FELLIG, 1899–1968)

Joy of Living, April 17, 1942
Gelatin-silver print, 16⅜ x 12½ in. (41.6 x 31.8 cm).
International Center of Photography, New York.
© Weegee/International Center of Photography/Getty Images

70

WILLIAM KLEIN (B. 1928)

Gun, Gun, Gun, New York, 1955
Gelatin-silver print, 15 3/4 x 19 5/8 in. (40 x 49.8 cm).
© William Klein, courtesy Howard Greenberg Gallery, New York

WILLIAM KLEIN (B. 1928)

Presentation, Ebbets Field, New York, 1955
Gelatin-silver print, 19⅝ x 23⅝ in. (49.8 x 60 cm).
© William Klein, courtesy Howard Greenberg Gallery, New York

72

GORDON PARKS (B. 1912)

Untitled (Man Preaching to Crowd), c. 1952
Vintage gelatin-silver print, 9 x 13¹/₂ in. (22.9 x 34.3 cm).
© Gordon Parks, courtesy Howard Greenberg Gallery, New York

73

WILLIAM KLEIN (B. 1928)

The Bars of a 2 by 4 Park. A Bench, Home for the Homeless, 1950s
Gelatin-silver print, 15 3/4 x 19 5/8 in. (40 x 49.8 cm).
© William Klein, courtesy Howard Greenberg Gallery, New York

74

LEON LEVINSTEIN (1910–1988)

Untitled, c. 1957
Gelatin-silver print, 10 ¹¹/₁₆ x 13 ¹/₄ in. (27.1 x 33.6 cm).
Private collection. © Stuart E. Karu

LEON LEVINSTEIN (1910–1988)

Mother and Child, Herald Square, c. 1955
Gelatin-silver print, 14 x 16¼ in. (35.6 x 41.3 cm).
© Stuart E. Karu, courtesy Howard Greenberg Gallery, New York

76

LEON LEVINSTEIN (1910–1988)

Times Square, New York, 1965
Vintage gelatin-silver print, 12³/₈ x 10³/₈ in. (31.6 x 26.2 cm).
The Dreyfus Corporation, New York. © Stuart E. Karu

77

78

MARY ELLEN MARK (B. 1940)

The Queen, 1968
Gelatin-silver print, 20 x 16 in. (50.8 x 40.6 cm).
© Mary Ellen Mark, courtesy of the artist

BRUCE GILDEN (B. 1946)

New York City, 1990
Gelatin-silver print, 16 x 20 in. (40.6 x 50.8 cm).
© Bruce Gilden/Magnum Photos, Inc., New York

GARRY WINOGRAND (1928–1984)

Rockefeller Victory Celebration, 1972
Gelatin-silver print, 16 x 20 in. (40.6 x 50.8 cm). Collection of
Eli Consilvio. Courtesy of Deborah Bell, New York. © The Estate of
Garry Winogrand, courtesy Fraenkel Gallery, San Francisco

81

BRUCE DAVIDSON (B. 1933)

East 100th Street, 1966
Gelatin-silver print, 20 x 16 in. (50.8 x 40.6 cm).
© Bruce Davidson/Magnum Photos, Inc., New York

BRUCE DAVIDSON (B. 1933)

Subway, 1980
Lambda Cibachrome print, 16 x 20 in. (40.6 x 50.8 cm).
© Bruce Davidson/Magnum Photos, Inc., New York

HELEN LEVITT (B. 1913)

New York, 1972
Dye transfer print, 16 x 20 in. (40.6 x 50.8 cm).
© Helen Levitt, courtesy Laurence Miller Gallery, New York

84

NAN GOLDIN (B. 1953)

Misty in Sheridan Square, New York City, 1991
Cibachrome print, 20 x 24 in. (50.8 x 61 cm).
© Nan Goldin, courtesy Matthew Marks Gallery, New York

NAN GOLDIN (B. 1953)

David with Butch Crying at Tin Pan Alley, New York City, 1982
Chromogenic color photograph, 20 x 24 in. (50.8 x 61 cm).
Collection of Marvin Heiferman, New York. © Nan Goldin,
courtesy Matthew Marks Gallery, New York

86

LARRY FINK (B. 1941)

George Plimpton, Jared Paul Stern, and Cameron Richardson,
Fashion Shoot, Elaine's, New York City, 1999
Gelatin-silver print, 14⁷/₈ x 14⁷/₈ in. (37.8 x 37.8 cm).
© Larry Fink, courtesy of the artist

87

LARRY FINK (B. 1941)

Edwardian Ball, Frick Museum, New York City, 2000
Gelatin-silver print, 14 3/4 x 18 1/4 in. (37.5 x 46.4 cm).
© Larry Fink, courtesy of the artist

JEFF MERMELSTEIN (B. 1957)

Untitled, New York City, 1995
Fujicolor crystal archive, 16 x 20 in. (40.6 x 50.8 cm).
© Jeff Mermelstein, courtesy of the artist

89

JEFF MERMELSTEIN (B. 1957)

Untitled, New York City, 1993
Fujicolor crystal archive, 16 x 20 in. (40.6 x 50.8 cm).
© Jeff Mermelstein, courtesy of the artist

JEFF JACOBSON (B. 1946)

Untitled, 1985
35mm Kodachrome original transparency, digital epson print,
20 x 30 in. (40.6 x 76.2 cm). © Jeff Jacobson, courtesy of the artist

91

JEFF JACOBSON (B. 1946)

Untitled, 1999
35mm Kodachrome original transparency, digital epson print,
20 x 30 in. (40.6 x 76.2 cm). © Jeff Jacobson, courtesy of the artist

92

93

94

ALEX WEBB (B. 1952)

Coney Island, New York, 1983
Lambda Cibachrome print, 16 x 20 in. (40.6 x 50.8 cm).
© Alex Webb/Magnum Photos, Inc., New York

95

ALEX WEBB (B. 1952)

Times Square, New York, 1996
Lambda Cibachrome print, 16 x 20 in. (40.6 x 50.8 cm).
© Alex Webb/Magnum Photos, Inc., New York

SYLVIA PLACHY (B. 1943)

Times Square, 1993
Archival gelatin-silver print, 15 x 15 in. (38.1 x 38.1 cm).
© Sylvia Plachy, courtesy of the artist

97

SYLVIA PLACHY (B. 1943)

Meat Market, 1997
Panoramic C-print, 12 x 29¹/₂ in. (30.5 x 74.9 cm).
© Sylvia Plachy, courtesy of the artist

98

BRUCE DAVIDSON (B. 1933)

Gay Pride, Central Park, 1992
Gelatin-silver print, 16 x 20 in. (40.6 x 50.8 cm).
© Bruce Davidson/Magnum Photos, Inc. New York

99

MEL ROSENTHAL (B. 1948)

Nelson Playing, Bathgate Avenue from *In the South Bronx of America*, 1976
Gelatin-silver print, 16 x 20 in. (40.6 x 50.8 cm).
© Mel Rosenthal, courtesy of the artist

100

LOU STOUMEN (1917–1991)

Sitting in Front of the Strand, Times Square, 1940
Vintage gelatin-silver print, 8¾ x 6⅞ in. (22.2 x 17.5 cm).
© Barry Singer Gallery, Petaluma, California

101

ANDREAS FEININGER (1906–1999)

On the Staten Island Ferry Approaching Downtown Manhattan, 1940
Gelatin-silver print, 12 15/16 x 10 15/16 in. (32.7 x 27.6 cm).
© Collection of The New-York Historical Society, New York

Artist Biographies

JOHANNA GOLDFELD

BERENICE ABBOTT (1898–1991)

Born in Springfield, Ohio, Berenice Abbott moved to Greenwich Village in 1918 to study journalism. In 1921, she went to Paris, planning to become a sculptor. Instead, she became a photographic assistant to Man Ray, and by 1925 she had her own portrait studio, where she photographed such artists and writers as Jean Cocteau, Marcel Duchamp, and James Joyce. Abbott admired Eugène Atget's photographs, which documented the streets and monuments of Paris. In 1929, she returned to the United States to take photographs of New York in a similar vein, and was integral in bringing Atget's work to the American public's attention. She worked for *Life* as well as for the New School for Social Research and became an active member of the Photo League. Beginning in the 1940s, Abbott explored and documented scientific principles in her work, photographing for the magazine *Science Illustrated* and for textbooks. The Museum of Modern Art held a major retrospective of Abbott's work in 1970, and her monograph *Berenice Abbott: Photographs* was published in the same year. In 1968, she relocated to Maine, where she lived and worked until her death.

ALEXANDER ALLAND (1902–1989)

Alexander Alland arrived in the United States at age twenty-one from Turkey, where he lived for three years after escaping civil war in Russia. He did not begin working exclusively as a photographer until the Federal Art Project commissioned him to make a photomural for the Newark Public Library in 1936. Alland cared deeply about the equality and unification of people regardless of ethnicity. He emphasized the value of a multicultural society in his books *Portrait of New York* (1939) and *American Counterpoint* (1943), the second of which included essays by Pearl Buck. Alland stopped working in the late 1940s when he was blacklisted because of his leftist views and affiliations. He became a historian, publishing several books on early photographers, including *Jacob A. Riis: Photographer and Citizen* (1973).

DIANE ARBUS (1923–1971)

Diane Arbus was born to a wealthy Jewish family on the Upper West Side of Manhattan and spent most of her life in New York. In the late 1940s, she produced advertising photographs for Russek's, her father's Fifth Avenue department store, with her husband, Allan Arbus. She studied with Lisette Model starting in 1957 and began the photographs for which she is best known: images depicting individuals on the periphery of society. In 1963 and 1966, Arbus won Guggenheim Fellowships, enabling her to work on a series of photographs documenting American customs. These were exhibited in *New Documents* (1967) at the Museum of Modern Art, which also featured works by New York photographers Garry Winogrand and Lee Friedlander. In 1972, the year after Arbus's suicide, the Museum of Modern Art mounted a major retrospective, and *Diane Arbus: An Aperture Monograph* was published.

LOU BERNSTEIN (B. 1911)

Lou Bernstein grew up in New York, and by 1928 he had established himself as a professional harmonica player, touring with the Harmonica Rascals. He returned to New York in the early 1930s, working as a shipyard steel mechanic into the 1940s. A recreational photographer, he joined the Brooklyn Camera Club in 1936 and a few years later joined the Photo League, remaining a member until 1951. From 1945 to 1973 he worked in camera stores in Manhattan and was included in a variety of group exhibitions. Since then, Bernstein, who lives in Brooklyn, has had retrospectives at the Queens Museum (1989) and the International Center of Photography (1981, 1992). His photographs of marine mammals in the Central Park Zoo were published in *Reflections on an Aquarium* in 1992, and in the same year his work was included in *Untamed Images* at the New York Zoological Society Gallery.

MARGARET BOURKE-WHITE (1904–1971)

Margaret Bourke-White grew up in the Bronx and attended several universities, where she initially intended to earn a degree in herpetology, the study of reptiles. A class with Clarence H. White in the early 1920s inspired her to become a photographer. Her industrial photographs earned her a position as staff photographer at *Fortune* in 1929, and in 1930 she set up her own studio in the Chrysler Building. *Fortune* and *Life* (her work appeared on the cover of the first issue) commissioned her to document conditions all over the world, from the dust bowl in the Midwest to the Soviet Union. In 1935 her book *You Have Seen Their Faces*, a collaboration with writer Erskine Caldwell, focused on the Depression. Her unique style led her to become a war correspondent in 1942, capturing images of the concentration camps during World War II. Bourke-White continued to travel the world, taking pictures, until her battle with Parkinson's disease led to her retirement in 1969.

BYRON COMPANY (1892–1942)

Joseph Byron (1847–1923) came from a family of photography studio proprietors in Nottingham, England. In the late 1880s, he moved with his wife and children to New York. Byron rapidly became known for his new methods of stage photography and soon established the Byron Company with his son Percy and his wife, who managed the printing department. The firm photographed celebrities, including Mark Twain and Ethel Barrymore, as well as the homes and businesses of New York's wealthiest citizens. In 1917, Percy Byron began photographing ships in New York Harbor, and he maintained the business until 1942, when most of the ships were sold to the government for use in World War II. He donated most of his archives that year to the Museum of the City of New York, where they remain today.

HENRI CARTIER-BRESSON (B. 1908)

Henri Cartier-Bresson grew up in France and studied painting with André Lhôte. In 1932 he made a transition to photography under the guidance of André Kertész and participated in his first exhibition at the Julien Levy Gallery in New York. In order to study with Paul Strand, he lived briefly in New York in 1935, then returned to France to work with Jean Renoir on several films. He joined the French army but in 1940 was captured and held as a prisoner of war in Germany for three years. After his escape in 1943, he worked to document the prisoners and soldiers in World War II with still photography and directed the film *Le Retour* (1945) for the U.S. Office of War Information. In collaboration with photographers Robert Capa, David (Chim) Seymour, and George Rodger, Cartier-Bresson established the Magnum cooperative in New York in 1947. With his influential publication *Images à la sauvette* (1952), Cartier-Bresson initiated the concept of "the decisive moment," which had a major impact on the future of photography. He spent the next twenty years traveling and documenting the world and in 1974 returned to Paris, where he still lives and works.

ALVIN LANGDON COBURN (1882–1966)

Alvin Langdon Coburn's mother, an amateur photographer, introduced him to the art of photography at a young age. In 1899, he traveled to London with his mother and cousin F. Holland Day, whom he helped to organize the exhibition *The New School of American Pictorial Photographers*. By 1903 he had become a member of the Photo-Secession, New York, and of London's Brotherhood of the Linked Ring. In New York, he photographed his friend George Bernard Shaw, among other figures, which resulted in both a solo exhibition at the Royal Photographic Society, London (1906), and the book *Men of Mark* (1913). With his teachers Gertrude Käsebier, Karl Struss, and Clarence H. White, he founded the Pictorial Photographers of America in 1915. Coburn exhibited his Vortographs, abstract photographs linked to Vorticism—the name coined by Ezra Pound for the Cubist-Futur-

ist movement in England—at the Goupil Gallery in London in 1917. After 1918, Coburn devoted himself to Freemasonry and spirituality, ultimately moving to North Wales. Most recently his work has been included in the retrospectives *Alvin Langdon Coburn: Photographs, 1900–1924*, at the George Eastman House, Rochester, New York (1999), and *The City Beautiful: Photogravures by Alvin Langdon Coburn, 1906–1910*, at the Philadelphia Museum of Art (2001).

TED CRONER (B. 1922)

Born in Baltimore, Ted Croner grew up in Charlotte, North Carolina, where he took pictures for his high school yearbook and the local newspaper. He planned to attend the University of North Carolina but instead became an aerial photographer in the South Pacific for the U.S. Army Air Corps during World War II. After the war, at the suggestion of Fernand Fonssagrives, a photographer for *Town and Country*, Croner moved to New York in 1946 and established Speed Graphics, a fashion photography studio, with Bill Helburn, a fellow air corps photographer. Frustrated with commercial photography, he enrolled in Alexey Brodovitch's Design Laboratory and developed his signature images of the New York streets at night. Brodovitch gave Croner his first assignments at *Harper's Bazaar* and introduced him to Edward Steichen, who included him in the Museum of Modern Art's exhibition *Four Photographers* (1948) with Bill Brandt, Henry Callahan, and Lisette Model. Croner continues to work both independently and commercially in New York City and in the past twenty years has been included in several exhibitions of twentieth-century photography.

BRUCE DAVIDSON (B. 1933)

Bruce Davidson began taking pictures as a teenager in Chicago. He studied photography and, with Josef Albers, graphic design at the Yale University School of Design in 1954. Stationed in France while in the army from 1955 to 1957, Davidson documented the streets of Paris and met one of his major influences, Henri Cartier-Bresson. On his return to New York, he joined Magnum in 1958 and spent the next decade working as both a commercial fashion photographer for magazines like *Vogue* and *Esquire* and a photojournalist documenting the civil rights movement in the South. He also worked on one of his best-known series, titled *East 100th Street*, which developed into a major exhibition at the Museum of Modern Art. He made several films in the late 1960s, including *Living Off the Land* (1969) and *Zoo Doctor* (1971), but returned to still photography in the mid-1970s. His work in the past twenty years has focused on New York, including such subjects as the subway and Central Park.

ROY DECARAVA (B. 1919)

Roy DeCarava was raised in Harlem by his mother, an immigrant from Jamaica. In his twenties he studied architecture, sculpture, painting, drawing, and printmaking at the Cooper Union Institute, Harlem Art Center, and George Washington Carver School, which prepared him for service as a topological draftsman in the U.S. Army and, on his return to New York, for several stints as a commercial artist. He supported himself working as a freelance photographer for publications including *Scientific American*, *Newsweek*, and *Life*. In 1952, he became the first African-American artist to earn a Guggenheim Fellowship, which he used to take photographs of Harlem that would be included in *The Sweet Flypaper of Life* (1955), a collaboration with poet Langston Hughes. From 1954 to 1956, DeCarava directed A Photographers Gallery, New York, which promoted photography as a fine art, and in 1963 he founded the Kamoinge Workshop to show the work of black photographers. He began teaching photography at Hunter College in 1975, and in 1996 his work was included in a major traveling retrospective organized by the Museum of Modern Art.

ARNOLD EAGLE (1910–1992)

Arnold Eagle immigrated to Brooklyn in 1929 from Budapest, where he had studied at an art academy. Because of a miscommunication arising from his poor English, he found himself working as a photo retoucher. After joining the Photo League in 1932, Eagle completed a photographic series on Orthodox Jews in New York. He also worked for the Works Projects Administration documenting the Lower East Side slums with fellow Photo League member David Robbins, for a project called *One Third of a Nation*. Shortly thereafter his work for the Standard Oil Project sent him across the United States photographing lumber and oil workers. Beginning in the 1940s and continuing for ten years, Eagle documented the Martha Graham Dance Company, deliberately posing and lighting the dancers solely for the photograph. He also worked as Dada artist Hans Richter's cinematographer for such films as *Dreams That Money Can Buy* (1947), a collaboration with several artists integral to the Dada movement. In 1955, Eagle began a long tenure as a professor at the New School for Social Research in New York.

MORRIS ENGEL (B. 1918)

Raised in Brooklyn, Morris Engel joined the Photo League as a teenager in the 1930s. There he met Paul Strand, who became a mentor and wrote the introduction to Engel's first solo exhibition at the New School for Social Research in 1939. In 1940, Ralph Steiner gave him a position on the photography staff of Marshall Field's liberal newspaper

PM. Engel left to join Edward Steichen's naval photographic unit during World War II and in 1945 returned to New York to do more documentary work for magazines and newspapers. In 1952 he and his future wife and fellow photographer, Ruth Orkin, directed *Little Fugitive*, a film about a boy wandering Coney Island, which was nominated for an Academy Award and which François Truffaut hailed as a major influence on the French New Wave. Engel works actively today in both film and video.

WALKER EVANS (1903–1975)

Born in Missouri, Walker Evans grew up in Kenilworth, Illinois, and in New York City. After studying at Williams College, Evans attended lectures and studied the works of Gustave Flaubert and Charles Baudelaire at the Sorbonne in Paris. His social and professional circle in Greenwich Village, where he lived and worked beginning in 1928, included dance executive and writer Lincoln Kirstein and artist Ben Shahn. By 1932, Evans had his first solo exhibition at the Julien Levy Gallery. His documentation of the Depression over the next ten years is represented by his work for the Farm Security Administration and the book *Let Us Now Praise Famous Men* (1941), a collaboration with James Agee about sharecroppers in Alabama. His twenty-year tenure as a writer and photographer at *Fortune* began in 1945, and in 1965 he became a professor at the Yale University School of Design, where he focused his work on interior photography. Since his death, his widely exhibited photographs have become icons of personal suffering during the Depression.

LOUIS FAURER (1916–2001)

Louis Faurer grew up in a Polish Jewish immigrant family in Philadelphia. Before attending the School of Commercial Art and Lettering in 1937, he earned money by drawing caricatures in Atlantic City, New Jersey, and in his spare time took photographs on the boardwalk. With the support of Walker Evans, Faurer began working for the *Harper's Bazaar* publication *Junior Bazaar*, and he became friends with Robert Frank, who allowed him to use his Manhattan loft and darkroom. While Faurer continued his freelance work at *Life*, *Vogue*, and *Flair* in the 1940s, Edward Steichen included his noncommercial works in several significant exhibitions at the Museum of Modern Art. Faurer's work gained recognition with his solo shows at the Limelight Gallery in 1959 and, after he spent several years in Europe, at the Marlborough Gallery in New York in 1977. In the late 1970s and early 1980s, Faurer received fellowships from the National Endowment for the Arts and the Guggenheim Foundation and taught at several universities.

ANDREAS FEININGER (1906–1999)

The son of painter Lyonel Feininger, Andreas Feininger was born in Paris. From 1922 to 1925, he attended the Bauhaus in Weimar, Germany, where his father directed the print-making workshop. After completing a degree in architecture and engineering at the Bauschule in Zerbst in 1929, Feininger worked as an assistant to Le Corbusier. He turned to photography in the 1930s, seeking realism in his work rather than the abstract ideals of the Bauhaus. He arrived in New York in 1939 and became a staff photographer for *Life* in 1942, a position he held for twenty years. The subjects of his photographs range from the vast panorama of the New York skyline to the minute details of the city streets and the natural world. Feininger's photographs have appeared in more than fifty books; his work is held by many museums, including the Smithsonian Institution, the Metropolitan Museum of Art, and the Victoria and Albert Museum.

LARRY FINK (B. 1941)

Larry Fink was born in New York and studied photography with Lisette Model and Alexey Brodovitch. His photographs of social scenes range from his work on the rich and famous in New York City to the residents of Martin's Creek, Pennsylvania, where he moved in 1980. He has done commercial work for corporations, including Nike and Adidas, and his celebrity photographs have been included in *W*, *GQ*, and *Vanity Fair*. In the 1980s, Fink earned several fellowships and began teaching photography at Bard College, a position he holds today. His books include *Social Graces* (1984), juxtaposing images of New York and Pennsylvania; *Boxing* (1997), focusing on the life of professional boxers; and *Runway* (2000), capturing New York's Fashion Week. Fink has had solo exhibitions at the Museum of Modern Art, Whitney Museum of American Art, and San Francisco Museum of Art.

LEONARD FREED (B. 1929)

The son of Eastern European Jewish immigrants, Leonard Freed grew up in Brooklyn. He aspired to be a painter but became a photographer with the informal guidance of Alexey Brodovitch and Edward Steichen. Committed to documenting social injustice, Freed published books and directed films focusing on subjects related to African Americans and Jews, including the civil rights movement, the world of Hasidic Jews, the Ku Klux Klan, and postwar Germany. After joining Magnum in 1972, Freed also worked as a freelance photographer on assignment for such publications as *Life*, *Der Spiegel*, and the *New York Times Magazine*. In 1980 he published *Police Work*, which contains striking examples of police brutality, a subject he continued to explore over the next decade. In the past twenty years, Freed has made several films for European television and has documented subjects including the Arab-Israeli conflict and the Romanian revolution.

RALPH GIBSON (B. 1939)

After growing up in Los Angeles, Ralph Gibson studied photography while at the Naval Training Center in Pensacola, Florida, in 1957. He continued his studies at the San Francisco Art Institute in 1961 and worked as an assistant to Dorothea Lange and, in 1967, to Robert Frank in New York. During the 1970s and 1980s, Gibson earned fellowships from several organizations, including the National Endowment for the Arts. His early books—*The Somnambulist* (1970), *Déjà-vu* (1973), and *Days at Sea* (1974), published by his own Lustrum Press—show the influence of Surrealism on his work. In 1975, Gibson joined Castelli Graphics and exhibited his works on architecture and the body as well as on life in France. Gibson has exhibited his photography at museums around the world, including the Whitney Museum of American Art (1996), the Leica Gallery (1996), and the Maison Européenne de la Photographie, Paris (1999). In 2001, he published *Ex Libris*, a book of photographs focusing on the written word.

GEORGE GILBERT (B. 1922)

Born George Gelberg in Brooklyn, Gilbert dropped out of Brooklyn College in 1940 to work for a photographer, then joined the Photo League in 1941 with the encouragement of Walter Rosenblum. He served in the U.S. Army Air Corps as a photogrammetrist during World War II. On his return to New York in 1945, he resumed teaching and writing for the Photo League and took on freelance photography assignments for the *New York Times*, *Newsweek*, and *Variety*. In 1951 he devoted himself to marketing, holding high-level positions in a variety of companies before establishing his public relations and marketing firm, George Gilbert and Associates, in 1972. In 1970, Gilbert founded the American Photographic Historical Society. He has published fifteen books on photography history and techniques, among them *Child Photography Made Easy*, the three-volume *Photographic Advertising from A to Z*, and *The Illustrated Worldwide Who's Who of Jews in Photography* (1996).

BRUCE GILDEN (B. 1946)

After studying sociology at Pennsylvania State University, self-taught photographer Bruce Gilden returned to his hometown of New York. While earning a living as a taxi driver, Gilden worked on projects revolving around the

New York streets and Coney Island that were influenced by the cinematic qualities of film noir. In 1984, he made the first of sixteen trips to Haiti, which he documented in several books, including *Haiti: Dreams and Nightmares* (1997). Now an associate at Magnum, Gilden has been the recipient of the European Award for Photography (1996) and fellowships from the National Endowment for the Arts (1980, 1982, 1984). More recently, Gilden has published *After the Off* (1999), capturing the Irish horse-racing scene, and *Go* (2000), documenting gangsters in Japan.

NAN GOLDIN (B. 1953)

Nan Goldin was born in Washington, D.C., and grew up in foster families in Massachusetts after running away from home at age thirteen. When she was eighteen, she began photographing her friends and relatives in New York, Boston, Provincetown, London, and Berlin, which culminated in her project *The Ballad of Sexual Dependency*. This work, which she originally exhibited as a slide show set to music, toured clubs, museums, and galleries in the early 1980s and was published in 1986. After spending time in a drug rehabilitation center in Boston in 1988, Goldin created self-portraits examining identity. Her success in the past decade has been due to her series documenting her friends, including those dying of AIDS, entitled *The Family of Nan* (1990–92), exhibited at the 1993 *Biennial* of the Whitney Museum of American Art, and to a collaboration with Japanese photographer Nobuyoshi Araki about bars and clubs in Japan called *Tokyo Love: Spring Fever* (1994). In 1996 the Whitney held a retrospective of her work, *I'll Be Your Mirror*, which was also published as a catalogue. Her recent book *Couples and Loneliness* (1999) is a compilation of photographs taken throughout her career that further explore the relationships of couples and her friends.

SAMUEL H. GOTTSCHO (1875–1971)

For the first half of his life, Samuel Gottscho worked as a traveling fabric salesman and part-time photographer. He began his full-time career in commercial photography in the mid-1920s, and in 1935 his son-in-law William H. Schleisner joined his practice, establishing the Gottscho-Schleisner firm, which lasted until Schleisner's death. The firm's photographs of middle- and upper-class homes and gardens were featured in architectural brochures and such publications as *House Beautiful*. When the demand for landscape photographers fell during the Depression, Gottscho developed a series of "sharp-focus" images of Manhattan's skyscrapers. He resumed his work with gardens in the 1940s, ultimately winning the New York Botanical Garden's Distinguished Service medal in 1967. Twenty-nine thousand of his prints are held in the Gottscho-Schleisner collection of the Library of Congress, and forty thousand are housed at the Museum of the City of New York.

SID GROSSMAN (1915–1955)

Sid Grossman spent his youth in New York. In 1936, he and Sol Libsohn co-founded the Photo League, where he played a major administrative, educational, and artistic role. Grossman led a War Production Group in 1942, and in 1943 he took pictures in Panama and Guatemala while in the U.S. Army. On his return to New York in 1946, he began to make his well-known photographs of Coney Island and Mulberry Street. During the 1940s, the government grew increasingly suspicious of the Photo League, which was listed as a subversive institution in 1947. The FBI placed Grossman under surveillance for being the supposed Communist leader of the League. By the time the League dissolved in 1951, Grossman had drifted from the group and toward less documentary work. He spent the rest of his life in New York and Provincetown, photographing the New York City Ballet and scenes in Cape Cod.

GEORGE GROSZ (1893–1959)

Born in Berlin, George Grosz grew up in Stolp, Pomerania. He studied drawing and painting first at the Akademie der Künst in Dresden from 1909 to 1911, then at the Kunstgewerbeschule with Emil Orlik in 1912, where he remained for a year before entering the Académie Colarossi in Paris. After volunteering for the German army in 1914, Grosz was discharged as being "unfit for service" and returned to Germany, where his art began to reflect his left-wing politics. He anglicized the spelling of his name—originally Georg— as an expression of his antinationalism, and he eventually joined the German Communist Party. In 1918 he became a major figure in the Berlin Dada movement with John Heartfield and Otto Dix. Known primarily as a painter and graphic artist, in 1932, Grosz accepted a visiting professorship at the Art Students League in New York, where he settled after being advised to leave Germany because of Hitler's increasing power. Grosz held his position at the Art Students League until 1955, drawing primarily caricatures and landscapes, until his return to West Berlin in 1959.

JOHN GUTMANN (1905–1998)

John Gutmann was born and raised in Breslau, Germany. He studied painting under Expressionist Otto Mueller at the Staatliche Akademie für Kunst und Kunstgewerbe from 1923 to 1927 and did postgraduate work at Humboldt Universität and the Berliner Akademie der Bildenden Künste. When

Hitler rose to power, Gutmann, anxious to leave Germany, taught himself how to use a Rolleiflex and, pretending to be a photojournalist, contracted with the Berlin agency Press-Photo to take photographs in the United States for European magazines. In 1936 he moved permanently to San Francisco, taking photographs for the Pix Inc. agency in New York City from 1939 to 1963 and doing freelance work for publications including the *Saturday Evening Post*, *Look*, *Life*, and *National Geographic*. He began teaching art at San Francisco State University in 1936, developed the graduate photography department in 1949, and retired in 1973. Between 1974 and 1997, Gutmann had solo exhibitions at several venues, including the San Francisco Museum of Modern Art (1976, 1989), Museum of Photographic Arts, San Diego (1985), Art Gallery of Ontario (1985), and San Francisco State University (1997). In 1994 he published *The Restless Decade: John Gutmann's Photographs of the Thirties*, with an introduction by Max Kozloff.

OTTO HAGEL (1909–1973)

At age fourteen, Otto Hagel left school in his hometown of Stuttgart to be an apprentice to a watchmaker. Shortly thereafter, he met Hansel Mieth, and the two traveled through Europe together, emigrating to the United States in 1928 and 1930, respectively. In San Francisco, they took jobs as migrant workers, documenting in photographs the lives of other laborers and longshoremen. In the late 1930s, Mieth took a staff position with *Life*, while Hagel worked as a freelance photographer in New York; they were married in 1940. After refusing to testify for the House Committee on Un-American Activities, Hagel and Mieth became chicken farmers, an experience they documented in a photo essay published in *Life* in 1955. While Mieth began focusing more on writing and painting in the early 1960s, Hagel worked extensively on the photography for and publication of *Men and Machines* (1963), for the International Longshoremen's and Warehousemen's Union. The couple began to collaborate again in the late 1960s on photo essays about children in a Head Start program and the lives of Pomo Indians in Sonoma County, California, among other subjects. In 1989, the Eye Gallery in San Francisco presented the first exhibition of their work in the United States, *A Lifetime of Concerned Photography*.

LEWIS HINE (1874–1940)

One of Lewis Hine's first jobs was as a factory worker in his hometown of Oshkosh, Wisconsin. He moved to New York and, after completing a master's degree in pedagogy at New York University, became a nature and geography teacher at the Ethical Culture School, where he also estab-lished a photography club for students. A self-taught photographer, he documented the arrival of immigrants at Ellis Island in his early work, which ultimately earned him several assignments from important government agencies. This experience culminated in his work for both the National Child Labor Committee, photographing and disseminating images of child workers, and the American Red Cross, traveling to the Balkans to report on the effects of World War I. On his return to New York, Hine completed one of his best-known series, *Men at Work* (1931), which depicted builders on the Empire State Building. After this time, his work drastically declined in popularity. Following the dissolution of the Photo League, Hine's student Walter Rosenblum maintained and exhibited his photographs until the George Eastman House, in Rochester, New York, acquired the collection of his works.

MORRIS HUBERLAND (B. 1909)

Born in Germany, Morris Huberland grew up in a Jewish ghetto in New York. He began taking photographs in New York neighborhoods and joined the Photo League in 1940, drawing inspiration from Eliot Elisofon's lectures and techniques. During World War II, Huberland worked for a Photo League War Production Group before joining the army himself in 1943, rising to the rank of corporal. On his return to New York in 1945, the Photo League exhibited his wartime photographs taken in Italy. This was the first of several of Huberland's projects that the League would exhibit in the 1940s. In 1989, the Friends of the Library at the Jewish Theological Seminary in New York presented *A Time to Remember: Jewish Life on the Lower East Side*, an exhibition of Huberland's work focusing on Jewish immigrants.

JEFF JACOBSON (B. 1946)

Jeff Jacobson was born in Des Moines, Iowa. Immediately after graduating from the University of Oklahoma, he attended Georgetown University Law Center. Giving up his civil rights law practice in 1974, Jacobson decided to become a full-time photographer, documenting the American presidential campaign in 1976. In 1981, after three years as an associate at Magnum, Jacobson left and founded Archive Pictures with photographers including Mary Ellen Mark, Burk Uzzle, and Charles Harbutt. Beginning in the early 1980s, he worked as a freelancer for publications including the *New York Times Magazine*, *Fortune*, and *Life* while also working on his monograph *My Fellow Americans* (1990), the photographs from which were exhibited internationally. Now living in Jersey City, New Jersey, Jacobson teaches workshops around the country and works as a commercial and freelance photographer. His recent series of photographs focuses on New York at night.

WILLIAM KLEIN (B. 1928)

William Klein left his studies in sociology at City College in his native New York in 1945 to become an army cartoonist. Remaining in Paris at the end of the war, Klein studied with Fernand Léger and, like his friend Ellsworth Kelly, painted geometric abstract works. Alexander Liberman, art director of *Vogue*, discovered Klein's experimental photography and sponsored him to return to New York in 1954 to photograph for the magazine. During this time, Klein also created street photographs for his book *Life Is Good and Good for You in New York: Trance Witness Revels*, which he published in France in 1956, earning the prestigious Prix Nadar. He created similar books about Rome, Moscow, and Tokyo. Beginning in 1958, Klein devoted himself to film, first producing *Broadway by Light* (1958) and then working with Louis Malle on *Zazie dans le Métro* (1960) and Jean-Luc Goddard on *Loin du Vietnam* (1967). Klein continues to live as an expatriate in France, working in both film and still photography. His films of the past forty years include *Qui êtes-vous, Polly Maggoo?* (1965–66), *Eldridge Cleaver, Black Panther* (1969), *Muhammed Ali, the Greatest* (1974), *Music City* (1978), *The Little Richard Story* (1980), and *The French* (1981).

ARTHUR LEIPZIG (B. 1918)

Arthur Leipzig instantly realized that he wanted to be a photographer when he started studying with Sid Grossman at the Photo League in his native New York in 1942. While a member of the League from 1942 to 1949, Leipzig was admitted to Paul Strand's advanced class and earned a living taking pictures for *PM* newspaper from 1942 to 1946. Leipzig left the League to pursue a freelance career and traveled the world as a photojournalist. Edward Steichen included his work in *The Family of Man* (1955) at the Museum of Modern Art and influenced his decision to begin a teaching career. In 1968, Leipzig joined the faculty of C. W. Post College at Long Island University, where he received numerous teaching awards, retiring in 1991.

SAUL LEITER (B. 1923)

Saul Leiter was born in Pittsburgh, where his father was a Talmudic scholar. Although expected to be a rabbi, Leiter abandoned his studies at the Cleveland Theological College to become a painter. He began experimenting with photography due to the influence of his friend Richard Pousette-Dart, the Abstract Expressionist painter, and was introduced to the work of the Photo League in its last years by photographer W. Eugene Smith. Edward Steichen recognized his work in 1953 by including twenty-five of Leiter's photographs in the exhibition *Always the Young Stranger* at the Museum of Modern Art. In 1957 *Esquire* published his

fashion photographs, which led to extensive assignments for *Elle*, *Harper's Bazaar*, and British *Vogue*. In the past twenty years, with the exception of portfolios for clothing designers Comme des Garçons (1990) and Alberto Aspesi (1991), Leiter has turned from commercial work to concentrate on his own photography and painting.

REBECCA LEPKOFF (B. 1916)

Born in New York, Rebecca Lepkoff earned her bachelor's degree from City College of New York while also studying at the Humphrey Weidman School of Modern Dance. She took photographs for the National Youth Administration under Arnold Eagle, who urged her to join the Photo League. There she studied with Sid Grossman, Paul Strand, and, perhaps her greatest influence, Walter Rosenblum. The majority of her work has focused on documenting immigrants on the Lower East Side, and she continues to take pictures today in both New York and Vermont. Naomi Rosenblum included Lepkoff's work in the catalogue *A History of Women Photographers* (1984), which became a traveling exhibition in 1996.

LEON LEVINSTEIN (1910–1988)

Leon Levinstein grew up in West Viginia and Baltimore in an Orthodox Jewish immigrant family and took classes at the Maryland Institute of Art. After serving as a mechanic in the U.S. Army for three years, he arrived in Greenwich Village in 1945 to begin a career as an art director for an advertising agency. In his mid-thirties, he began studying painting with Stuart Davis and photography with Alexey Brodovitch at the New School for Social Research; he sought further instruction from Sid Grossman at the Photo League. Levinstein's work was influenced by that of fellow Grossman student Lisette Model, and he continued to pursue his interest in painting by attending the workshop of her husband, Evsa Model. The popularity of Levinstein's work in the 1950s, supported by Edward Steichen at the Museum of Modern Art and Helen Gee at the Limelight Gallery, was short-lived because of his failure to continue to promote his own photographs. Since his death, his work has resurfaced and was included in a retrospective at the National Gallery of Canada (1995).

HELEN LEVITT (B. 1913)

A Brooklyn native, Helen Levitt is associated with the loosely defined New York School of Photography. Her unique street photography capturing the daily life of Yorkville and Harlem was dramatically influenced by the work of her friends and mentors Henri Cartier-Bresson and Walker Evans. In the 1940s Beaumont Newhall, Nancy Newhall, and later, Edward Steichen, photography curators at the Museum of

Modern Art, took a particular interest in Levitt's work, installing her first solo exhibition in 1943. Also at that time she collaborated with writer James Agee on a book of her photographs entitled *A Way of Seeing* (published in 1965) and on the films *The Quiet One* (1947), which earned first prize at the Venice Film Festival, and *In the Street* (1951). Levitt has earned several fellowships, from the Museum of Modern Art (1946), the Guggenheim Foundation (1959, 1960), and the National Endowment for the Arts (1976). She currently lives and works in New York.

SOL LIBSOHN (1914–2001)

Sol Libsohn was born in Harlem to Polish immigrants. After spending four years attending night classes at City College in New York and working for the Works Progress Administration, he founded the Photo League with Sid Grossman in 1936. Over the next fifteen years, Libsohn organized production groups for the League, including Chelsea Document (1938), Housing Document (1939–40), and a War Production Group (1943), was a staff photographer for *Look* (1940–43), and collaborated with photographers Gordon Parks, Todd Webb, and others on a project for the Standard Oil Company of New Jersey, *There Is a Drop of Oil in the Life of Everyone* (1944–50). After the dissolution of the Photo League, Libsohn continued his freelance career with assignments from publications including *Fortune* and *Ladies Home Journal*. Beginning in the summer of 1965, Libsohn taught at Princeton University, where he also held a position on the technical staff of the Visual Arts Program from 1969 to 1973. He continued to live in Roosevelt, New Jersey, until his death.

MARY ELLEN MARK (B. 1940)

Raised in Philadelphia, Mary Ellen Mark earned a bachelor of fine arts and a master's degree in communications from the University of Pennsylvania. Her photographs from her journey to Turkey as a Fulbright scholar in 1965 resulted in the first of many documentary projects that distinguish her career. Her work has focused on subjects that include Western youths in Asia, Protestant and Catholic women during the conflict in Northern Ireland, women in the Oregon State Mental Hospital, pregnant teenagers in America, and diverse aspects of India. The Academy Award–nominated film *Streetwise* (1984), directed by her husband, Martin Bell, was based on her 1982 *Life* photo essay about runaway children in Seattle. Mark has also been published in the *New York Times Magazine*, *Vogue*, and *Rolling Stone* and has been the recipient of the International Center of Photography's Cornell Capa Award, several fellowships from the National Endowment for the Arts, and an honorary degree from the University of Pennsylvania (1994). Her

photographs taken in the United States over the past thirty-five years were included in the traveling exhibition *American Odyssey* (2001), organized by the Aperture Foundation.

JEFF MERMELSTEIN (B. 1957)

Jeff Mermelstein grew up in the suburbs of New Jersey and earned a bachelor's degree from Rutgers University in 1978. He began exhibiting his work in galleries in the early 1980s and has photographed for numerous publications including the *Village Voice*, the *New York Times Magazine*, *Vanity Fair*, *PHOTO* (France), and *MODA* (Italy). In 1991, he earned the Aaron Siskind Foundation Individual Photographer's Fellowship. Mermelstein has been on the faculty of the International Center of Photography since 1988. He won the European Publisher's Award in 1999 for *Sidewalk* (2000), his book of photographs documenting life on the streets of New York.

GJON MILI (1904–1984)

Born in southern Albania, Gjon Mili immigrated to the United States in 1923 and earned a B.S. in electrical engineering at the Massachusetts Institute of Technology in 1927. During his employment as a lighting research engineer for the Westinghouse Electrical and Manufacturing Company, Mili, with his teacher Dr. Harold E. Edgerton, worked on the development of the tungsten filament bulb, the stroboscopic electronic flash, and high-speed photography. His ability to photograph the fast action of sporting events, dance, and theater earned him many freelance assignments for *Life*, beginning in the late 1930s. Statuary and celebrity portraits are prevalent subjects in his photography. Mili's work documenting artists and musicians includes the films *Raoul Dufy Paints, New York* (1950), *Salvador Dali* (1951), *Stomping for Mili, Brubeck Jazz Quartet* (1955), *Henri Cartier-Bresson, Photographer* (1958), and *Homage to Picasso* (1967) and the books *The Magic of the Opera* (1960) and *Picasso's Third Dimension* (1970).

LISETTE MODEL (1906–1983)

Raised by a wealthy Jewish Austro-Czech father and an Italian mother in Vienna, Lisette Model studied music with Arnold Schoenberg in 1920 and with Polish soprano Marya Freund in Paris in 1922. In the early 1930s, she turned to photography, capturing trademark images of the wealthy on the beachfront Promenade des Anglais in Nice and of the poor on the streets of Paris. She moved to New York with her husband, abstract painter Evsa Model, in 1938. Model joined the Photo League and began working closely with Alexey Brodovitch, the art director who published her photographs in *Harper's Bazaar*, and with Weegee. In the 1940s, Model had solo exhibitions at the Photo League, the Art Institute of Chicago, and the California Palace of the Legion of Honor in San Francisco. She took a teaching position at the New School for Social Research in New York with her friend Berenice Abbott in 1951, and Diane Arbus became her student in 1957. Model continued to teach, photograph, and exhibit her work until her death.

FRITZ NEUGASS (1899–1979)

Fritz Neugass grew up in a Protestant-Jewish family in Baden, Germany. He studied art and archaeology, earning his doctorate in Heidelberg in 1924. In 1926 he moved to Paris, where he was an art correspondent for German and Swiss newspapers and art magazines until the mid-1930s, when his work was no longer accepted in Germany. He continued to work for American, French, and British periodicals under the pseudonyms François Neuville and Friedrich Brenatano until 1939, when he was interned at a French detention camp. Immigrating to the United States through Casablanca in 1941, Neugass worked as a nurse and a swimming instructor before joining the Volunteer Service Photographers during the war. At war's end he established a career writing and photographing for American and European publications including the *New Yorker*, *Handelsblatt*, *Staats Zeitung*, and *Art News*. Neugass continued to photograph until his death in 1979, upon which Goethe House held a memorial exhibition of his work in New York.

RUTH ORKIN (1921–1985)

Born in Boston, Ruth Orkin spent her childhood surrounded by the glamour of Hollywood, where her mother, Mary Ruby, was a silent film actress and her father owned a toy boat company. She moved to New York in 1943 and became a freelance photographer, shooting celebrities for publications including the *New York Times*, *Life*, and *Cosmopolitan*. On trips to Israel and then to Italy in the early 1950s, Orkin captured some of her most famous images. Shortly after her return to the United States in 1952, Orkin married Morris Engel, and in that same year directed the Academy Award–nominated *Little Fugitive* with him, a film that François Truffaut credited as a major influence on the French New Wave. In that decade she achieved great success: Edward Steichen included her work in *The Family of Man* (1955) at the Museum of Modern Art, and in 1959 the Professional Photographers of America named her one of the "Top Ten Women Photographers in America." Her work in the last twenty years of her life focused on the views outside her Central Park West apartment, which culminated in the book *A World Through My Window* (1978), and on her children.

GORDON PARKS (B. 1912)

Gordon Parks used photography to protest the extreme racism and poverty he grew up with in Fort Scott, Kansas, and Saint Paul, Minnesota. Awarded the first fellowship from the Julius Rosenwald Foundation, which supported black artists, the self-taught Parks worked for the Farm Security Administration and, subsequently, for the Office of War Information, where he documented the training of the first African-American Air Corps. By 1948 he had earned a position at *Life*, photographing the civil rights movement, gang violence, and social injustice as well as fashion, later moving to Paris to photograph artists, intellectuals, and celebrities throughout Europe. Parks pushed his work beyond the limits of photography: he directed films including *Shaft* (1971) and wrote books such as *The Learning Tree* (1964), an autobiographical novel, and *Moments Without Proper Names* (1975), which incorporated his poems and photographs. Parks continues to live and work in New York. His retrospective *Half Past Autumn: The Art of Gordon Parks* (1997) originated at the Corcoran Museum of Art in Washington, D.C., and traveled to ten other cities.

SYLVIA PLACHY (B. 1943)

Sylvia Plachy immigrated to the United States from Budapest in 1958. After earning a bachelor of fine arts degree from Pratt Institute, she embarked on a successful freelance career. Her work has been included in *Artforum*, *Life*, *Doubletake*, the *New Yorker*, the *Village Voice*, and *Wired*. Her first book, *Unguided Tour* (1990), was recognized by the International Center of Photography as the best publication of 1990 with its Infinity Award. More recently she completed *Red Light: Inside the Sex Industry* (1996), a collaboration with James Ridgeway, and *Signs and Relics* (2000), which includes a foreword by the film director Wim Wenders. Plachy earned a Guggenheim Fellowship in 1977 and has had solo exhibitions in New York at the Palladium, Pennsylvania Station, the Whitney Museum of American Art at Philip Morris, the Queens Museum, and galleries around the country.

WALTER ROSENBLUM (B. 1919)

Walter Rosenblum's parents were Romanian Jewish immigrants living on New York's Lower East Side. He joined the Photo League in the late 1930s and studied photography with his two greatest influences, Lewis Hine and Paul Strand, while pursuing freelance assignments. His active involvement in the League, leading up to his presidency from 1947 to 1952, was interrupted by his service as a photographer in the U.S. Army Signal Corps from 1943 to 1945. In 1952 he joined the faculty of the Yale Summer School of Music and Art, Norfolk, Connecticut, and from 1956 to 1965 he was a professor of photography at Cooper Union. In 1979,

Rosenblum used his Guggenheim Fellowship to create *People of the South Bronx*, a photographic series that traveled to several venues. After the collapse of the Photo League, Rosenblum and his wife, Naomi Rosenblum, maintained Lewis Hine's archive for several years, also organizing a retrospective at the Brooklyn Museum of Art.

MEL ROSENTHAL (B. 1948)

After earning a doctorate from the University of Connecticut in 1967, Mel Rosenthal taught literature and journalism at Vassar College for seven years. His position as a medical photographer in Tanzania initiated his photography career, and in 1975 he became a distinguished professor of art and director of photography programs at the Empire State College of the State University of New York, a position he holds today. His photographs, including several from his first three books—*Villa Sin Miedo, Presente!* (1991), documenting a utopian community in Puerto Rico, *Beyond Homelessness* (1992), and the *Silverwolf Homeless Project* (1995)—have been exhibited at galleries and art centers in Latin America and the United States. His work has been published in magazines and newspapers including *Newsweek*, *Artforum*, *Rolling Stone*, and the *Village Voice*, and in 1993 he became the photography editor for *culturefront*, the magazine of the New York Council for the Humanities. Rosenthal's recent book *In the South Bronx of America* (2001) consists of portraits taken between 1975 and 1983, documenting the "planned shrinkage" of the South Bronx to allow for urban renewal.

BEN SHAHN (1898–1969)

Ben Shahn's Orthodox Jewish family was reunited in 1906 when he and his mother emigrated from Lithuania to New York, where his father had fled from Siberia after being exiled for his political activities. Shahn served as an apprentice to a lithographer and, forgoing a scholarship to study zoology at Wood's Hole, Massachusetts, he attended the National Academy of Design in New York. In the early 1930s, Shahn gained recognition for his socially conscious paintings: he exhibited *The Passion of Sacco and Vanzetti* and his *Dreyfus* series, and he worked with Diego Rivera on his mural at Rockefeller Center, which was subsequently destroyed. He shared a studio with Walker Evans, photographing the streets of New York, and earned an assignment to photograph workers in America during the Depression for the Resettlement Administration and the Farm Security Administration. In the 1940s and 1950s, Shahn returned to commercial work and graphic design: he painted public murals, created pamphlets for the Office of War Information and the reelection campaign of Franklin D. Roosevelt, and

designed sets for the Jerome Robbins Ballet. His work as a printmaker and painter, as well as a photographer, was widely shown during his life, and most recently in the exhibitions *Common Man, Mythic Vision: The Paintings of Ben Shahn* (1998), at The Jewish Museum, New York, and *Ben Shahn's New York: The Photography of Modern Times* (2000), organized by the Fogg Art Museum at Harvard University, which houses a large collection of his photographic archives.

AARON SISKIND (1903–1991)

As an English teacher and recreational photographer in New York, where he grew up in a Jewish family, Aaron Siskind first encountered an exhibition of the Film and Photo League in 1930. He established a branch of the Photo League, the Feature Group, in 1936 and organized a project to photograph the street life of Harlem. Ultimately called *Harlem Document*, this project was not published in its entirety until 1981. In the early 1940s, Siskind adapted Surrealist concepts in his work and distanced himself from the Photo League, working on photographic series including *Tabernacle City*, about the religious community in Martha's Vineyard. By the end of the decade, Siskind's photographs shared subject matter and themes with the paintings of the Abstract Expressionists, including Franz Kline and Willem de Kooning, with whom he became acquainted through the Egan Gallery in New York. In 1951, he became a photography professor at the Illinois Institute of Technology, beginning a teaching career that would last for twenty years. During the 1960s, Siskind earned several awards, published numerous books, and became co-editor of *Choice*, a literary and photographic magazine. In 1984, he established the Aaron Siskind Foundation, which donates the proceeds from his vintage photographs to contemporary photographers.

EDWARD STEICHEN (1879–1973)

Edward Steichen emigrated with his family from Luxembourg in infancy and grew up in Hancock, Michigan, and Milwaukee, Wisconsin, where he studied painting, drawing, and photography at the Art Students League. Steichen founded the Photo-Secession with Alfred Stieglitz in 1902 and, living in both Paris and New York, played an integral role in bringing such artists as Paul Cézanne, Constantin Brancusi, Auguste Rodin, and Henri Matisse to The Little Galleries of the Photo-Secession (also known as 291). As his and Stieglitz's work progressed in different directions, Steichen moved to Voulangis, France, in 1908, where he bred his award-winning delphiniums, and in 1911 he took on a four-year commission to paint murals titled *In Exaltation of Flowers* for the home of Agnes and Eugene Meyer. The outbreak of World War I prompted him to return to

New York, and he joined the U.S. Army's aerial photography division in 1917. As chief photographer for Condé Nast from 1923 to 1948, he produced famous portraits of many celebrities, including Noël Coward, Gloria Swanson, and Charlie Chaplin. After several years in naval photography during World War II, Steichen became director of the Department of Photography at the Museum of Modern Art from 1947 to 1962, curating notable exhibitions including *The Family of Man* (1955). His work has been the subject of retrospectives at the Museum of Modern Art (1963), the George Eastman House, Rochester, New York (1971), and the Whitney Museum of American Art (2000).

ALFRED STIEGLITZ (1864–1946)

Alfred Stieglitz was the eldest of six children in a Jewish family in Hoboken, New Jersey. When the family moved to Germany in 1881, Stieglitz studied engineering at the Technische Hochschule in Berlin and then photochemistry with scientist Hermann Wilhelm Vogel. His earliest inspiration was British naturalist photographer P. H. Emerson. On arriving in New York in 1890, Stieglitz began taking photographs in the Pictorialist style. In 1902, he established the Photo-Secession with Edward Steichen, and through the publication *Camera Work* and the 291 gallery promoted the work of European and American modernists including Pablo Picasso, Marcel Duchamp, Marsden Hartley, John Marin, and Elie Nadelman. After closing 291 in 1917, Stieglitz focused on his own work for the next twenty years, taking photographs of Lake George and New York City as well as portraits of his wife, Georgia O'Keeffe, while continuing to promote work by American modernists at the Intimate Gallery and at his last gallery, An American Place. After his death, O'Keeffe donated his works to major museums, including the National Gallery of Art, Washington, D.C., and the Metropolitan Museum of Art, both of which have held major retrospectives of his work.

LOU STOUMEN (1917–1991)

Born in Springtown, Pennsylvania, Lou Stoumen moved to New York in 1939 to study photography with Sid Grossman at the Photo League. His documentary work in the 1940s included assignments for the National Youth Association in Puerto Rico, the United States Public Health Service, and the U.S. Army. After studying film, television, and photography at the University of Southern California in the early 1950s, Stoumen wrote, directed, and produced *The Naked Eye* (1956), an Academy Award–nominated documentary featuring Edward Weston, Alfred Eisenstadt, and Weegee. His next two films, *The True Story of the Civil War* (1956) and *Black Fox: The True Story of Adolf Hitler* (1963), both

won Academy Awards. In 1966, he became professor of motion pictures and television at the University of California, Los Angeles, a position he held for twenty-two years. He published several books of text and photographs, among them *Times Square, 1940: A Paper Movie* (1977), *Journey to Land's End: A Paper Movie* (1988), and *Ablaze with Light and Life* (1992), an autobiographical book of photographs and text published after his death.

PAUL STRAND (1890–1976)

Paul Strand was born on Manhattan's Upper West Side to a Jewish family from Bohemia. While attending the Ethical Culture School, he met Lewis Hine, who fostered his interest in photography and introduced him to the work of the Photo-Secession. By 1916, Alfred Stieglitz was exhibiting Strand's photographs at 291 (the gallery of the Photo-Secession) and publishing his gravures in *Camera Work*. During the 1920s, Strand photographed both urban and natural landscapes throughout the United States and actively exhibited his work at the Camera Club and other New York galleries. Beginning in 1935, he devoted himself to filmmaking, and from 1937 to 1943 he was president of Frontier Films, a leftist organization that developed from the Photo League. He relocated to France in 1950 and through the 1970s traveled in Europe and Africa documenting the individuals and natural surroundings of each place that he visited. Since his death, his work has been the subject of numerous monographs and exhibitions.

KARL STRUSS (1886–1981)

Raised in New York, Karl Struss studied photography with Clarence H. White at Columbia University while simultaneously working at his father's bonnet-wire factory. In his late twenties, Struss worked as a commercial and freelance photographer for *Harper's Bazaar*, *Vanity Fair*, and the Bermuda Government Tourist Board before becoming a photographer in the Air Corps during World War I. He was accepted into the Photo-Secession in 1912, and when it dissolved, he established the Pictorial Photographers of America with Alvin Langdon Coburn, Gertrude Käsebier, and Clarence H. White. Arriving in Hollywood in 1919, Struss began his career in film shooting production stills for Cecil B. DeMille. Over the next three decades, he won awards for cinematography for films including *Ben-Hur* (1925), *Dr. Jekyll and Mr. Hyde* (1932), *The Great Dictator* (1940), and *Limelight* (1952). He won the Academy Award for his cinematography of *Sunrise* (1927), directed by F. W. Murnau, which employed the Struss Pictorial Lens, his invention that allowed for soft-focus images. In the 1960s, Struss began working on television commercials in California, and his photographs continued to be shown in Pictorialist exhibitions.

JAMES VAN DER ZEE (1886–1983)

James Van Der Zee was born in Lenox, Massachusetts, where his parents worked as servants in the homes of affluent New England families. He established his first portrait studio, Guaranty Photos, in 1916, when he moved to Harlem, and his second, GGG Studios, in 1932. His photographs of prominent figures of the Harlem Renaissance such as Langston Hughes, Bill "Bojangles" Robinson, and Duke Ellington, as well as those of weddings, funerals, and parades, created a dignified image of Manhattan's African-American community during the 1920s and 1930s. In 1924, Marcus Garvey chose him to be the official photographer for the Universal Negro Improvement Organization. Van Der Zee's work remained unnoticed for decades by the mainstream art community until 1969, when Reginald McGhee, a photography researcher at the Metropolitan Museum of Art, brought his work to the public's attention with the exhibition *Harlem on My Mind*. Since then, his popularity has increased dramatically, and his work has been recognized in books, films, and exhibitions, including a retrospective at the National Portrait Gallery in Washington, D.C., in 1993.

ALEX WEBB (B. 1952)

Alex Webb was born in San Francisco and studied history and literature at Harvard University (B.A. 1974). While at Harvard, he studied at the Carpenter Center for Visual Arts and attended the Apeiron Workshop in Millerton, New York, in 1972. Webb published his photographs in the *New York Times Magazine*, *Life*, and *Geo* before joining Magnum in 1976, when he began to photograph the American South, Latin America, Africa, and the Caribbean. The images he created during these travels resulted in his books *Hot Light/Half-Made Worlds: Photographs from the Tropics* (1986), *Under a Grudging Sun: Photographs from Haiti Libéré* (1989), *From the Sunshine State: Photographs of Florida* (1996), and *Amazon: From the Floodplains to the Clouds* (1997). In the past twenty years, he has received several grants as well as the Leopold Godowsky Color Photography Award (1988) and the Leica Medal of Excellence (2000).

WEEGEE (B. ARTHUR FELLIG, 1899–1968)

Weegee, the second of seven children in a religious Jewish family, came to New York from Poland at age eleven. After stints as a commercial studio assistant, he began working in the darkroom at Acme Newspictures. By 1935, Weegee was a successful freelance photographer published in the *New York Herald Tribune* and *New York Post*, and in 1940 he joined the staff of *PM* newspaper. The police radio installed in his car gave him his almost supernatural, "Ouija-like" ability to arrive at crime scenes before the police, likely earning him his nickname, although the name might also have derived

from his early work as a photo assistant using a "squeegee" to dry prints. Throughout the 1940s, he showed his work with the Photo League. Weegee published several books, including *Naked City* (1945), which contained pictures of New York's seamy underside, and *Naked Hollywood* (1953), featuring portraits of celebrities. While in Hollywood, Weegee served as a consultant on special effects for films including Stanley Kubrick's *Dr. Strangelove*. Major exhibitions of Weegee's work since his death include *Weegee the Famous* at the International Center of Photography in 1977 and *Weegee and the Human Comedy* at the San Francisco Museum of Modern Art in 1984.

DAN WEINER (1919–1959)

Dan Weiner was born in New York and studied painting at the Art Students League and Pratt Institute. In order to support himself, he assisted commercial photographer Valentino Sarra from 1940 to 1942 and simultaneously joined the Photo League. During World War II, he served as an air force photographer, and in 1946 he returned to New York to establish a commercial studio. Switching to photojournalism in 1949, Weiner traveled to Eastern Europe, to the American South to document the civil rights movement, and to South Africa to collaborate with Alan Paton, with whom he had worked on assignment for *Collier's* and on a book entitled *South Africa in Transition* (1956). While on assignment in 1959, Weiner was killed in a plane crash in Kentucky. In 1967, Cornell Capa included Weiner with six other photojournalists in the traveling exhibition *The Concerned Photographer*.

GARRY WINOGRAND (1928–1984)

After studying painting for several years in his hometown of New York, where he was raised in a Jewish family, Garry Winogrand began studying photography at Alexey Brodovitch's Design Laboratory at the New School for Social Research. Beginning in 1954, he completed freelance assignments for *Collier's* and *Sports Illustrated*. His exhibition at the Image Gallery in 1960 was the first of numerous gallery shows, and major retrospectives followed at the Museum of Modern Art (1969, 1977, and 1988), Bibliothèque Nationale, Paris (1980), and the Photographers' Gallery, London (2000). He received his first of many fellowships from the Guggenheim Foundation in 1964 and spent the next twenty years traveling and teaching at several universities. Among his books of photographic series published during this time were *The Animals* (1969), capturing humans and animals in New York City zoos, and *Stock Photographs: Fort Worth Fat Stock Show and Rodeo* (1980). Winogrand won acclaim for his photographs of the 1970s and 1980s concentrating on New York nightlife.

Exhibition Checklist

BERENICE ABBOTT (1898–1991)
Lyric Theater; Third Avenue
Between 12th and 13th Street from
Changing New York, 1936
Gelatin-silver print
8 x 10 in. (20.3 x 25.4 cm)
Photography Collection, Miriam and
Ira D. Wallach Division of Art, Prints &
Photographs, The New York Public Library.
Astor, Lenox and Tilden Foundations

ALEXANDER ALLAND (1902–1989)
Untitled, c. 1938
Vintage gelatin-silver print
9³/₄ x 7⁷/₈ in. (24.8 x 20 cm)
Howard Greenberg Gallery, New York

ALEXANDER ALLAND (1902–1989)
Chinatown, 1938
Vintage gelatin-silver print
14 x 11 in. (35.6 x 27.9 cm)
Howard Greenberg Gallery, New York

ANONYMOUS
The Lower East Side, 1900
Photochrome process print
12¹/₂ x 16¹/₂ in. (31.8 x 41.9 cm)
Collection of Lisa Ades, New York

DIANE ARBUS (1923–1971)
Girl with a Cigar in Washington
Square Park, New York City, 1965
Gelatin-silver print
11 x 10¹/₄ in. (27.9 x 26 cm)
The Museum of Modern Art, New York.
Lily Auchincloss Fund
exhibition only

DIANE ARBUS (1923–1971)
The Jewish Giant at Home with
His Parents, Bronx, New York, 1970
Gelatin-silver print
20 x 16 in. (50.8 x 40.6 cm)
The Jewish Museum, New York. Museum
purchase, Photography Acquisition
Committee Fund and the Horace W.
Goldsmith Foundation, 1999-3
exhibition only

LOU BERNSTEIN (B. 1911)
Landlord and His Wife, New York City
(Man and Wife), 1941
Gelatin-silver print
13¹⁵/₁₆ x 10¹⁵/₁₆ in. (35.4 x 27.8 cm)
The Museum of Fine Arts, Houston. Gift
of Wolf Associates, 82.546.1

MARGARET BOURKE-WHITE (1904–1971)
Untitled (Sergei Eisenstein Having a
Shave on the Terrace of
Margaret Bourke-White's Studio), 1930
Gelatin-silver print
13³/₈ x 9¹/₂ in. (34 x 24.1 cm)
Margaret Bourke-White Papers,
Syracuse University Library,
Department of Special Collections

BYRON COMPANY (1892–1942)
Hester Street, 1898
Gelatin-silver print
14 x 19 in. (35.6 x 48.3 cm)
Museum of the City of New York, Byron
Collection, 93.1.1.18122

BYRON COMPANY (1892–1942)
Indians and Their Teepees on the
Roof of the Hotel McAlpin, 1913
Gelatin-silver print
10¹/₂ x 13³/₁₆ in. (26.7 x 33.7 cm)
Museum of the City of New York,
Byron Collection, 93.1.1.4468

HENRI CARTIER-BRESSON (B. 1908)
New York, 1946
Gelatin-silver print
20 x 16 in. (50.8 x 40.6 cm)
Magnum Photos, Inc., New York

ALVIN LANGDON COBURN (1882–1966)
The Tunnel Builders, 1908
Photogravure
7⁵/₈ x 6¹/₈ in. (19.4 x 15.7 cm)
George Eastman House, Rochester,
New York

TED CRONER (B. 1922)
Untitled, c. 1947
Vintage gelatin-silver print
14 x 11 in. (35.6 x 27.9 cm)
Howard Greenberg Gallery, New York

TED CRONER (B. 1922)
Untitled, c. 1947
Vintage gelatin-silver print
11⁷/₈ x 10¹/₂ in. (30.2 x 26.7 cm)
Howard Greenberg Gallery, New York

BRUCE DAVIDSON (B. 1933)
East 100th Street, 1966
Gelatin-silver print
20 x 16 in. (50.8 x 40.6 cm)
Magnum Photos, Inc., New York

BRUCE DAVIDSON (B. 1933)
Gay Pride, Central Park, 1992
Gelatin-silver print
16 x 20 in. (40.6 x 50.8 cm)
Magnum Photos, Inc., New York

BRUCE DAVIDSON (B. 1933)
Subway, 1980
Lambda Cibachrome print
16 x 20 in. (40.6 x 50.8 cm)
Magnum Photos, Inc., New York

ROY DECARAVA (B. 1919)
Man on Subway Stairs, 1952
Gelatin-silver print
19³/₁₆ x 12⁷/₈ in. (48.8 x 32.7 cm)
International Center of Photography,
New York. Photography in
the Fine Arts Collection, 1981
exhibition only

ARNOLD EAGLE (1910–1992)
New York, 1937
Gelatin-silver print
14 x 11 in. (35.6 x 27.9 cm)
Howard Greenberg Gallery, New York

ARNOLD EAGLE (1910–1992)
On the Elevated—Sailor, Newspaper, 1941
Vintage gelatin-silver print
10¹/₄ x 12¹/₄ in. (26 x 31.1 cm)
Howard Greenberg Gallery, New York

MORRIS ENGEL (B. 1918)
Harlem Merchant, 1937
Gelatin-silver print
11 x 14 in. (27.9 x 35.6 cm)
Howard Greenberg Gallery, New York

MORRIS ENGEL (B. 1918)
Shoeshine Boy with Cop, 1947
Vintage gelatin-silver print,
mounted on masonite
13¹/₄ x 10¹/₄ in. (33.7 x 26 cm)
The Jewish Museum, New York.
Museum purchase, Photography
Acquisitions Committee Fund, 2000-63

WALKER EVANS (1903–1975)
Untitled (Subway Passengers), 1938
Gelatin-silver print
3¹³/₁₆ x 5¹/₄ in. (9.6 x 13.3 cm)
The Museum of Modern Art,
New York. Purchase

LOUIS FAURER (1916–2001)
Staten Island Ferry, 1946
Gelatin-silver print
11 x 14 in. (27.9 x 35.6 cm)
The Jewish Museum, New York.
Museum purchase with funds provided
by Judith and Jack Stern, 2000-57

LOUIS FAURER (1916–2001)
New York City, 1950
Gelatin-silver print
16 x 20 in. (40.6 x 50.8 cm)
Collection of Deborah Bell, New York

LOUIS FAURER (1916–2001)
New York City, 1950
Gelatin-silver print
11 3/8 x 7 7/8 in. (28.9 x 18.7 cm)
Addison Gallery of American Art, Phillips
Academy, Andover, Massachusetts.
Gift of Deborah Bell

ANDREAS FEININGER (1906–1999)
*On the Staten Island Ferry Approaching
Downtown Manhattan*, 1940
Gelatin-silver print
12 15/16 x 10 15/16 in. (32.7 x 27.6 cm)
The New-York Historical Society,
New York

ANDREAS FEININGER (1906–1999)
Noon Rush Hour on Fifth Avenue, 1949
Gelatin-silver print
13 5/8 x 10 3/4 in. (34.6 x 27.3 cm)
The New-York Historical Society,
New York

LARRY FINK (B. 1941)
*George Plimpton, Jared Paul Stern,
and Cameron Richardson, Fashion Shoot,
Elaine's, New York City*, 1999
Gelatin-silver print
14 7/8 x 14 7/8 in. (37.8 x 37.8 cm)
Courtesy of the artist

LARRY FINK (B. 1941)
*Edwardian Ball, Frick Museum,
New York City*, 2000
Gelatin-silver print
14 3/4 x 18 1/4 in. (37.5 x 46.4 cm)
Courtesy of the artist

LEONARD FREED (B. 1929)
New York, 1954
Gelatin-silver print
20 x 16 in. (50.8 x 40.6 cm)
Magnum Photos, Inc., New York

LEONARD FREED (B. 1929)
New York, USA from *The Dance
of the Pious*, 1954
Gelatin-silver print
10 1/4 x 6 7/8 in. (26 x 17.5 cm)
The Jewish Museum, New York.
Museum purchase with funds provided
by Mimi and Barry J. Alperin, 2000-73

RALPH GIBSON (B. 1939)
Untitled from *The Gotham Chronicles*, 1999
Chromogenic print
24 x 20 in. (61 x 50.8 cm)
Courtesy of the artist

GEORGE GILBERT (B. 1922)
Untitled from *American Faces*, 1942
Gelatin-silver print
14 x 11 in. (35.6 x 27.9 cm)
Courtesy of the artist

BRUCE GILDEN (B. 1946)
New York City, 1990
Gelatin-silver print
16 x 20 in. (40.6 x 50.8 cm)
Magnum Photos, Inc., New York

NAN GOLDIN (B. 1953)
*David with Butch Crying at
Tin Pan Alley, New York City*, 1982
Chromogenic color photograph
20 x 24 in. (50.8 x 61 cm)
Collection of Marvin Heiferman, New York

NAN GOLDIN (B. 1953)
*Misty in Sheridan Square,
New York City*, 1991
Cibachrome print
20 x 24 in. (50.8 x 61 cm)
Courtesy of the artist and Matthew Marks
Gallery, New York

SAMUEL H. GOTTSCHO (1875–1971)
Times Square at Forty-fourth Street, 1932
Gelatin-silver print
16 x 20 in. (40.6 x 50.8 cm)
Museum of the City of New York.
Gift of Samuel H. Gottscho, 34.102.10

SID GROSSMAN (1915–1955)
New York, 1947
Vintage gelatin-silver print
7 3/4 x 8 1/8 in. (19.7 x 20.6 cm)
Howard Greenberg Gallery, New York

SID GROSSMAN (1915–1955)
Coney Island, 1947–48
Vintage gelatin-silver print
8 1/4 x 7 1/2 in. (21 x 19.1 cm)
Howard Greenberg Gallery, New York

SID GROSSMAN (1915–1955)
Mulberry Street, 1948
Vintage gelatin-silver print
13 3/16 x 10 1/2 in. (33.5 x 26.7 cm)
The Jewish Museum, New York. Museum
purchase; Lillian Gordon Bequest, 2000-78

GEORGE GROSZ (1893–1959)
A Face in the Crowd from
First Landing, 1932
Gelatin-silver print
5 1/4 x 7 3/16 in. (13.3 x 19.7 cm)
Kimmel Cohn Photography Arts, New York

JOHN GUTMANN (1905–1998)
Guns for Sale, 1936
Gelatin-silver print
7 5/8 x 6 7/8 in. (19.3 x 17.5 cm)
The Metropolitan Museum of Art, New
York. Gift of the artist, 2000 (2000.651.4)

OTTO HAGEL (1909–1973)
New York Stock Exchange, 1938
Gelatin-silver print
12 1/2 x 10 3/8 in. (34.2 x 26.4 cm)
Center for Creative Photography, Tucson

LEWIS HINE (1874–1940)
Climbing into America, 1905
Gelatin-silver print
6 1/2 x 4 5/8 in. (16.6 x 11.9 cm)
George Eastman House, Rochester,
New York

LEWIS HINE (1874–1940)
Bowery Mission Bread Line 2 A.M., 1907
Gelatin-silver print
4 9/16 x 5 7/8 in. (11.5 x 14.9 cm)
The Museum of Modern Art,
New York. Purchase

LEWIS HINE (1874–1940)
Mendicants, New York City, 1910
7 x 5 in. (17.8 x 12.7 cm)
National Archives, Still Pictures Branch,
College Park, Maryland

LEWIS HINE (1874–1940)
Steelworker, Empire State Building, 1931
Gelatin-silver print
6 3/4 x 4 3/4 in. (16.9 x 11.9 cm)
George Eastman House, Rochester,
New York

MORRIS HUBERLAND (B. 1909)
Bocce Players, c. 1940
Gelatin-silver print
8 1/2 x 11 in. (21.6 x 27.9 cm)
The New-York Historical Society,
New York

MORRIS HUBERLAND (B. 1909)
Outdoor Meeting, c. 1940
Gelatin-silver print
7 1/2 x 7 1/2 in. (19.1 x 19.1 cm)
The New-York Historical Society,
New York

JEFF JACOBSON (B. 1946)
Untitled, 1985
35mm Kodachrome original transparency,
digital epson print
20 x 30 in. (40.6 x 76.2 cm)
Courtesy of the artist

JEFF JACOBSON (B. 1946)
Untitled, 1999
35mm Kodachrome original transparency,
digital epson print
20 x 30 in. (40.6 x 76.2 cm)
Courtesy of the artist

WILLIAM KLEIN (B. 1928)
Presentation, Ebbets Field, New York, 1955
Gelatin-silver print
19 5/8 x 23 5/8 in. (49.8 x 60 cm)
Howard Greenberg Gallery, New York

WILLIAM KLEIN (B. 1928)
Gun, Gun, Gun, New York, 1955
Gelatin-silver print
15 3/4 x 19 5/8 in. (40 x 49.8 cm)
Howard Greenberg Gallery, New York

WILLIAM KLEIN (B. 1928)
*The Bars of a 2 by 4 Park. A Bench,
Home for the Homeless*, 1950s
Gelatin-silver print
15 3/4 x 19 5/8 in. (40 x 49.8 cm)
Howard Greenberg Gallery, New York

ARTHUR LEIPZIG (B. 1918)
Coney Island—Steeplechase, 1952
Vintage gelatin-silver print
10 1/2 x 10 1/4 in. (26.7 x 26 cm)
Howard Greenberg Gallery, New York

SAUL LEITER (B. 1923)
New York, 1950s
Gelatin-silver print
14 x 11 in. (35.6 x 27.9 cm)
Howard Greenberg Gallery, New York

SAUL LEITER (B. 1923)
Barbershop 75¢, 1950s
Fujicolor crystal archive
14 x 11 in. (35.6 x 27.9 cm)
Howard Greenberg Gallery, New York

REBECCA LEPKOFF (B. 1916)
Henry Street, Manhattan, 1946–47
Vintage gelatin-silver print
12 1/8 x 10 1/2 in. (30.8 x 26.7 cm)
Howard Greenberg Gallery, New York

LEON LEVINSTEIN (1910–1988)
Mother and Child, Herald Square, c. 1955
Gelatin-silver print
14 x 16 1/4 in. (35.6 x 41.3 cm)
Howard Greenberg Gallery, New York

LEON LEVINSTEIN (1910–1988)
Untitled, c. 1957
Gelatin-silver print
10 5/8 x 13 1/4 in. (27.1 x 33.6 cm)
Private collection

LEON LEVINSTEIN (1910–1988)
Times Square, New York, 1965
Vintage gelatin-silver print
12 3/8 x 10 3/8 in. (31.6 x 26.2 cm)
The Dreyfus Corporation, New York

HELEN LEVITT (B. 1913)
New York, c. 1940
Gelatin-silver print
11 x 14 in. (27.9 x 35.6 cm)
The Jewish Museum, New York.
Museum purchase; Lillian Gordon
Bequest, 2000-56

HELEN LEVITT (B. 1913)
New York, c. 1939
Gelatin-silver print
11 x 14 in. (27.9 x 35.6 cm)
Laurence Miller Gallery, New York

HELEN LEVITT (B. 1913)
New York, 1972
Dye transfer print
16 x 20 in. (40.6 x 50.8 cm)
Laurence Miller Gallery, New York

HELEN LEVITT (B. 1913)
Untitled (Finger Pointing in Window),
c. 1938
Gelatin-silver print
4 3/4 x 7 13/16 in. (12.1 x 19.9 cm)
The Metropolitan Museum of Art. Purchase, The Horace W. Goldsmith Foundation Gift, 1991 (1991.1146)

SOL LIBSOHN (1914–2001)
Hester Street, c. 1938
Gelatin-silver print
10 x 9 7/8 in. (25.4 x 25.1 cm)
Howard Greenberg Gallery, New York

MARY ELLEN MARK (B. 1940)
The Queen, 1968
Gelatin-silver print
20 x 16 in. (50.8 x 40.6 cm)
Courtesy of the artist

MARY ELLEN MARK (B. 1940)
Coney Island, 1994
Gelatin-silver print
16 x 20 in. (40.6 x 50.8 cm)
Courtesy of the artist

JEFF MERMELSTEIN (B. 1957)
Untitled, New York City, 1993
Fujicolor crystal archive
16 x 20 in. (40.6 x 50.8 cm)
Courtesy of the artist

JEFF MERMELSTEIN (B. 1957)
Untitled, New York City, 1995
Fujicolor crystal archive
16 x 20 in. (40.6 x 50.8 cm)
Courtesy of the artist

GJON MILI (1904–1984)
Café Society, New York, 1943–47
Gelatin-silver print
19 3/4 x 15 5/16 in. (50.1 x 38.8 cm)
The Museum of Modern Art, New York.
Purchase

LISETTE MODEL (1906–1983)
Reflection, New York, 1939–45
Gelatin-silver print
12 3/4 x 10 3/8 in. (32.5 x 26.5 cm)
The Metropolitan Museum of Art, New
York. Purchase, Gift of Various Donors
and Matching Funds from The National
Endowment for the Arts, 1981 (1981.1040)

LISETTE MODEL (1906–1983)
Untitled (New York City), 1940
Gelatin-silver print
13 7/16 x 10 5/16 in. (34.2 x 26.5 cm)
San Francisco Museum of Modern Art.
Byron Meyer Fund Purchase

LISETTE MODEL (1906–1983)
Asti's, New York, 1946
Gelatin-silver print
13 3/8 x 10 13/16 in. (34 x 27.4 cm)
The J. Paul Getty Museum, Los Angeles

FRITZ NEUGASS (1899–1979)
Untitled, 1940s
Gelatin-silver print
6 3/8 x 4 5/8 in. (16.2 x 11.7 cm)
Keith de Lellis Gallery, New York

RUTH ORKIN (1921–1985)
Times Square, V-E Day, NYC, 1945
Gelatin-silver print
16 x 20 in. (40.6 x 50.8 cm)
Ruth Orkin Photo Archive, New York

GORDON PARKS (B. 1912)
Untitled (Man Preaching to Crowd),
c. 1952
Vintage gelatin-silver print
9 x 13 1/2 in. (22.9 x 34.3 cm)
Howard Greenberg Gallery, New York

SYLVIA PLACHY (B. 1943)
Meat Market, 1997
Panoramic C-print
12 x 29 1/2 in. (30.5 x 74.9 cm)
Courtesy of the artist

SYLVIA PLACHY (B. 1943)
Times Square, 1993
Archival gelatin-silver print
15 x 15 in. (38.1 x 38.1 cm)
Courtesy of the artist

WALTER ROSENBLUM (B. 1919)
Group in Front of Fence, 1938
Gelatin-silver print
11 x 14 in. (27.9 x 35.6 cm)
Courtesy of the artist

WALTER ROSENBLUM (B. 1919)
Block Party, New York East Side, 1942
Gelatin-silver print
7³/₈ x 9³/₈ in. (18.7 x 23.8 cm)
The Museum of Modern Art, New York.
Extended loan from the photographer

MEL ROSENTHAL (B. 1948)
Nelson Playing, Bathgate Avenue from
In the South Bronx of America, 1976
Gelatin-silver print
16 x 20 in. (40.6 x 50.8 cm)
Courtesy of the artist

BEN SHAHN (1898–1969)
Untitled (Seward Park, New York City),
1932–35
Gelatin-silver print
6¹/₄ x 9¹/₂ in. (15.8 x 24 cm)
Fogg Art Museum, Harvard University
Art Museums, Cambridge, Massachusetts.
Gift of Bernarda Bryson Shahn

BEN SHAHN (1898–1969)
*Untitled (New York General Post
Office, Eighth Avenue and Thirty-third
Street, New York City)*, 1932–35
Vintage gelatin-silver print
6¹/₄ x 9¹/₈ in. (15.9 x 23.2 cm)
Howard Greenberg Gallery, New York

AARON SISKIND (1903–1991)
The Wishing Tree from
Harlem Document, 1937
Gelatin-silver print
11 x 14 in. (27.9 x 35.6 cm)
The Jewish Museum, New York. Museum
purchase; Lillian Gordon Bequest, 2000-58

AARON SISKIND (1903–1991)
Most Crowded Block from *Most
Crowded Block in the World*, 1938–39
Gelatin-silver print
7³/₈ x 6³/₈ in. (18.8 x 16.2 cm)
George Eastman House, Rochester,
New York. Gift of Aaron Siskind

EDWARD STEICHEN (1879–1973)
In a New York Penthouse, 1931
Vintage gelatin-silver print
9¹/₂ x 7¹/₂ in. (24.1 x 19.1 cm)
Howard Greenberg Gallery, New York

ALFRED STIEGLITZ (1864–1946)
The City of Ambition, 1910, printed c. 1913
Photogravure
13¹/₄ x 10¹/₄ in. (33.8 x 26 cm)
The Metropolitan Museum of Art,
New York, Alfred Stieglitz Collection,
1949 (49.55.19)

LOU STOUMEN (1917–1991)
*Sitting in Front of the Strand,
Times Square*, 1940
Vintage gelatin-silver print
8³/₄ x 6⁷/₈ in. (22.2 x 17.5 cm)
Barry Singer Gallery, Petaluma, California

PAUL STRAND (1890–1976)
Wall Street, New York, 1915
Platinum palladium print
11 x 13⁷/₈ in. (27.9 x 35.2 cm)
Whitney Museum of American Art,
New York. Gift of Michael E. Hoffman in
honor of Sondra Gilman, 91.102.2

PAUL STRAND (1890–1976)
*Portrait, Five Points Square,
New York*, 1916
Platinum print
12³/₈ x 7¹/₂ in. (31.4 x 19.1 cm)
Museum of Fine Arts, Boston.
Sophie Friedman Fund, 1997.776

KARL STRUSS (1886–1981)
*Trolley, Horse-drawn Vehicle & El.,
N.Y.C.*, 1911
Platinum print
3³/₁₆ x 4¹/₈ in. (7.9 x 10.5 cm)
Amon Carter Museum, Fort Worth, Texas,
P1983.23.3

KARL STRUSS (1886–1981)
Back of Public Library, 1912
Platinum print
4¹/₄ x 3³/₄ in. (10.8 x 9.5 cm)
Amon Carter Museum, Fort Worth, Texas,
P1983.23.2

JAMES VAN DER ZEE (1886–1983)
Manhattan Temple B.C. Lunch, 1936
Gelatin-silver print
12¹/₈ x 10¹/₂ in. (30.8 x 26.7 cm)
The Metropolitan Museum of Art,
New York. Gift of The James Van Der Zee
Institute, 1970 (1970.539.53)

ALEX WEBB (B. 1952)
Coney Island, New York, 1983
Lambda Cibachrome print
16 x 20 in. (40.6 x 50.8 cm)
Magnum Photos, Inc., New York

ALEX WEBB (B. 1952)
Times Square, New York, 1996
Lambda Cibachrome print
16 x 20 in. (40.6 x 50.8 cm)
Magnum Photos, Inc., New York

WEEGEE (B. ARTHUR FELLIG, 1899–1968)
*Crowd at Coney Island, temperature 89
degrees . . . They came early
and stayed late*, July 22, 1940
Gelatin-silver print
11 x 14 in. (27.9 x 35.6 cm)
International Center of Photography,
New York. Gift of Wilma Wilcox, 1993

WEEGEE (B. ARTHUR FELLIG, 1899–1968)
Ballet Rehearsal, c. 1940s
Gelatin-silver print
14 x 11 in. (35.6 x 27.9 cm)
International Center of Photography,
New York

WEEGEE (B. ARTHUR FELLIG, 1899–1968)
Joy of Living, April 17, 1942
Gelatin-silver print
16³/₈ x 12¹/₂ in. (41.6 x 31.8 cm)
International Center of Photography,
New York

DAN WEINER (1919–1959)
San Gennaro Festival, 1952
Gelatin-silver print
14 x 11 in. (35.6 x 27.9 cm)
Museum of the City of New York.
Gift of Sandra Weiner, 99.127.1

DAN WEINER (1919–1959)
*Harold Arlen (Partly Hidden),
Marlene Dietrich, and
Truman Capote at El Morocco*, 1955
Gelatin-silver print
11 x 14 in. (27.9 x 35.6 cm)
Collection of Sandra Weiner

GARRY WINOGRAND (1928–1984)
Park Avenue, New York, 1959
Gelatin-silver print
22¹/₄ x 14⁷/₈ in. (56.7 x 37.8 cm)
The Museum of Modern Art, New York.
Gift of the photographer

GARRY WINOGRAND (1928–1984)
Rockefeller Victory Celebration, 1972
Gelatin-silver print
16 x 20 in. (40.6 x 50.8 cm)
Collection of Eli Consilvio.
Courtesy of Deborah Bell, New York

Bibliography

Alinder, James, ed. *Roy DeCarava: Photographs.* Essay by Sherry Turner DeCarava. Carmel, Calif.: Friends of Photography, 1981.

Appel, Alfred, Jr. *Signs of Life.* New York: Knopf, 1983.

Arbus, Diane. *Diane Arbus.* Exh. cat. New York: The Museum of Modern Art and Aperture, 1972.

Arnold, Eve, et al. *The Fifties: Photographs of America.* Intro. by John Chancellor. New York: Pantheon, 1985.

Avedon, Richard, and James Baldwin. *Nothing Personal.* New York: Atheneum, 1964.

Barth, Miles, ed. *Weegee's World.* Exh. cat. New York: International Center of Photography; Boston: Little, Brown, 1997.

Beauvoir, Simone de. *America Day by Day.* Trans. Patrick Dudley. New York: Grove, 1953.

Bendavid-Val, Leah. *Propaganda and Dreams: Photographing the 1930s in the U.S.S.R. and the U.S.* Zurich: Editions Stemmler, 1999.

Bezner, Lili Corbus. *Photography and Politics in America: From the New Deal into the Cold War.* Baltimore: Johns Hopkins University Press, 1999.

Blom, Benjamin. *New York: Photographs, 1850–1950.* New York: Amaryllis, 1982.

Bosworth, Patricia. *Diane Arbus: A Biography.* New York: Knopf, 1984.

Burns, Ric, James Sanders, and Lisa Ades. *New York: An Illustrated History.* New York: Knopf, 1999.

Byron, Joseph. *New York Life at the Turn of the Century in Photographs: From the Byron Collection of the Museum of the City of New York.* Text by Albert K. Baragwanath. New York: Museum of the City of New York and Dover, 1985.

Byron, Joseph. *Photographs of New York Interiors at the Turn of the Century: From the Byron Collection of the Museum of the City of New York.* Text by Clay Lancaster. New York: Museum of the City of New York and Dover, 1976.

Chiarenza, Carl. *Aaron Siskind: Pleasures and Terrors.* Exh. cat. Boston: Center for Creative Photography and Little, Brown, 1982.

Christopher, Nicholas. *Somewhere in the Night: Film Noir and the American City.* New York: Free Press, 1997.

Coleman, A. D. "Diane Arbus, Lee Friedlander, and Garry Winogrand at Century's End." In *The Social Scene: The Ralph M. Parsons Foundation Photography Collection at the Museum of Contemporary Art, Los Angeles.* Exh. cat. Los Angeles: Museum of Contemporary Art, 2000. 30–38.

Coleman, A. D. "No Pictures: Some Thoughts on Jews in Photography." *Photo Review* 23, no. 1 (Winter 2000): 1–6.

Conrad, Peter. *The Art of the City: Views and Versions of New York.* New York: Oxford University Press, 1984.

Coplans, John. *Weegee's New York.* Munich: Schirmer/Mosel, 1982.

Corn, Wanda A. "The New New York." *Art in America* 61 (1973): 58–65.

Cuddihy, John Murray. *The Ordeal of Civility: Freud, Marx, Lévi-Strauss, and the Jewish Struggle with Modernity.* New York: Basic Books, 1974.

Culturefront 6, no. 3 (Winter 1998). Special issue: "Gotham at 100."

Davidson, Bruce. *Brooklyn Gang.* Santa Fe, N.Mex.: Twin Palm, 1999.

Davidson, Bruce. *Bruce Davidson.* New York: Pantheon; Paris: Centre National de la Photographie, 1986.

Davidson, Bruce. *Bruce Davidson Photographs.* New York: Agrinde/Summit, 1978.

Davidson, Bruce. *East 100th Street.* Cambridge, Mass.: Harvard University Press, 1970.

Davidson, Bruce. *Subway.* New York: Aperture, 1986.

DeCarava, Roy, and Langston Hughes. *The Sweet Flypaper of Life.* New York: Simon and Schuster, 1955.

Dickstein, Morris. "The City as Text: New York and the American Writer." *TriQuarterly* 83 (1991–92): 183–205.

Douglas, Ann. *Terrible Honesty: Mongrel Manhattan in the 1920s.* New York: Farrar, Straus, and Giroux, 1995.

Einzig, Barbara. *Louis Stettner's New York: 1950s–1990s.* New York: Rizzoli, 1996.

Engel, Morris. *Early Works.* New York: Ruth Orkin Photo Archive, 1999.

Evans, Martin Marix, and Amanda Hopkinson, eds. *Contemporary Photographers.* 3d ed. New York: St. James Press, 1995.

Evans, Walker. *First and Last.* New York: Harper and Row, 1978.

Evans, Walker. *Walker Evans at Work.* Essay by Jerry L. Thompson. New York: Harper and Row, 1982.

Ewing, William A. *America Worked: The 1950s Photographs of Dan Weiner.* New York: Abrams, 1989.

Fink, Larry. *Social Graces: Photographs by Larry Fink.* New York: Aperture, 1984.

Frank, Robert. *The Americans.* New York: Aperture, 1978.

Freed, Leonard. *Leonard Freed: Photographs, 1954–1990.* New York: Norton, 1992.

Fulton, Marianne. *Mary Ellen Mark: Twenty-five Years.* Boston: Bulfinch, 1991.

Galassi, Peter. *Roy DeCarava: A Retrospective.* Exh. cat. Essay by Sherry Turner DeCarava. New York: Museum of Modern Art, 1996.

Gee, Helen. *Limelight: A Greenwich Village Photography Gallery and Coffeehouse in the Fifties.* Albuquerque: University of New Mexico Press, 1997.

Gibson, Ralph. *Deus ex Machina*. Cologne: Taschen, 1999.

Gilbert, George. *The Illustrated Worldwide Who's Who of Jews in Photography*. Riverdale, N.Y.: George Gilbert, 1996.

Gilden, Bruce. *Facing New York*. Manchester: Cornerhouse, 1992.

Goldberg, Vicki. *Lewis W. Hine: Children at Work*. Munich and New York: Prestel, 1999.

Goldin, Nan. *The Ballad of Sexual Dependency*. Ed. Marvin Heiferman, Mark Holborn, and Suzanne Fletcher. New York: Aperture, 1986.

Goldin, Nan. *The Other Side*. Ed. David Armstrong and Walter Keller. Exh. cat. New York and Berlin: Scalo; Berlin: D.A.A.D. Artists-in-Residence Programme, 1993.

Green, Jonathan. ed. *Camerawork: A Critical Anthology*. Millerton, N.Y.: Aperture, 1973.

Greenough, Sarah, and Philip Brookman. *Robert Frank: Moving Out*. Exh. cat. Washington, D.C.: National Gallery of Art, 1994.

Grundberg, Andy. *Alexy Brodovitch, 1898–1971*. New York: Abrams, 1989.

Hales, Peter Bacon. *Silver Cities: The Photography of American Urbanization, 1839–1915*. Philadelphia: Temple University Press, 1984.

Hambourg, Maria Morris. *Paul Strand Circa 1916*. New York: Metropolitan Museum of Art, 1998.

Hambourg, Maria Morris, Jeff Rosenheim, Douglas Eklund, and Mia Fineman. *Walker Evans*. Exh. cat. New York: Metropolitan Museum of Art, 2000.

Hannigan, William. *New York Noir*. New York: Rizzoli, 1999.

Harrison, Martin. *Louis Faurer*. Paris: Photo Poche, 1992.

Hertzberg, Arthur. *The Jews in America*. New York: Columbia University Press, 1997.

Howe, Irving. *World of Our Fathers*. New York: Harcourt Brace Jovanovich, 1976.

Jacobs, Jane. *The Death and Life of Great American Cities*. New York: Modern Library, 1993.

Judt, Tony. *Past Imperfect: French Intellectuals, 1944–1956*. Berkeley: University of California Press, 1992.

Kao, Deborah Martin, Laura Katzman, and Jenna Webster. *Ben Shahn's New York: The Photography of Modern Times*. Exh. cat. Cambridge, Mass.: Fogg Art Museum, Harvard University Art Museums; New Haven and London: Yale University Press, 2000.

Kao, Deborah Martin, and Charles A. Meyer, eds. *Aaron Siskind: Towards a Personal Vision, 1935–1955*. Exh. cat. Chestnut Hill, Mass.: Boston College Museum of Art, 1994.

Kaplan, Daile. *Lewis Hine in Europe*. New York: Abbeville, 1988.

Kazin, Alfred. *A Walker in the City*. New York: Harcourt Brace, 1951.

Keller, Ulrich F. "The Myth of Art Photography: A Sociological Analysis." *History of Photography* 8 (October–December 1984): 24–25.

Keller, Ulrich F. "The Myth of Art Photography: An Iconographical Analysis." *History of Photography* 9 (January–March 1985): 1–38.

Klein, William. *New York, 1954–55*. Manchester: Dewi Lewis, 1995.

Klein, William. *Photographs, Etc.: New York and Rome, Also Moscow and Tokyo, Also Elsewhere*. Essay by John Heilpern. New York: Aperture, 1981.

Kozloff, Max. *Lone Visions, Crowded Frames: Essays on Photography*. Albuquerque: University of New Mexico Press, 1994.

Kozloff, Max. "Lost Baggage: *The Family of Man* Reconsidered." In *Family, Nation, Tribe, and Community*. Ed. Frank Wagner. Berlin: Neue Gesellshaft für Bildende Kunst, 1996. 168–70.

Kozloff, Max. "Mass Hysteria: The Photography of Weegee." *Artforum* 36, no. 7 (March 1998): 76–82.

Kozloff, Max. *The Privileged Eye: Essays on Photography*. Albuquerque: University of New Mexico Press, 1987.

Kozloff, Max. *The Restless Decade: John Gutmann's Photographs of the Thirties*. Ed. Lew Thomas. New York: Abrams, 1984.

Kozloff, Max. "Service in a Minefield: American Social Documentary Photography, 1966–1994." In *The Social Scene: The Ralph M. Parsons Foundation Photography Collection at the Museum of Contemporary Art, Los Angeles*. Exh. cat. Los Angeles: Museum of Contemporary Art, 2000. 8–20.

Kozloff, Max. "Skyscrapers, the Late Imperial Mob." *Artforum* 30, no. 4 (December 1990): 96–102.

Kozloff, Max. "Time Stands Still: The Photographs of Roy DeCarava." *Artforum* 34, no 9 (May 1996): 78–124.

Kozloff, Max. "The Uncanny Portrait: Sander, Arbus, Samaras." *Artforum* 11, no. 10 (June 1973): 58–67.

Kozloff, Max. "William Klein and the Radioactive Fifties." *Artforum* 19, no. 9 (May 1981): 34–42.

Lancaster, Clay. *Joseph Byron: Photographs of New York Interiors at the Turn of the Century*. New York: Dover, 1976.

Lane, Anthony. "The Shutterbug." *New Yorker*, May 21, 2001, 78–85.

Langer, Freddy. *Lewis W. Hine: The Empire State Building*. Munich: Prestel, 1998.

Leipzig, Arthur. *Growing Up in New York: Photographs*. Boston: Godine, 1995.

Levin, Gail, and Judith Tick. *Aaron Copland's America: A Cultural Perspective*. New York: Watson-Guptill, 2000.

Levitt, Helen. *A Way of Seeing*. Essay by James Agee. Durham, N.C.: Duke University Press, 1989.

Livingston, Jane. *The New York School of Photographs, 1936–1963*. New York: Stuart Tabori Chang, 1992.

Lopate, Phillip, ed. *Writing New York: A Literary Anthology*. New York: Library of America, 1998.

Lord, Catherine. "What Becomes a Legend Most: The Short, Sad Career of Diane Arbus." In *The Contest of Meaning: Critical Histories of Photography*. Ed. Richard Bolton. Cambridge, Mass.: MIT Press, 1989. 112–23.

Mayer, Grace M. *Once Upon a City*. New York: Macmillan, 1958.

Mellow, James R. *Walker Evans*. New York: Basic Books, 1999.

Mermelstein, Jeff. *Sidewalk*. Stockport, U.K.: Dewi Lewis, 1999.

Miller, Russell. *Magnum: Fifty Years at the Front Line of History: The Story of the Legendary Photo Agency*. New York: Grove, 1997.

Model, Lisette. *Lisette Model*. Preface by Berenice Abbott. Millerton, N.Y.: Aperture, 1979.

Mora, Gilles, and John T. Hill. *Walker Evans: The Hungry Eye*. New York: Abrams, 1993.

Morris, Jan. *Manhattan '45*. New York: Oxford University Press, 1987.

Mumford, Lewis. *The City in History: Its Origins, Its Transformations, and Its Prospects*. New York: Harcourt, Brace, and World, 1961.

Munby, Jonathan. *Public Enemies, Public Heroes: Seeing the Gangster from "Little Caesar" to "Touch of Evil."* Chicago: University of Chicago Press, 1999.

Norman, Dorothy. *Alfred Stieglitz: An American Seer*. New York: Random House, 1973.

O'Connell, Shaun. *Remarkable, Unspeakable New York: A Literary History*. Boston: Beacon, 1995.

Parks, Gordon. *Half Past Autumn: A Retrospective*. Essay by Philip Brookman. Exh. cat. Washington, D.C.: Corcoran Gallery of Art; Boston: Bulfinch, 1997.

Phillips, Sandra S. *Life Is Good and Good for You in New York: Trance Witness Revels: William Klein*. Exh. cat. San Francisco: Museum of Modern Art, 1995.

Phillips, Sandra S., and Maria Morris Hambourg. *Helen Levitt*. Exh. cat. San Francisco: San Francisco Museum of Modern Art, 1991.

Plachy, Sylvia. *Unguided Tour*. New York: Aperture, 1990.

Pratt, Davis, ed. *The Photographic Eye of Ben Shahn*. Cambridge, Mass.: Harvard University Press, 1975.

Rathbone, Belinda. *Walker Evans: A Biography*. Boston: Houghton Mifflin, 1995.

Rice, Shelley. "Essential Differences: A Comparison of the Portraits of Lisette Model and Diane Arbus." *Artforum* 18, no. 9 (May 1980): 66–73.

Rice, Shelley, and Naomi Rosenblum. *Walter Rosenblum: Photographer*. Dresden: Verlag der Kunst, 1990.

Roegiers, Patrick. *Diane Arbus, ou Le Rêve du naufrage*. Paris: Chêne, 1985.

Rosenthal, Mel. *In the South Bronx of America: Photographs by Mel Rosenthal*. Willimantic, Conn.: Curbstone, 2000.

Sachar, Howard M. *A History of the Jews in America*. New York: Knopf, 1992.

Sandeen, Eric J. *Picturing an Exhibition: The Family of Man and 1950s America*. Albuquerque: University of New Mexico Press, 1995.

Sante, Luc. *Evidence*. New York: Farrar, Straus, and Giroux, 1992.

Schloss, Carol. *In Visible Light: Photography and the American Writer, 1840–1940*. New York: Oxford University Press, 1987.

Schoener, Allon, ed. *Harlem on My Mind: Cultural Capital of Black America, 1900–1968*. New York: Random House, 1968.

Shamis, Bob, and Max Kozloff. *Leon Levinstein: The Moment of Exposure*. Exh. cat. Ottawa: National Gallery of Canada, 1995.

Silverman, Jonathan. *For the World to See: The Life of Margaret Bourke-White*. New York: Viking, 1983.

Simmel, Georg. "The Metropolis and Mental Life." In *The Sociology of Georg Simmel*. Ed. and trans. Kurt H. Wolff. New York: Free Press, 1964.

Simmons, Peter. *Gotham Comes of Age: New York Through the Lens of the Byron Company, 1892–1942*. Exh. cat. New York: Museum of the City of New York; San Francisco: Pomegranate, 1999.

Siskind, Aaron. *Harlem Document: Photographs, 1932–1940*. Ed. Ann Banks. Providence, R.I.: Matrix, 1981.

Smith, Terry. *Making the Modern: Industry, Art, and Design in America*. Chicago: University of Chicago Press, 1993.

Sontag, Susan. *On Photography*. New York: Farrar, Straus, and Giroux, 1977.

Stange, Maren. *Symbols of Ideal Life: Social Documentary Photography in America, 1890–1950*. Cambridge: Cambridge University Press, 1989.

Stange, Maren, ed. *Paul Strand: Essays on His Life and Work*. New York: Aperture, 1990.

Steichen, Edward. *The Family of Man*. Exh. cat. New York: Museum of Modern Art, 1955.

Steichen, Edward. *A Life in Photography*. New York: Doubleday, 1963.

Steichen, Joanna. *Steichen's Legacy: Photographs, 1895–1973*. New York: Knopf, 2000.

Steinfoth, Karl, ed. *Alvin Langdon Coburn*. Munich: Editions Stemmler, 1999.

Stettner, Louis. "Cézanne's Apples and the Photo League: A Memoir." *Aperture* 112 (Fall 1988): 14–36.

BIBLIOGRAPHY

Stettner, Louis, ed. *Weegee.* New York: Knopf, 1977.

Stott, William. *Documentary Expression and Thirties America.* New York: Oxford University Press, 1973.

Stoumen, Lou. *Times Square: Forty-five Years of Photography.* New York: Aperture, 1985.

Stourdzé, Sam, Helen Gee, and A. D. Coleman. *Leon Levinstein: Obsession.* Exh. cat. Paris: Centre Photographique d'Île-de-France, Pontault-Combault, and Leó Schneer, 2000.

Sundell, Michael G. *Berenice Abbott: Documentary Photography of the 1930s.* Exh. cat. Cleveland: New Gallery of Contemporary Art, 1980.

Sussman, Elizabeth. *Nan Goldin: I'll Be Your Mirror.* Exh. cat. Ed. Nan Goldin, David Armstrong, and Hans Werner Holzwarth. New York: Whitney Museum of American Art; Zurich: Scalo, 1996.

Sussman, Elizabeth, and John Handhardt. *City of Ambition: Artists and New York, 1900–1960.* Exh. cat. New York: Whitney Museum of American Art; Paris: Flammarion, 1996.

Szarkowski, John. *Walker Evans.* New York: Museum of Modern Art, 1971.

Szarkowski, John. *Winogrand: Figments from the Real World.* Exh. cat. New York: Museum of Modern Art; Boston: Little, Brown, 1988.

Thézy, Marie de. *La Photographie humaniste, 1930–1960: Histoire d'un mouvement en France.* Paris: Contrejour, 1992.

Thomas, Ann. *Lisette Model.* Exh. cat. Ottowa: National Gallery of Canada, 1990.

Tonelli, Edith A., and John Gossage. *Louis Faurer: Photographs from Philadelphia and New York, 1937–1973.* College Park: University of Maryland Art Gallery, 1981.

Trachtenberg, Alan. *America and Lewis Hine.* New York: Aperture, 1977.

Trachtenberg, Alan. *Reading American Photographs: Images as History: Matthew Brady to Walker Evans.* New York: Hill and Wang, 1989.

Tucker, Anne Wilkes, Claire Cass, and Stephen Daiter. *This Was the Photo League: Compassion and the Camera from the Depression to the Cold War.* Exh. cat. Chicago: Stephen Daiter Gallery; Houston: John Cleary Gallery, 2001.

Vestal, David. *Berenice Abbott: Photographs.* New York: Horizon, 1970.

Von Hartz, John. *Andreas Feininger: New York in the Forties.* New York: Dover, 1978.

Walzer, Michael. *On Toleration.* New Haven and London: Yale University Press, 1997.

Weegee. *Naked City.* New York: Da Capo, 1985.

Weegee. *Weegee: An Autobiography.* New York: Da Capo, 1975.

Weiner, Dan. *Dan Weiner.* Ed. Cornell Capa and Sandra Weiner. New York: Grossman, 1974.

Westerbeck, Colin. "Night Light: Brassaï and Weegee." *Artforum* 15, no. 4 (December 1976): 34–45.

Westerbeck, Colin, and Joel Meyerowitz. *Bystander: A History of Street Photography.* Boston: Bulfinch, 1994.

Whitfield, Stephen J. *American Space, Jewish Time.* New York: Anchor, 1988.

Yochelson, Bonnie. *The Committed Eye: Alexander Alland's Photography.* Exh. cat. New York: Museum of the City of New York, 1991.

Yochelson, Bonnie. "What Are the Photographs of Jacob Riis?" *Culturefront* 3, no. 3 (Fall 1994): 28–39.

Yochelson, Bonnie, Barbara McCandless, and Richard Koszarski. *New York to Hollywood: The Photography of Karl Struss.* Albuquerque: University of New Mexico Press, 1995.

Zurier, Rebecca, Robert W. Snyder, and Virginia M. Mecklenburg. *Metropolitan Lives: The Ashcan Artists and Their New York.* Exh. cat. Washington, D.C.: National Museum of American Art; New York: Norton, 1995.

Index

Page numbers in italics refer to illustrations